Growth Rates of The Internet Worldwide

July 1992 — July 1993

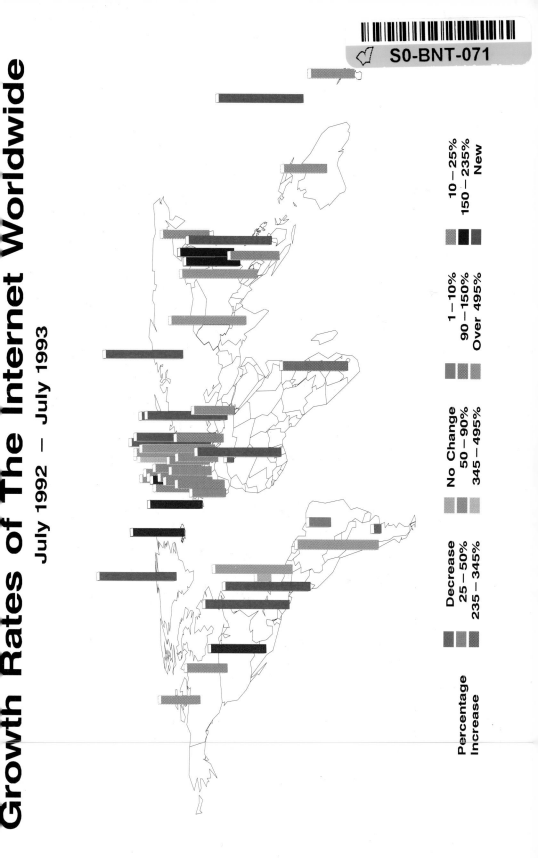

Percentage Increase

Decrease
25 — 50%
235 — 345%

No Change
50 — 90%
345 — 495%

1 — 10%
90 — 150%
Over 495%

10 — 25%
150 — 235%
New

The Internet Connection

System Connectivity and Configuration

John S. Quarterman

Smoot Carl-Mitchell

Texas Internet Consulting
tic@tic.com

 Addison-Wesley Publishing Company

Reading, Massachusetts • Menlo Park, California • New York
Don Mills, Ontario • Wokingham, England • Amsterdam • Bonn
Sydney • Singapore • Tokyo • Madrid • San Juan • Milan • Paris

This book is in the **Addison-Wesley UNIX and Open Systems Series**
Series Editors: Marshall Kirk McKusick and John S. Quarterman

Deborah R. Lafferty: Sponsoring Editor
Thomas Stone: Senior Editor
Patsy DuMoulin: Associate Production Supervisor
Bob Donegan: Marketing Manager
Roy E. Logan: Senior Manufacturing Manager
Jaap Akkerhuis: Troff Macro Designer
Laura K. Michaels: Copy Editor

Library of Congress Cataloging-in-Publication Data

```
Quarterman, John S.
     The Internet connection : system connectivity and
  configuration / by John S. Quarterman, Smoot Carl-Mitchell.
       p.   cm.
     Includes bibliographical references and index.
     ISBN 0-201-54237-4
     1. Internet (computer network).  I. Carl-Mitchell, Smoot.
  II. Title.
  TK5105.875.I57Q37   1994                          93-30530
  384.3--dc20                                            CIP
```

The programs and applications presented in this book have been included for their instructional value. They have been tested with care, but are not guaranteed for any particular purpose. The publisher does not offer any warranties or representations, nor does it accept any liabilities with respect to the programs or applications.

UNIX is a registered trademark of UNIX System Laboratories in the United States and other countries. Many of the designations used by manufacturers and sellers to distinguish their products are claimed as trademarks. Where those designations appear in this book, and Addison-Wesley was aware of a trademark claim, the designations have been printed in initial caps or all caps.

2 3 4 5 6 7 8 9 10–MA–9594

To our parents

Series Foreword

Marshall Kirk McKusick

John S. Quarterman

Addison-Wesley is proud to publish the **UNIX and Open Systems Series.** The primary audience for the Series will be system designers, implementors, administrators, and their managers. The core of the series will consist of books detailing operating systems, standards, networking, and programming languages. The titles will interest specialists in these fields, as well as appeal more broadly to computer scientists and engineers who must deal with open-systems environments in their work. The Series comprises professional reference books and instructional texts.

Open systems allow users to move their applications between systems easily; thus, purchasing decisions can be made on the basis of cost-performance ratio and vendor support, rather than on which systems will run a user's application suite. Decreasing computer hardware prices have facilitated the widespread adoption of capable multiprocess, multiuser operating systems, UNIX being a prime example. Newer operating systems, such as Mach and Chorus, support additional services, such as lightweight processes. The Series illuminates the design and implementation of all such open systems. It teaches readers how to write applications programs to run on these systems, and gives advice on administration and use.

The Series treats as a unified whole the previously distinct fields of networking and operating systems. Networks permit open systems to share hardware and software resources, and allow people to communicate efficiently. The exponential growth of networks such as the Internet and the adoption of protocols such as TCP/IP in industry, government, and academia have made network and system administration critically important to many organizations. This Series will examine many aspects of network protocols, emphasizing the interaction with operating systems. It will focus on the evolution in computer environments and will assist professionals in the development and use of practical networking technologies.

Standards for programming interfaces, protocols, and languages are a key concern as networks of open systems expand within organizations and across the globe. Standards can be useful for system engineering, application programming, marketing, and procurement; but standards that are released too late, cover too little, or are too narrowly defined can be counterproductive. This series will encourage its readers to participate in the standards process by presenting material that details the use of specific standards to write application programs, and to build modern multiprocess, multiuser computing environments.

Newer operating systems are implemented in object-oriented languages, and network protocols use specialized languages to specify data formats and to compile protocol descriptions. As user interfaces become increasingly sophisticated, the level at which they are programmed continues to evolve upward, from system calls to remote procedure call compilers and generic description environments for graphical user interfaces. The effects of new languages on systems, programs, and users are explored in this series.

Preface

This book explains how to connect your computer or network to the world's largest computer network and community of computer users: the Internet.

The Internet

The Internet is the largest computer network in the world, consisting of more than 13,000 networks and more than 1,776,000 machines as of July 1993. It has been growing approximately 100 percent annually for the last five years. The TCP/IP protocols used in the Internet are very capable, but are not plug and play. The pool of knowledgeable TCP/IP engineers is not growing as fast as the Internet itself. This book addresses that gap in knowledge.

There is no Internet, Inc. to call for service like the old telephone monopoly. The Internet is a worldwide decentralized distributed cooperative interconnection of numerous underlying technologies and organizations with no overall goals, management, or pricing structure. Like the current telephone system, there are many suppliers of Internet connectivity and services, some competing, some complementary. Just as the local telephone company usually does not do the wiring inside your house, your Internet connectivity provider will not set up the environment inside your local host machine or your local network. This book tells you how to do it yourself.

The Internet is not like television. When you join the Internet, you become a participant, able to post mail and news; to publish files, documents, and software; and to make your machines directly accessible to others, if you wish. Your machine or network becomes a part of the distributed Internet mail system, and can become a server of many other kinds of information. This book tells you how to join the Internet community.

The Book

This book shows how to connect to the Internet, step by step, from finding a connection through registering a domain and a network number, through configuring your TCP/IP protocols, to running your own domain server and setting up your mail and news systems. Security techniques are described, for use either with or without a router. The most common new Internet services, netfind, archie, WAIS, and gopher, are covered. Access information for network connectivity providers, for domain and IP network number registries, and for other books, is included.

Much of the material in this book is applicable to any software platform, because it is about the TCP/IP protocols, which were designed to work with any platform. Single-process personal computer operating systems such as MS-DOS and MacOS are most frequently used as clients of network services. The book includes information on where to get TCP/IP software packages for IBM compatibles and Macintoshes. Multi-process operating systems such as UNIX commonly run both clients and servers. Most of the detailed information in the book on setting up and configuring network application servers is about UNIX software.

This book is about setting up communications between your host or network and the Internet. That is, it is about communications with the outside world. We must address some internal LAN issues in dealing with external connectivity, but we avoid discussion of issues solely related to LANs, just as we avoid discussion of issues of system administration, unless they also are related to external connectivity.

The book includes brief overviews of Internet services and protocols, and it briefly describes what the Internet is and is not, and how it differs from other networks. However, we assume the reader already knows about those other networks, knows about Internet services, and already wants to connect to the Internet. This book shows how to do that.

Organization

The book begins with two overview chapters, about services and networks.

- Chapter 1, *Internet Services* gives a motivational overview of what you can do with the Internet, and then describes the size and growth of the Internet. The bulk of the chapter describes specific Internet services, their facilities and advantages, and the TCP/IP protocols that support them on the Internet.

- Chapter 2, *The Internet and Other Networks* gives an overview of the history, protocols, and politics of the Internet and other networks, such as FidoNet, UUCP, BITNET, USENET, that together form the global Matrix of computers that exchange electronic mail.

These contextual chapters set the stage and define the terms for the rest of the book. If you are already familiar with the Internet, you may want to skip forward to the other chapters, but there is an amazing amount of disinformation about the Internet in circulation, and these chapters are short and, we hope, accurate.

Before you can use the Internet you have to decide how to connect, and you may need to register organizational names and network addresses.

- Chapter 3, *Types of Internet Access* categorizes types of access to the Internet, ranging from public hosts to direct fiber optic connections at hundreds of megabits per second. The chapter includes a very brief refresher on protocol layering models and Internet protocol layers.

- Chapter 4, *Registering Domain Names and IP Numbers* tells exactly how to register a domain name and a network number, and where to get the registration forms by electronic mail, or on paper or CD/ROM.

The rest of the chapters show how to set up Internet services, and are presented approximately in the order you are likely to need the services they describe.

- Chapter 5, *Setting Up IP*

- Chapter 6, *Setting Up the Domain Name System*

- Chapter 7, *Setting Up Internet Electronic Mail*

- Chapter 8, *Setting Up USENET News*

- Chapter 9, *Security Issues*

- Chapter 10, *Setting Up Resource Discovery Services*

These chapters do not attempt to describe all possibilities in great generality (we've already done that in another book, *Practical Internetworking with TCP/IP and UNIX*). Instead, they give the short and direct path to getting what you're most likely to need set up as quickly and painlessly as possible.

The appendices provide names and addresses for sources of information.

- Appendix A, *Internet Providers* lists Internet providers, from public login hosts to dialup and direct IP connectivity providers.

- Appendix B, *Registration Templates* includes the actual text of example registration templates for domains and IP network numbers, and the addresses to send them to.

- Appendix C, *Software and Other Information* tells where to get the software (often over the Internet itself; sometimes for free; sometimes from commercial suppliers).

- Appendix D, *Further Reading* is a brief reading list of books about the Internet and other networks.

There is a brief glossary, and a brief index.

The cover shows a view of the world from above the north pole, with each of four networks glowing in its own color light. Similar maps appear on four of the endpapers,* showing the whole world, Eurasia, and most of Canada and the United States. As the legends indicate, wide orange ellipses are for UUCP, tall violet ellipses are for FidoNet, blue squares are for BITNET, EARN, and other NJE networks, and green circles are for the Internet; these four networks are the largest distributed networks in the Matrix, and they are described briefly in Chapter 2. The size of an icon indicates the number of host computers near the center of the icon.

For example, the map of Eurasia shows the Internet green as the most prevalent in the north and west of Europe, and BITNET (or other NJE network) blue as the most widespread in the middle east. In eastern Europe, Internet green fades into FidoNet and UUCP violet and orange in central Asia, until east Asia suddenly shows all four networks again. However, the Internet is following behind those two access networks, and green Internet circles are visible in Talinn, St. Petersburg, Kiev, Moscow, Novosibirsk, New Delhi, Bombay, and Accra, Ghana.

The fourth endpaper shows growth rates of the Internet alone in each country of the world. Much of the world is already connected, from Antarctica to Siberia, from Greenland to Ecuador, from Australia to Austria. The newest countries are growing the fastest, but even the longest connected and most densely networked countries are adding new hosts at exponential rates.

Readers

This book is for readers who know they want a connection to the Internet, not to a different network. It is for anyone who wants to connect a single machine or a network to the Internet. Such a machine might be in someone's house or office, in a company or a university. Such a network might be in a company office or a university department.

Managers and executives can use the book to get a good idea of what is really involved in setting up an Internet connection. Technical people can use the book to actually set up a connection.

In 1993 more than a million new machines and ten thousand more networks are expected to connect to the Internet. That is more people confused by technology than all the TCP/IP consultants in the world can help directly. This book can assist many of those people in doing their own basic IP connection configuration. In 1994, two million more machines and twenty thousand more networks are expected.

These numbers are just for the Internet proper. There are probably at least as many machines in private IP networks inside companies, and more are forming all

---

* The growth map was drawn by Gretchen Phillips of the University at Buffalo, using SAS/Graph from SAS, Inc. The detailed host maps were drawn by John S. Quarterman of Matrix Information and Directory Services (MIDS), using the GMT map projection software from the University of Hawaii, plus custom software by MIDS. For more maps of this kind, contact *mids@tic.com* about *Matrix Maps Quarterly*.

the time. Many of these enterprise networks then connect to the Internet, either as full participants, or through one of the kinds of firewalls described in this book. Every company or department considering making such a connection has at least one potential reader. Every engineer involved in setting up the connection, the engineer's manager, and many of the engineer's users, are potential readers.

The person wanting to connect may already have electronic mail access to some other network, such as UUCP, FidoNet, or BITNET, or may be a complete newcomer to wide area networking. Even if you work in a place with many network experts, it is very easy to spend a lot of time finding the right person to ask for basic information about a variety of topics. This book answers most of the basic questions, and points you at sources for appropriate registrars, software, and vendors. The book is aimed more at newcomers, but will also be of use to engineers familiar with LANs who want the quick path to setting up wide area Internet services.

Most specific details are drawn from the Internet in the United States. Most details are the same in other countries. Where there are major differences, we describe them. The Internet itself is still mostly (60%) in the United States, but already reaches at least 50 other countries, and is growing even more rapidly in some of them than the overall 100% annual growth rate. Thus readers of this book may be anywhere in the world.

Terminology and Typography

This book is written in American English. We have avoided idioms that might be hard for other English readers to understand. We have also avoided overly formal or academic phrasing, while attempting to maintain clarity.

Jargon words and important terms are defined in the glossary, and also appear in the index. Glossary definitions are necessarily brief, and isolated. Definitions of the same terms in the text are often longer, and are always given in context, so you may want to use the index to locate these embedded definitions, as well. Defined terms, whether words, phrases, or acronyms, appear in boldface where they are defined in the text, and sometimes in other places where they are important.

Most networking concepts depend on other networking concepts, leading to circular definitions. For this reason, many terms are introduced briefly at the outset, and defined more properly later. For example, major network services are introduced in Chapter 1 and many of them are defined or discussed in more detail in later chapters. Similarly, basics of packet switching are explained in the ARPANET section in Chapter 2, leading into the discussion of network protocol layering in Chapter 3, the discussion of routing in Chapter 5, and the discussion of types of gateways in Chapter 9.

Acronyms present some interesting issues. Traditionally in English an acronym is a short sequence of letters, pronounceable or not, derived from a sequence of words, perhaps by taking the first letter of each word. In computing and networking jargon acronyms are not always derived from a longer form; often the reverse is true. That is, frequently an interesting, euphonic, or punning acronym is constructed and later an expansion is produced to fit it. Such expansions serve merely as mnemonics and rationalizations, not as derivations. In addition, many network protocols and networking organizations are known almost exclusively by their acronyms, not by a longer name. For these reasons, we do not follow the usual English convention of always introducing an acronym in parentheses after the longer form of the name. Sometimes we instead give the acronym first, followed by the longer form in parentheses. In addition, it is customary in English to introduce an acronym along with its longer form once only in a text. We also do not follow this custom, since readers may not be reading this book in strict page number order, and even readers who do may easily have forgotten a complicated acronym introduced at the beginning of the book by the time it recurs in a later chapter. Instead we reintroduce an acronym whenever we think it might have been forgotten. All acronyms that are given in the text with an expansion appear in the index, and most also appear in the glossary.

Network protocol names are usually given in uppercase, whether they are acronyms or not, as in RLOGIN. UNIX commands are given in lowercase and italics, as in *rlogin*. Pathnames are given in italics, as in */etc/hosts.equiv*.

Acknowledgments

We would like to acknowledge the invaluable assistance of Eric Allman, Michael L. Barrow, Kurt Baumann, Steve Cisler, Peter Deutsch, Ole Jacobsen, Brewster Kahle, Glenn Kowack, Debbie Lafferty, Doug McCallum, Eric McKinney, Kirk McKusick, Laura Michaels, Gretchen Phillips, Prentiss Riddle, Luis German Rodriguez, Rich Salz, Michael Schwartz, Barry Shein, Jose Silvio, Jose Soriano, Henry Spencer, Tom Stone, Toru Takahashi, Clifford A. Wilkes, and anyone else we may have neglected to name.

Contents

Chapter 1   Internet Services   **1**

1.1   Uses of the Internet   2
1.2   Growth of the Internet   5
1.3   Communications   7
1.4   Resource Sharing   10
1.5   Resource Discovery   13
1.6   Naming   15
1.7   Classes of Service   16

Chapter 2   The Internet and Other Networks   **19**

2.1   The ARPANET   19
2.2   Internet Protocols   24
2.3   Internet History   25
2.4   The Internet and the Matrix   28
2.5   The Internet Now   32

Chapter 3   Types of Internet Access   **39**

3.1   Overview of Access Types   39
3.2   Overview of Internet Protocols   42
3.3   Mail Networks   46
3.4   Conferencing Systems   47
3.5   Public Internet Hosts   48
3.6   Packaged Dialup Software and Services   49
3.7   Dialup IP Connections   50
3.8   Direct Connections   50
3.9   Connectivity Providers   53
3.10 Acceptable Use Policies   55
3.11 Checklist   56

Chapter 4   Registering Domain Names and IP Numbers   **59**

4.1   What, Where, and How to Register   60
4.2   Anonymous FTP   65
4.3   The InterNIC   67
4.4   Mail Document Servers   68

Chapter 5   Setting Up IP   **73**

5.1   Connectivity Options   73
5.2   Packet Routing   74
5.3   Dedicated Connectivity   77
5.4   Dialup Connectivity   77

Chapter 6   Setting Up the Domain Name System   **81**

6.1   DNS Basics   81
6.2   Zone Databases   83
6.3   Nameserver Cache   88
6.4   Bootstrap File   89
6.5   Typical Internet Server Arrangement   90
6.6   SOA Record Parameters   92
6.7   Complete Examples of DNS Database Files   93
6.8   Hints and Tidbits   96
6.9   Checking It Out   97

Chapter 7   Setting Up Internet Electronic Mail   **99**

7.1   Mail Architecture   99
7.2   Mail Envelopes and Contents   101
7.3   Internet Mail Addresses   102
7.4   Internet Mail and DNS MX Records   103
7.5   Example Mail System   104
7.6   The Post Office Protocol   113
7.7   MIME: Multipurpose Internet Mail Extensions   114
7.8   Mail User Agents   116
7.9   Checking It Out   117

Chapter 8   Setting Up USENET News   **119**

8.1   Overview of USENET News   120
8.2   News Software   124
8.3   News Feeds and News Costs   127
8.4   INN: InterNet News   129
8.5   Outgoing News (nntplink)   133

8.6   A News User Agent (trn)   133
8.7   News Administration   135
8.8   Checking It Out   140

Chapter 9   Security Issues   141

9.1   Air Gapping   141
9.2   Passwords   142
9.3   Hiding Information   143
9.4   Dangerous Services   144
9.5   Kerberos   145
9.6   CERT   145
9.7   Host Connection Protection: tcpd   146
9.8   Packet Filtering   153

Chapter 10   Setting Up Resource Discovery Services   163

10.1   Finding People   163
10.2   Finding Files   166
10.3   Finding Documents   170
10.4   Front Ends   175
10.5   Checking It Out   180

Appendix A   Internet Providers   183

A.1   Internet Connectivity Providers   183
A.2   Other   234

Appendix B   Registration Templates   235

B.1   Domain Registration   235
B.2   IP Network Number Registration   237
B.3   IP Number to Domain Registration   239

Appendix C   Software and Other Information   241

C.1   Archie   241
C.2   Software Access List   242

Appendix D   Further Reading   247

Glossary   249

Index   265

CHAPTER 1

Internet Services

With the Internet, you can

- Exchange textual and other messages with any of millions of people in business, academia, government, and other organizations in more than fifty countries.

- Retrieve software, documents, pictures, weather maps, library catalogs, and other information from any of thousands of repositories worldwide.

- Use communications and shared resources to collaborate with people in the same office or on another continent; to complete old tasks such as correspondence more quickly and conveniently; and to perform tasks not possible at all before the Internet.

The community of users of the Internet is the most important reason for connecting to the Internet. That community is supported by a spectrum of services, such as electronic mail, file transfer, and file locators, the most important of which we describe in Chapter 2, *The Internet and Other Networks*. One of these services, electronic mail, extends into many other networks, such as BITNET, UUCP, and FidoNet. All computer networks that exchange electronic mail form the Matrix, which we describe in Chapter 2. Matrix users can participate in some Internet communications. Internet users have access to many more services, and the Internet is the core and main support of the Matrix. Join the Internet and you join the center of the networked world.

In this chapter, we first discuss uses and users of the Internet, followed by its size and growth. Then we describe some of the specific services you will actually use on the Internet. The network services we emphasize in this chapter are the ones we explain how to set up later in the book. We do not attempt to list all the many Internet services here. Instead, we give a brief description of major services: what each does, some advantages of each, and some comparisons among them. We also mention the TCP/IP protocols that are used in the Internet to support these services.

This chapter introduces many topics that are treated in more detail later in the book. Most networking concepts depend on other networking concepts, leading to circular definitions. For this reason, many terms are introduced briefly at the outset, and defined more properly later.

1.1   Uses of the Internet

The Internet supports a global business, academic, and personal community of more than ten million people in more than fifty countries. Its users include artists, academics, and administrators, business people, bureaucrats, and bedfellows, non-profits and monopolies, the U.S. Congress, NATO, and the former KGB. The offices of the governor of Texas and of the president of the United States are now on the Internet; they use it to access worldwide resources and to communicate with constituents. They, like the Internet's traditional academic users, and like its newer business users (who are now in the majority), don't want to do without this global information utility and online community. The Internet has become popular in the press recently, appearing everywhere from technical trade publications to a cartoon in the *New Yorker*, as the public discovers the utility of this network and the value of its community. Many Internet users wouldn't take a job that did not include Internet access, and many employers seek employees familiar with the Internet. Why do all these people use the Internet?

Communications

The Internet is a communications tool; some of its communications services are sketched in Fig. 1.1 and some of their uses are described in this section.

The most popular use of the Internet is to exchange messages among people with electronic mail. You can communicate with tens of millions of people worldwide, with the clarity of a letter and much of the immediacy of the telephone, yet without having to stamp an envelope or play telephone tag. We write a lot of articles, and we can tell you the difference between a publication that accepts submissions by electronic mail and one that doesn't is often the difference between a few months to publication and a year to publication; this is an example of the degree to which online communications can increase efficiency. Also, a week's worth of business paper correspondence can be written, sent, and delivered in a day with electronic mail, without retyping, printing, stamps, express mail fees, or waiting a week for delivery. Even within a department, among workers in the same building, electronic mail is quicker, cheaper, and more convenient than paper memos, and less disturbing to productive work than telephone calls.

You can exchange electronic mail from other networks in the global Matrix of computers that exchange mail, but mail over the Internet is faster. Many other networks charge per message or per byte for mail, but Internet service providers traditionally charge for speed of access (bandwidth), and perhaps by connect time, not specifically for mail. With this speed and charging model, you can carry on mail conversations with people in other states or countries with only seconds

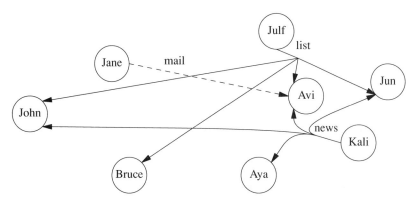

Figure 1.1 Communications Among People.

between sending a message and its receipt on the other end. In addition, Internet mail has a standard way of communicating still images, audio, video, and assorted rich text formats. Access to the Matrix makes you part of the global online community, but access to the Internet makes you part of the core of that community.

With electronic mailing lists, you can send a message to dozens or thousands of people at the same time, without photocopying memos or making multiple fax telephone calls. Thousands of such mailing lists discuss subjects ranging from genealogy to investment in petroleum companies. Some mailing lists carry online newsletters and journals. Some of the journals are refereed, and are just as good as traditional academic paper journals, but faster. Mailing lists are distributed from various parts of the Matrix, but many of the most interesting and largest mailing lists are distributed from the Internet.

For even larger discussions, USENET news permits tens or hundreds of thousands of participants, providing true many-to-many conferencing, a service that does not exist in traditional media. This service is like four thousand newspapers consisting entirely of columnists and letters to the editor, or like television with two thousand channels where everyone has a transmitter as well as a receiver, or like a meeting of two million people where everyone can not only speak at once, but can also be heard. In addition to the public newsgroups (discussion topics), there are for-pay business newsgroups that provide wire service news, stock market quotes, and specialized newsletters. USENET news is carried on many networks, but the fastest and largest part of USENET is carried on the Internet.

Resource Sharing

The Internet connects computers and facilitates sharing resources among those computers, as shown in Fig. 1.2.

Over the Internet, you can retrieve software, essays, data, and programs from thousands of distribution points across the world. To many companies, the free software available over the Internet is alone worth the cost of connection. Many companies provide free software over the Internet as marketing, or as a service to

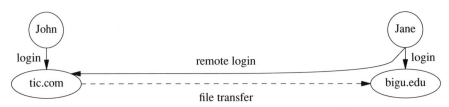

Figure 1.2 Resource Sharing Among Computers.

their customers. A growing number of companies provide for-pay services over
the Internet, as well. You can retrieve information with other networks, too, but
usually only more slowly, often only through mail, sometimes only from one
machine, and usually less conveniently.

You can connect across the Internet to a computer in another room, department, or country, and log in there as if you were directly connected. With proper
permission on each end, you can use this service to access supercomputers or to
log into your own office computer from your home or while you are travelling.
You can't do this at all on many networks, and when you can you often can't do
anything else. The Internet is a general purpose network, with multiple services
multiplexed over the same links for multiple users.

This concept of distributed resource sharing is new to many personal computer or mainframe users. You don't need a wheelbarrow to carry floppy disks
around to isolated PCs anymore. Instead, you can make the information available
over the Internet, where anyone who needs it can get it.

Resource Discovery

Finding an appropriate file, document, host, or person among millions of hosts and
many gigabytes of public repositories can be a problem. Fortunately, Internet
resource discovery services have been developed in recent years to help solve this
problem. Internet resource discovery services include:

- An online index of thousands of repositories

- Full-document keyword lookup to thousands of other repositories

- Hundreds of major library catalogs, including the Library of Congress and many
  major university catalogs

- Online bookstores

- Dozens of specialized databases

The Internet has a distributed menu-oriented front end to many of these other services, and also a hypertext front end. All these mechanisms permit the Internet
user to find information among tens of thousands of information servers. Many
people, including librarians and reporters, now use Internet resource discovery
services.

The Community

People use the Internet to get free software, to communicate with each other, to use supercomputers and databases, and for many other purposes. The capabilities, speed, and variety of Internet services and resources, although hard to explain to non-users, ensure that few people ever leave the Internet once they try it.

Internet services for communication, resource sharing, and resource discovery make the Internet an excellent vehicle for coordination and collaboration. A group working on the same project can exchange messages without all members having to be present at the same time or place, can exchange files to work on, and can even (given appropriate permissions) use each other's computers directly. All the users of the Internet together form a larger community.

The advantage of the Internet is the community of people that use it, not any specific service or piece of information. These people and their organizations and computers each add value to the Internet, so that the result is larger than any single organization could supply [Quarterman 1993].

1.2   Growth of the Internet

Most businesses consider ten percent annual growth to be good. The Internet has been growing approximately one hundred percent a year since about 1988, whether measured in numbers of users, hosts, or networks. This annual doubling promises to continue for some time yet.

The approximate numbers of hosts on the Internet from 1981 to 1993 are shown in Fig. 1.3 [Lottor 1992; MIDS 1993]. The numbers shown for dates since late 1986 were produced by looking at the distributed Domain Name System (DNS) database on the Internet. They exclude domains that have only mail connectivity via UNIX to UNIX CoPy (UUCP) or some other non-TCP/IP protocol. Domains included have associated IP addresses, although whether they are actually directly connected to the Internet isn't known (to find out would require actually attempting to exchange traffic with each host). However, it is reasonable to assume that most are connected and that these numbers are probably accurate to within a factor of 3 for the size of the Internet; that is, the numbers shown could be as much as 3 times larger than the real numbers of hosts on the Internet at the given dates. They certainly demonstrate the extraordinarily strong and undiminished growth of the Internet.

The number estimated for July 1993 was 1,776,000 hosts. Given a factor of 5 to 10 users per host (plausible in an era of more PCs, workstations, and fileservers than large timesharing machines), this means approximately 8.9 to 17.8 million Internet users worldwide, a figure consistent with estimates from other sources and calculation methods [Partridge 1991]. So if we say the number of users is 13 million and more or less doubling each year, this means 26 million (more than the population of the largest city) in July 1994, 52 million (bigger than all but 15 countries) in 1995, 104 million (bigger than Germany) in 1996, 208 million (bigger than Japan) in 1997, 416 million (bigger than the United States) in 1998, 1.664

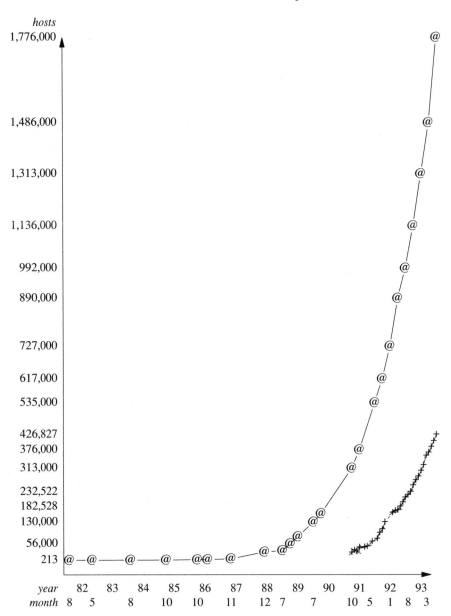

@   Worldwide (see RFC 1296), by Mark Lottor <mkl@nisc.sri.com>.
+   Europe, for RIPE (see RFC 1181), by Marten Terpstra <terpstra@ripe.net>.

Figure 1.3 Internet hosts, worldwide and in Europe.
*Adapted from Quarterman, "Sizes of Four Networks in the Matrix," Matrix News,
Vol. 2, No. 2, MIDS, Austin, mids@tic.com, July 1992. Copyright © 1992 MIDS.
Reprinted with permission.*

billion (bigger than China) in 2000, and more than 6 billion by 2002, that is, more than the expected total human population of the planet. If the current estimates are high by a factor of 4, add two to each of the years above.

This is, of course, a naive projection, and we don't expect the real figures to match in the years listed. Such rapid growth must slow down eventually, and it is interesting to speculate on whether the limiting factor will be computers, communications, people, or something else. Nonetheless, with only a few more years of this kind of exponential growth the Internet will connect a sizeable fraction of the population of the most developed countries, and will reach most of the world [Quarterman 1992].

1.3   Communications

The most widespread use of computer networks, including the Internet, is communication among people. Services for that purpose are known in the academic literature as **Computer Mediated Communication (CMC).** Because this whole book is about computers, we just call them communication services. Some classes of these services are listed in Table 1.1.

Electronic Mail

The most commonly used network service is **electronic mail (email),** also known as **e-mail,** or simply as **mail.** Mail permits network users to send textual messages to each other. Computers and networks handle delivering the mail, so that communicating mail users do not have to handle details of delivery, and do not have to be present at the same time or place. Electronic mail eliminates telephone tag, removes much of the inconvenience of time zones, avoids the necessity to be in the office all the time, and provides access to tens of millions people worldwide. We discuss mail in detail in Chapter 7, *Setting Up Internet Electronic Mail.*

As shown in Fig. 1.4, to compose, send, or read a mail message, you need a **user agent (UA).** Many of these are available for UNIX, including */bin/mail*,

Table 1.1 Communication Services.

Type		Interactive		Batch	
		Service	Example	Service	Example
1–1	person-to-person	chat	talk	mail	SMTP
1–n	one-to-many (broadcast)	discuss	phone	lists	aliases
n–n	many-to-many	confer	IRC	news	NNTP

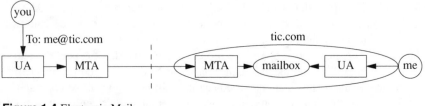

Figure 1.4 Electronic Mail.

Berkeley *Mail*, *MH*, *mush*, *elm*, and *pine*. To transfer the mail message, the UA must communicate with a **message transfer agent (MTA),** also called a **mailer.** Several MTAs are popular for use with UNIX, including *upas*, *smail*, *zmailer*, and *sendmail*. For difficult situations, the de facto standard UNIX mailer is still *sendmail*, which was originally introduced with 4.2BSD [Leffler *et al.* 1989]. An MTA delivers an electronic mail message to a **mailbox,** for each addressee. That person then uses a UA to read the mail. The mailbox is often a file, and the MTA and UA use a common convention for its name and location.

SMTP: Simple Mail Transfer Protocol. SMTP (Simple Mail Transfer Protocol) is the Internet Standard mail protocol. MTAs on the Internet, whether running on UNIX or not, use SMTP.

MIME: Multipurpose Internet Mail Extensions. A set of Multipurpose Internet Mail Extensions (MIME) have been specified recently and their use on the Internet is spreading rapidly. MIME permits sending more than just the plain 7-bit ASCII text of traditional Internet mail. It does so by providing conventions for marking part of a message as a non-ASCII encoding, such as a European or Asian character set, a sound file, a PostScript description of a typeset page, a fax format image, a still video image, or a moving image.

Mailing Lists

Mail can also be addressed to an **alias,** which is a name that has special meaning to the MTA. An alias can cause mail to be sent to a single user, or to many users. In the latter case, the alias implements a **mailing list.** Such a mailing list may expand to many mailboxes or even to other aliases. Software automatically forwards a message to each address on the list. Mailing lists provide ongoing forums for discussion of relatively specific topics, in medium scale discussion groups, with control over who can participate. Using such a list is much more convenient than typing in each address every time you want to send a message to the same group of people. Keeping the list of addresses in a single place ensures that everyone who sends mail to the list will reach the same group of people; most list users do not even need to know who is on the list. A list administrator can usually add new people or remove others by simply updating the list alias. A user usually subscribes or unsubscribes to a mailing list by sending mail to a related alias (such as *listalias-request* for list *listalias*). The subscription alias may forward to a human

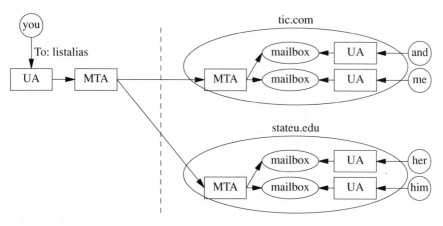

Figure 1.5 Mailing Lists.

list maintainer, or to a program, either of which then updates the list alias. There are hundreds of such lists on the Internet [SRI 1992]. Figure 1.5 shows an example of this process, in which mail to the list *listalias* distributes automatically to four people on two machines.

USENET News

USENET news provides discussion groups ranging in numbers of participants from few very may people, and with aggregate readership of at least 2,000,000 people worldwide. A news message is called an **article.** A news article looks much like a mail message, but is handled quite differently, as in Fig. 1.6. A news

Figure 1.6 USENET News.

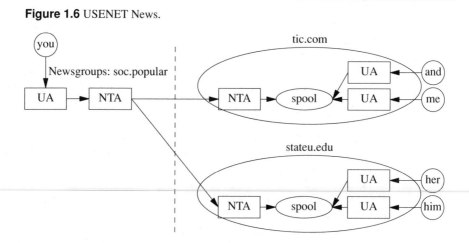

article is posted in a discussion topic, called a **newsgroup.** For example, Fig. 1.6 shows a user posting an article in the newsgroup *soc.popular,* causing the article to be distributed to two machines. In Fig. 1.5 we saw that each user subscribed to a mailing list gets a copy of a mail message in a separate mailbox. But, as shown in Fig. 1.6, only one copy of a news article is kept per computer. This reduction in copies of messages is one of the keys to the efficiency of news, allowing news-groups to reach larger numbers of people than is practical with mailing lists. Once news is set up on a host, users of that host can access newsgroups even more read-ily than mailing lists. There is no need to send mail to subscribe or unsubscribe to a newsgroup; simply tell your news UA which newsgroups you want to read. We discuss news in detail in Chapter 8, *Setting Up USENET News.*

NNTP: Network News Transfer Protocol. The usual protocol for delivering and accessing USENET news over the Internet is NNTP (Network News Transfer Protocol). News servers use NNTP to transfer news among themselves. News clients use it to read and post news through a news server.

News Readers. Just as you need a mail UA to read or send mail, you need a news UA, or news reader, to read or post news. There are many news readers, including *vnews*, *rn*, *trn*, *xrn*, *nn*, and *tin.* All of the ones just mentioned have screen-oriented interfaces, some for character-cell displays and some for bitmapped displays. Several also organize messages into threads of conversation and present them in menus.

IRC: Internet Relay Chat

IRC (Internet Relay Chat) supports interactive discussions among more than two people.

1.4   Resource Sharing

Communications services may be more widely used, but resource sharing services are equally important. Resource sharing is remote access to resources like super-computers and file servers through a network.

Resource sharing services are classified in Table 1.2. The traditional "big three" (most-used) Internet services are the communication protocol SMTP, which we've already mentioned, and two resource sharing protocols we describe in this section: File Transfer Protocol (FTP) and Virtual Terminal Protocol (TEL-NET). These are all Internet Standards and are required for Internet hosts. The basic Internet resource sharing services, TELNET and FTP, are ordinarily config-ured by default in the process of setting up IP and DNS so we discuss them only briefly in Chapter 9, *Security Issues.*

In addition, 4.2BSD and 4.3BSD supplied several UNIX-specific protocols, including RCP (remote copy), RLOGIN (remote login), and RSH (remote shell). These R* (pronounced "R star") protocols provide functionality similar to the Internet Standard protocols (RCP and FTP do file transfer and RLOGIN and

Table 1.2 Resource Sharing Services.

Type	Interactive	Batch
remote *login*	**TELNET** rlogin SUPDUP X Window System	
remote job *execution*	rsh	UUCP NJE
file *transfer*	**FTP** rcp	BFTP
transparent *file* *access (TFA)*	AFS NFS RFS Prospero Alex	

TELNET perform remote login). But the R* protocols are quite specific to UNIX, in that they make no allowances for different text line terminators or file formats. Their purpose was to extend basic UNIX functionality across a LAN of UNIX machines. The advantages of the R* protocols include simplified and convenient authentication and, in the case of RLOGIN, passing of more initialization parameters. We discuss these and other resource sharing services next.

File Transfer

The simplest way to access a file on another host is to copy it across the network to your local host. FTP or RCP can do this.

FTP: File Transfer Protocol. The Internet Standard for file transfer is the File Transfer Protocol (FTP). It requires little setup; in fact, most vendors deliver machines with FTP already configured.

A special FTP convention called **Anonymous FTP** requires more configuration. Ordinary FTP requires a remote user to have a normal user account on the FTP server host. Anonymous FTP permits any user on the Internet to access a carefully protected filesystem subtree using FTP. We discuss how to use anonymous FTP in Chapter 4, *Registering Domain Names and IP Numbers* and how to set it up in Chapter 10, *Setting Up Resource Discovery Services*. Anonymous FTP is particularly useful for retrieving information from the large number of Internet archive sites.

RCP: Remote Copy Protocol. 4.2BSD introduced RCP (Remote Copy Protocol) in the *rcp* command, whose user syntax is much like that of the UNIX file copy command, *cp*. The RCP facility is designed to transfer files inside a department or organization in which all machines have equivalent access to each other. Although convenient in such a situation, for security reasons it's not widely used across WANs.

Remote Login

To access a resource of a remote host, it can be convenient to actually log in on the remote host as if it were local. This can be done using TELNET or RLOGIN.

TELNET: Virtual Terminal Protocol. The Internet Standard for remote login is TELNET (Virtual Terminal Protocol). Like FTP, TELNET is usually preconfigured by most OS vendors.

RLOGIN: Remote Login Protocol. 4.2BSD also introduced RLOGIN (Remote Login Protocol). The UNIX *rlogin* command is the client side of this protocol and provides convenient local network login access. When properly configured, rlogin permits a user to log in on another host without typing a password. Access is controlled by several parameter files, which should be carefully configured to avoid security problems. Terminal type is also passed through automatically by the RLOGIN protocol.

TFA: Transparent File Access

Protocols that access files from remote servers but make them appear to the end-user application as if they were local provide Transparent File Access (TFA). Here we mention two traditional TFA protocols: NFS and AFS. This class of service fades into resource discovery, and we mention it again later in that context. NFS and AFS are used more on LANs than across WANs, so we do not discuss them further in this book. We do describe how to set up some TFAs that are designed for WAN access, in Chapter 10, *Setting Up Resource Discovery Services*.

NFS: Network File System. The **Network File System (NFS)** from **Sun Microsystems, Inc. (SMI)** was designed for use over LANs and is widely used in such environments. It also was designed for use with many operating systems, not just UNIX. DOS and Macintosh NFS clients are widely used to access files on UNIX NFS servers.

AFS: Andrew File System. The **Andrew File System (AFS)** from **Carnegie-Mellon University (CMU)** and Transarc, Inc. was designed for efficiency over WANs, and also for use across heterogenous operating systems.

Table 1.3 Resource Discovery Services.

Type	Machines	People	Files	Documents
resource *discovery*	X.500 /etc/hosts NIS DNS	X.500 WHOIS finger KIS netfind netdig	X.500 archie Prospero Alex Gopher WWW Z39.50	X.500 WAIS
retrieval			FTP NFS AFS Prospero	WAIS Gopher Z39.50
selection				WAIS Gopher Z39.50

1.5   Resource Discovery

The Internet has become so big that finding a file, document, resource, or person can be a huge problem. Fortunately, resource discovery services have been implemented on the Internet in the past few years. Following are some examples, which are also classified in Table 1.3. Chapter 10, *Setting Up Resource Discovery Services* tells how to set up some popular resource discovery services, including archie, WAIS, and Gopher.

Finding People

Electronic mail is useful but only if you know the address of the person you want to reach. Many services have been developed to find people's mail addresses.

WHOIS: A centralized user database server. The WHOIS service uses a centralized database to maintain information on people who ask to be listed. This information usually includes a person's electronic mail address, telephone number, and postal address. This service is convenient, but it is intended to list host, network, and domain administrators, so only a small fraction of the millions of Internet users is listed.

finger: A local user database server. The finger protocol allows remote users to query information about users on a specific host. This service distributes the information as locally as possible but addresses neither the problem of ensuring that everyone is listed nor that of finding the host a person uses.

netfind: A person locator. The netfind facility uses finger, SMTP, DNS, and other protocols to try to locate an electronic mail address, given keywords about a person and an organization. Netfind uses the structure of the Internet itself rather than the kind of separate database that WHOIS uses.

X.500: Directory and Name Service. X.500 is the ISO-OSI Directory and Name Service. It is implemented in several forms on the Internet.

Finding Files

Resource sharing protocols like FTP are very useful but only if you first know the resource's location.

archie: An archive index. Hundreds of gigabytes of information are available on the Internet by anonymous FTP. But how do you find the right anonymous FTP server? With **archie,** which polls thousands of FTP servers monthly, compiles a composite index, and makes that index accessible to users.

Prospero: Transparent anonymous FTP access. The Prospero protocol permits anonymous FTP servers to be used as if the files on them were local to the user's host. It also permits building both temporary and permanent classifications of files and directories.

Alex. **Alex** maps anonymous FTP accesses into a virtual filesystem that can then be mounted via NFS. It caches files, so that they do not need to be transferred every time they are accessed locally.

Finding Documents

Finding files is often not enough. Finding documents, or passages within documents, is often more useful.

WAIS: Wide Area Information Servers. WAIS (Wide Area Information Servers) is one approach to finding documents. WAIS supports keyword searches of arbitrary textual databases without requiring markup of the documents before searching.

Other. Some services that provide document location, such as Gopher and WWW, also act as general front ends to a variety of services, so we describe them in the next section.

Front Ends

Each resource discovery service has its strong points; unfortunately each also usually has a user interface and uses a different protocol. The same problem applies to the more traditional services, such as FTP and TELNET. Many resources are accessible only through TELNET to idiosyncratic, locally designed user interfaces; library catalogs are particularly notorious for this kind of gratuitous variation. The average user, however, just wants to find and use the resources. Fortunately, there are Internet services to address this problem of excess diversity.

Gopher: An interactive menu-oriented front end. So far, the most popular solution to finding diverse resources through diverse interfaces and protocols is Gopher. This service is sometimes called "duct tape for the Internet," because it glues together many other services. A Gopher server provides menus of resources for display by Gopher clients. Menu items can refer to other Gopher servers. Gopher also can call archie, WAIS, TELNET, or FTP, with appropriate parameters, so that the user does not have to do so.

Veronica: A Gopher server index. Given hundreds of Gopher servers, how do you know which one you want? You can walk through hierarchical menus from server to server until you stumble over the right one, or you can use Veronica. Veronica, available through Gopher, is an index of the names of Gopher servers, much as archie is an index of filenames.

WWW: World Wide Web. World Wide Web (WWW) is a networked hypertext protocol and user interface. It provides access to multiple services and documents like Gopher does but is more ambitious in its methods. WWW permits users to select words or phrases within a document that then retrieve other documents, in hypertext fashion. Unlike WAIS, WWW requires documents to have keywords marked with **Simplified Generic Markup Language (SGML).**

1.6   Naming

Most high-level Internet services require mapping of textual domain names to numeric IP addresses. This can be done using either the Domain Name System or the Network Information Service.

DNS: Domain Name System

The Internet Standard DNS (Domain Name System) maps host names, such as *tic.com,* to IP addresses, such as 192.135.128.129. DNS is also designed to map domain names to network resources other than IP addresses. It is the most widely distributed service in the Internet, and we describe it in detail in Chapter 4, *Registering Domain Names and IP Numbers* and Chapter 6, *Setting Up the Domain Name System.*

The DNS namespace is partitioned hierarchically into a tree. Redundant nameservers accept requests from clients to map resource names to resource values. Its protocol specifications define how DNS clients ask DNS servers for mappings and how DNS servers communicate with each other.

An organization without an IP connection can still arrange to have its domain recognized for exchange of mail with the Internet.

Table 1.4 Internet Service Classes.

Service Classes
resource discovery
communication   resource sharing
naming

NIS: Network Information Service

The NIS (Network Information Service) from Sun Microsystems provides another method of mapping domain names to addresses. It also can handle other mappings, such as user names to userids. It has some advantages over DNS on LANs but was not designed to deal with WANs. DNS, not NIS, should be used for domain nameservice across the Internet, and DNS is in fact required for that purpose.

1.7   Classes of Service

Naming supports communications and resource sharing services, which in turn support resource discovery services, as shown in Table 1.4. Actual services aren't as neatly delineated as the picture, but to build services we do need to start at the bottom of Table 1.4 and work up, as we do in this book. We discuss IP and other infrastructure first, in Chapter 5, then naming, in Chapter 6, then mail in Chapter 7 and news in Chapter 8, followed by security, in Chapter 9, and finally resource discovery services, in Chapter 10.

References

Leffler et al. 1989.   Leffler, Samuel J., McKusick, Marshall Kirk, Karels, Michael J., & Quarterman, John S., *The Design and Implementation of the 4.3BSD UNIX Operating System,* Addison-Wesley, Reading, MA (1989).

Lottor 1992.   Lottor, Mark, "Internet Growth (1981-1991); RFC1296," *Network Working Group Request for Comments* (RFC1296), Network Information Systems Center, SRI International (January 1992).

MIDS 1993.   MIDS, "Matrix Size Estimates for Spring 1993: FidoNet, UUCP, BITNET, and the Internet," *Matrix News* **3**(8), pp. 10-12, MIDS (August 1993).

Partridge 1991.   Partridge, Craig, "How Many Users are on the Internet," *Matrix News* **1**(3), p. 1, Matrix Information and Directory Services, Inc. (MIDS) (June 1991).

Quarterman 1992.   Quarterman, John S., "Sizes of Four Networks in the Matrix," *Matrix News* **2**(7), pp. 5–9, MIDS (July 1992).

Quarterman 1993.   Quarterman, John S., "What can businesses get out of the Internet?," *COMPUTERWORLD* (22 February 1993).

SRI 1992.   SRI, *Internet: Mailing Lists,* SRI International, Menlo Park, CA (1992).

CHAPTER 2

The Internet and Other Networks

Technology, social history, and politics are inextricably intertwined in networking, particularly in the Internet. To understand the Internet, you must know a little about its history, its protocols, and how it is related to other networks.

This chapter is organized in roughly historical order. We begin with the ARPANET, which was the predecessor of the Internet; we discuss packet switching technology in the same section. The TCP/IP protocols were developed to support the Internet, and the Internet protocol suite is commonly known by the name TCP/IP, after the names of the first two protocols developed; we describe the most basic TCP/IP protocols. We provide a brief history of the Internet, including some of its major backbone networks, such as NSFNET. We discuss how the Internet fits as part of the Matrix, describing FidoNet, UUCP, BITNET, and USENET in some detail. We end the chapter with a look at the Internet today, including a glance at some plans for the future, involving NREN, CIX, CoREN, NII, and GIX.

2.1 The ARPANET

Before the Internet, there was the ARPANET (1969–1990). The **Advanced Research Projects Agency (ARPA)** of the U.S. **Department of Defense (DoD)** created the ARPANET as an experiment in packet-switched computer networking [Quarterman 1990]. Although the ARPANET was the precursor to the Internet, the two are not the same. The first protocols used on the ARPANET were not TCP/IP; rather the TCP/IP protocols were invented using the ARPANET. The ARPANET, however, was the first transcontinental backbone network in the Internet. Decommissioned in 1990, it was made obsolete by the newer network technologies it in part helped create.

ARPANET Services

ARPA was funding supercomputers at a few research institutions and had many requests for more supercomputers at other locations. Rather than buying more supercomputers, the government considered a network that could permit researchers to access supercomputers remotely might be more cost-effective. The first four nodes of the ARPANET were communicating with each other by 1969. Resource sharing, in the form of remote login and file transfer, was thus one of the earliest goals of the ARPANET.

Electronic mail was not in the original plans for the ARPANET, although early forms of it on single timesharing computers had been around since the late 1960s. However, ARPANET researchers were distributed across several time zones, and soon tired of attempting to catch each other on the telephone to discuss their research. By 1972 or 1973, they had implemented distributed electronic mail across the network so that they could easily communicate across time zones without such telephone tag. Mail quickly became the most popular service on the ARPANET.

Researchers tend to work in groups, not pairs. Electronic mail permitted the user to supply multiple addresses to reach more than one person with the same message, but required the user to type each address in every time. To simplify group communications, ARPANET researchers invented techniques for supporting electronic mailing lists, so that groups of people could have ongoing discussions. Communications, in the form of mail and lists, was thus one of the earliest practical products of the ARPANET; some other early networks, such as CYCLADES, did not have these services [Quarterman 1990].

The combination of resource sharing (remote login and file transfer) and communication (mail and lists) made the ARPANET a convenient and useful platform and tool for collaboration. Researchers in many geographical locations could work on the same project at once. Convenient distributed collaboration was perhaps the most profound contribution of the ARPANET; a contribution the Internet has made much more widely available.

Surviving a Nuclear War

The ARPANET was a direct product of the Cold War. ARPA itself was formed in response to the launching of the Sputnik satellite by the Soviet Union in 1957. It was intended to ensure the U.S. got ahead in military research and stayed there. As DoD urgently wanted military command and control networks that could survive a nuclear war, ARPA was charged with inventing a technology that could get data to its destination reliably even if arbitrary parts of the network disappeared without warning as a result of a nuclear attack. Traditional telephone technology, called **circuit switching,** was considered too fragile for the purpose, because it involved allocation of cables, buffers, and other resources in a path between two communicating entities, as indicated in Fig. 2.1. Any of these resources could be destroyed in a war, breaking the connection, and requiring reconstruction of a path. Alternate paths might not be available, since circuit switching providers

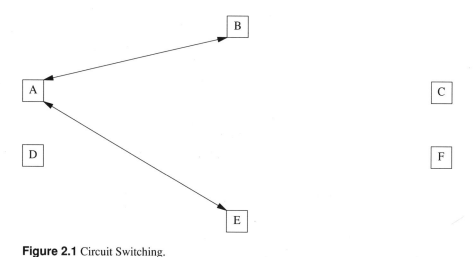

Figure 2.1 Circuit Switching.

tend to concentrate the underlying physical circuits (cables, satellite links, etc.) in order to save money. So the ARPANET used a different kind of technology, called **packet switching.** Packet switching was the most basic technological contribution of the ARPANET. Packet switching is also the basis of the protocols used in the Internet. To understand how TCP/IP works, you must understand the basics of packet switching.

Packet Switching

Readers familiar with TCP/IP will probably already know about packet switching. We place this discussion here for readers not familiar with the technology and terminology. In addition, some networking concepts have several current names, and some terms have several meanings, so we must define the terms used in this book. In the interest of brevity, we avoid discussing link-layer protocols such as Ethernet and packet radio, in favor of concepts directly related to TCP/IP, such as routing. In addition, in networking, technology is history and history is technology.

In packet switching, data to be sent over a network is divided into many discrete chunks of data, each usually not more than a few thousand bytes long and each called a **packet.** Each packet is self-contained and holds all the information required to send it to its final destination. Each packet is routed from one computer to the next across the network until it reaches its final destination. Dedicated computers are normally used to route packets from place to place, much like a smart relay; each of these computers is called a **router.**

Routers are connected to each other by a physical data carrier, such as a copper cable, a fiber optic cable, or a microwave relay. This physical connection between two routers is called a **link.** Each networked computer that people actually use directly is called a **host.** A host is connected to the network in the same way as a router is, except that a host usually has a single link to one network, while a router has several links to different networks. In the ARPANET, for example, each host was connected to a single local router, so the host needed to know only how to send data to the router; it wasn't involved in the packet routing decisions.

A networked computer that is not used directly by people but that provides some sort of service, such as providing large amounts of disk space, is called a **server.** The same machine can be both a host and a server, so for simplicity we will use the term host when we don't need to be more specific.

A general term for a computer that may be a router, host, or server is **node.** Each network node has an **address,** which is a type of identifier, usually numeric. (IP addresses actually identify interfaces of links to nodes, not the nodes themselves, but most nodes have only one interface, so let's ignore that distinction for the moment.) A node that wants to send a packet to another node uses the address of the destination node to tell the intervening routers where the packet should go. As a packet travels through the network, it traces a **path,** or **route,** among the nodes of the network. A router decides which link to send a packet on next.

Once data are divided into packets, the packets can be routed to their destinations in one of two ways: through virtual circuits or as datagrams.

Virtual Circuits. A **virtual circuit** is a connection that is established when one node begins to send packets to another node. All packets between the two nodes pass over the same route as long as that connection lasts, as indicated in Fig. 2.2. The figure shows two links selected from many in order to form a path between two nodes, E and B, going from E to A to B and back, with all traffic for the virtual circuit passing through that path in either direction. A host and a router are also labelled in the figure. The other nodes may be either routers or simply hosts or servers with more than one link. A protocol that implements a virtual circuit is

Figure 2.2 Virtual Circuit.

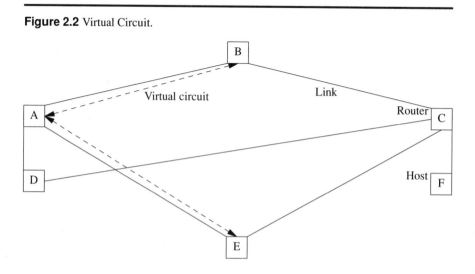

called a **connection-oriented protocol.** Virtual circuit technology and connection-oriented protocols have been advocated by large segments of industry, academia, and government worldwide, especially by telephone companies. This is the kind of technology used in X.25 and other **ISO (International Organization for Standardization) OSI (Open Systems Interconnection)** protocols, which we will discuss briefly in Chapter 3, *Types of Internet Access.*

Datagrams. However, a fast, efficient, dependable virtual circuit becomes none of those things when a node or link along its path fails, as either hardware circuit switching or virtual circuits will, particularly if failures are unpredictable in location, extent, or duration, as one would expect in a war. So ARPA chose to route packets individually, each as a datagram. A **datagram** is a packet with sufficient addressing information that it can be routed independently, as indicated in Fig. 2.3. The figure shows datagrams taking different paths at different times and in different directions. A protocol that uses datagrams without virtual circuits is called a **connectionless protocol.**

Intervening nodes don't usually allocate resources specific to datagrams traveling between a pair of nodes because any given packet might take a different route, thus bypassing a node that other packets traversed. This sounds inefficient, but it need not be. Packets can be rerouted for reasons other than node or link failures. For example, a link or node might become overloaded. A router then can choose to reroute some packets around the heavily loaded link. Use of datagrams thus permits load balancing throughout the network. This kind of dynamic reconfiguration is useful not only when nodes or links degrade or fail due to enemy action, but also when this occurs as a result either of ordinary hardware or software overloads or failures, or of simple human error. The ARPANET was mostly built out of datagram technology because of its inherent fault tolerance.

Figure 2.3 Datagrams.

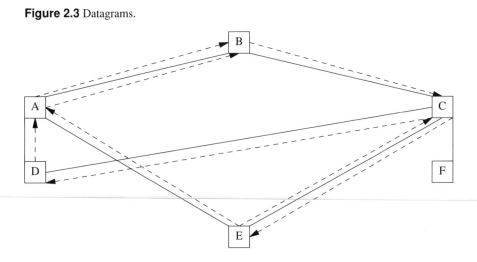

Connections or Datagrams?. Advocates of connection-oriented protocols with virtual circuits and advocates of connectionless protocols with datagrams have had an ongoing controversy for more than thirty years now. These adversaries have grouped themselves to some extent into two camps, around OSI and TCP/IP. The battle lines are not that simple, however. IP uses datagrams, but TCP implements a kind of virtual circuit over IP. Understanding the basic strategies of these protocols will help you in installing and administering them.

2.2   Internet Protocols

The basis of the Internet, and the most basic reason for its success, is its communication protocols. The Internet also uses other protocols, but it is primarily based on the **TCP/IP** (**Transmission Control Protocol / Internet Protocol**) protocol suite.

IP: (Internet Protocol)

There are more than 100 TCP/IP protocols, but the key one is the Internet Protocol (IP), which provides a uniform address space and routing across diverse underlying physical networks, including Ethernets, token rings, leased lines, and others.

Transport Protocols

IP attempts to get data to the intended destination, but does not make any guarantees about how much of the data arrives, when, or in what order. Different services have different needs for data delivery, so TCP/IP provides a class of transport protocols for use with IP. There are two main TCP/IP transport protocols: TCP and UDP.

TCP: Transmission Control Protocol. When you use remote login, you want every character you type to arrive on the remote machine in the order you typed it, and you want every character sent from the remote machine to reach you across the Internet. When you transfer a file, you do not want to lose pieces of the program, document, or other information the file contains, and you do not want duplicate information. The transport protocol for these situations is TCP (Transmission Control Protocol). TCP provides a reliable two-way byte stream and is the most popular transport protocol. It's used by mail, file transfer, and remote login protocols. It ensures that bytes are delivered reliably, in order, and without duplication. TCP is a connection-oriented protocol, since it establishes a virtual circuit for transmitting data between two processes.

UDP: User Datagram Protocol. Voice and video services need speed much more than they need every piece of data to arrive in exactly the order it was sent, and even if some data do not arrive these services will experience only a transient imperfection that the user will hardly notice. Occasional static is preferable than slow video or doppler-shifted sound. Other services want to send an occasional information request and get one response back each time; such a service may be willing to try again if it receives no answer. The transport protocol for these kinds of services is UDP (User Datagram Protocol). UDP is an unreliable datagram protocol and is deliberately rudimentary. The standard Internet name service, DNS, uses UDP, as do some transparent file access mechanisms. Packets sent with UDP may arrive out of order, more than once, or not at all. One process uses UDP to send datagrams to another process, and the receiving process uses UDP to retrieve messages that survive passage across the Internet. UDP is a connectionless protocol, which does not establish virtual circuits. It is especially useful on networks that are reliable without further protocol help, for services that do their own error recovery, and for services such as voice and video where speed is more important than extreme reliability.

TCP/IP Implementations

TCP/IP is implemented for almost every computer platform and thus can support a very high degree of interoperability between computers and software of the same or different types. This flexibility, together with the services provided and the sheer size of the Internet, permits and promotes collaboration among users. This collaboration is the main benefit of the Internet. Users can be full participants, providing information rather than just consuming it, and cooperating with other users to produce joint outcomes more effectively than each user alone could.

2.3   Internet History

The Internet evolved from the ARPANET, and sometimes people still confuse the ARPANET with the Internet. This confusion results probably because the ARPANET was the first backbone network of the early Internet and remained a part of the Internet until it was retired in 1990. But the Internet has always interconnected other networks and other kinds of networks.

Early Internet Experiments

New networking technologies, such as Ethernet and packet radio, were developed by industry and government during the 1970s. In 1973, **Defense Advanced Research Projects Agency (DARPA)** (as ARPA had been renamed; the D was dropped again in early 1993) began a research program to investigate techniques and technologies for interconnecting various kinds of packet networks. DARPA wanted protocols that could tie together networks built out of these various technologies so that they would appear to participating computers as a single virtual network: an **internet.** This was called the Internetting project, and the main internet that resulted from it was called **the Internet** [Cerf 1992a].

The first workable system was demonstrated in 1977. This first implementation of the Internet involved four networks: a packet satellite network, a packet radio network, the ARPANET, and an Ethernet at the XEROX research center in Palo Alto, California [Cerf 1992b].

Although the TCP/IP protocols and the Internet built from them are usually associated with the U.S. research community, this research has never been limited to one country. Norway and the United Kingdom were connected from the earliest days of IP development, and considerable technical input for IP and TCP came from France and the United Kingdom. For example, the original TCP retransmission algorithm was known as the **RSRE (Royal Signals and Radar Establishment)** algorithm, after the organization in the United Kingdom that developed it [Partridge 1992].

The Early Internet

By 1983, the ARPANET had become so successful that DARPA no longer considered it experimental and so passed operational control of it to the **Defense Communications Agency (DCA),** now known as the **Defense Information Systems Agency (DISA).** A nonexperimental internet known as the ARPA Internet began in January, 1983, when DCA required all nodes to use TCP/IP. Simultaneously, DCA mandated the split of the original ARPANET into two networks: ARPANET (for continued research) and MILNET (for military operations).

Much of the early popularity of TCP/IP can be traced to the implementation of the TCP/IP protocols in the **4.2BSD (Fourth.2 Berkeley Software Distribution)** version of the UNIX operating system. 4.2BSD was funded in part by DARPA to develop an operating system to serve as a research platform. Other funding came from the State of California, since 4.2BSD was developed at the **University of California at Berkeley (UCB)** by its **Computer Systems Research Group (CSRG).** Because of the public source of its funding, 4.2BSD was made available at the cost of its distribution and so its use spread quickly. Coincidentally, the 4.2BSD implementation became available at the same time as inexpensive microprocessors such as the Motorola 680x0 series and the Intel 80x86 chip sets. Both startup and established companies took advantage of the combination of available software and hardware to build systems, mainly workstations, incorporating both the newly available inexpensive processors and 4.2BSD. Consequently, the development of UNIX and TCP/IP became intimately intertwined.

The operating system used on most Internet hosts is probably UNIX, but the Internet is not a UNIX network. TCP/IP is implemented on nearly every known operating system, and computers running most such operating systems are connected to the Internet; in particular, there are large numbers of MS-DOS and Macintosh machines.

As mentioned previously, ARPANET and MILNET were the two early transcontinental national backbones in the developing Internet. Others were added by government agencies such as the **National Aeronautics and Space Agency (NASA).** As the participation of other government agencies increased, the name of this composite internet changed from ARPA Internet to the Federal Research Internet to TCP/IP Internet and finally to its current name of just the Internet.

NSFNET

In 1984, **National Science Foundation (NSF)** established an office for networking and implemented several versions of its NSFNET national backbone network: in 1986 (DS-0, 56Kbps), 1988 (T-1, 1.544Mbps), and 1990 (T-3, 45Mbps). In addition to NSFNET, NSF provided seed money for the NSFNET mid-level networks that are commonly known as the NSFNET regionals. These regional networks (now all mostly self-supporting) provide extensive connectivity for campus networks at educational institutions, government agencies, and commercial businesses.

Meanwhile, interexchange carriers and telephone companies had laid many miles of fiber optic cable, causing fiber optic bandwidth to become much more available and much less expensive. The NSFNET backbone, the regionals, and other networks took advantage of this availability of higher speeds. High bandwidth wide area networks thus became much less expensive to build and as a result more of them were built.

Internet Growth, Again

All these factors combined to produce exponential growth of the Internet:

- The reference implementation of TCP/IP in the 4.2BSD version of the UNIX operating system in 1983 (later updated in 4.3BSD and 4.4BSD). This reference implementation became the basis for all subsequent implementations of TCP/IP on machines ranging from PCs to supercomputers.

- Inexpensive microprocessors (available beginning around 1983). These made possible relatively low-cost workstations and increased the demand for distributed computing.

- Inexpensive long distance fiber-optic bandwidth (available beginning around 1984). This made high-speed wide area networking more affordable and practical.

- The NSFNET backbone and regional networks (beginning in 1986). These became the first wide area network infrastructure.

- The deployment of DNS (in 1986). This allowed the distribution of resource naming on a large scale.

None of these factors was enough alone to cause rapid growth. However, all came together in about 1986, thus causing the Internet to grow exponentially.

2.4   The Internet and the Matrix

The Internet is not the only computer network in the world. It is related to, and often confused with, several other networks. The ARPANET became so popular and useful to researchers that several networks, such as CSNET, BITNET, UUCP, USENET, and FidoNet, sprang up partly in imitation of it. In this section, we explain how the Internet is related to and differs from these networks.

Electronic Mail

The most basic and widely implemented computer network service is electronic mail. It is the characteristic service of the Matrix, which is all computer networks that exchange mail. Given mail, it is a long conceptual step but a short technical step to implementing mailing lists for ongoing discussions among a relatively stable group of people. We discussed in the section on the ARPANET how both these services were invented on the ARPANET.

Many networks do not have resource sharing, since it usually requires an interactive connection. This is a major reason that communications services, especially mail, are so important. In addition, mail is perhaps simply the most generally useful network service.

CSNET. CSNET (Computer Science Network) was established in January, 1981, to facilitate research and advanced development in computer science and engineering by providing a means for increased collaboration among people working in those fields. Most CSNET hosts didn't use TCP/IP; instead, many were connected by telephone dialup protocols that permitted essentially only one service: mail. Because they had mail, they could also use ARPANET mailing lists.

BITNET. BITNET (Because It's Time Network) was formed in May 1981 and uses the **Network Job Entry (NJE)** protocol and software that had been developed by IBM employees for internal use, principally as a part of the VM/370 operating system. The most common implementation of NJE is **Remote Spooling Communications Subsystem (RSCS).** RSCS and NJE are often confused, and people frequently say RSCS when they mean NJE, since many people know of no other implementation of NJE.

NJE supports several services, including mail, sending files, and relaying brief interactive messages. BITNET, like CSNET, interconnects mostly universities. But while CSNET tended to go to computer science departments, BITNET usually links computer centers. In 1989, BITNET and CSNET merged administratively under the name **Corporation for Research and Education Networking (CREN)** and CSNET was subsequently retired when the NSFNET regionals subsumed its function. BITNET and CREN continue, however. There are other NJE networks in other parts of the world, such as the **European Academic and Research Network (EARN)** in Europe, GULFNET in the Arabian Gulf countries, BITNET-J in Japan, and NetNorth in Canada. These NJE networks all use a common node list and exchange services with one another, forming a worldwide network that we call, for lack of a better name, BITNET [Quarterman 1992a].

UUCP. The UUCP mail network began in its earliest form in 1978. Named after its protocol, **UNIX to UNIX CoPy (UUCP),** which was first distributed with **UNIX Seventh Edition** in 1978, it since has come packaged with most versions of UNIX. UUCP is usually used over ordinary dialup telephone lines and is therefore very inexpensive to implement; all you need is a phone line and a modem. Under favorable conditions and with similar versions of UNIX, you can actually transfer files through several UUCP links. However, the only service you can really depend on getting through the UUCP network is mail.

USENET. USENET (Users' Network), began in 1979. It isn't really a network. Instead, USENET is all computers that carry USENET news. Originally, USENET was carried solely over UUCP. USENET and UUCP are often confused, but they are not the same. USENET news is currently also carried over BITNET, FidoNet, the Internet, and probably other networks. Most USENET hosts are now on the Internet. Newsgroups were invented in imitation of ARPANET mailing lists; however, they are much more efficient and can reach much larger groups of people.

FidoNet. FidoNet was invented in 1983 to connect computers running the MS-DOS operating system. It uses the **Fido** protocols, which have many of the functions of UUCP but which are, in comparison, completely different internally and more efficient. The name, Fido, is not an acronym; it is a common pet name for a family dog. The network was intended to reach the masses with their personal computers. Fido, like UUCP, usually is used for telephone dialup connections, although either Fido or UUCP can be used over dedicated connections [Quarterman 1992b].

FidoNet was invented somewhat in imitation of UUCP and USENET, which were invented somewhat in imitation of the ARPANET, so the ARPANET has at least one unexpected grandchild.

DNS. The Internet also is often confused with the hosts and networks that use the Internet Domain Name System (DNS), which defines and implements domain names like *tic.com,* so that (among other functions) mail to addresses like *tic@tic.com* works.

DNS is intended primarily to map between domain names and IP addresses for use by machines that are directly connected to the Internet. The deployment of DNS in 1986 was important because it freed the Internet from dependence on the old centralized ARPANET host table that had previously been used to map hostnames to addresses. However, DNS also can support domain names for machines that are not on the Internet. For such a machine, DNS can provide a domain name of a **mail forwarder** that *is* on the Internet and that knows how to reach the machine that is *not* on the Internet. The forwarder may send the mail on to its destination by UUCP, FidoNet, or some other means; the sending host and user doesn't have to know or care how.

DNS names are widely used on UUCP, BITNET, FidoNet, and other networks. One name for all computers that use DNS names and that interchange mail is the **DNS Mail System.** Although the DNS Mail System is closely related to the Internet, it is not the Internet. It is larger, and many of the hosts on it cannot provide Internet services such as FTP for file transfer or TELNET for remote login. Another name sometimes used is the **Internet Mail System;** however, this name is too easily confused with the Internet itself. Such confusion leads people on mail-only networks to expect Internet services, such as FTP or TELNET, that they can't get.

The Matrix

The existence of all these networks can create confusion, but each has its own niche and each serves a purpose [Quarterman 1991]. All, taken together, plus other networks and computers, form the Matrix. The Matrix consists of all inter-connected computer networks that exchange mail.

Figure 2.4 The Matrix.
Adapted from Quarterman, "Matrix Size Estimates for Spring 1993," Matrix News, *Vol. 3, No. 8, MIDS, Austin, mids@tic.com, August 1993. Copyright © 1993 MIDS.*
Reprinted with permission.

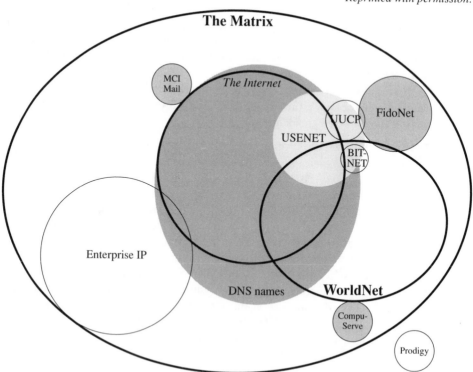

The Internet is often confused with the Matrix. The Internet is the largest and perhaps the fastest growing network in the Matrix, but it is not the Matrix, which also includes UUCP, FidoNet, BITNET, thousands of enterprise IP networks within corporations, and numerous other entities [MIDS 1993]. Figure 2.4 shows the relative sizes of some of these networks according to estimates of their numbers of users as of April 1993 (the numbers for MCI Mail, CompuServe, and Prodigy are arbitrarily and generously set to 500,000 each). As you can see, the Internet is by far the largest of these networks. The figure is a Venn diagram, and shows approximately the amounts of overlap among the networks shown. For example, USENET is shown partly on top of FidoNet, UUCP, BITNET, and especially the Internet. The large dark shaded ellipse indicates networks that use DNS domain names. It covers not only all of the Internet, but also parts of UUCP, BITNET, and enterprise IP networks. An **enterprise IP network** is a TCP/IP network inside a corporation that is used for the business of the corporation. The lighter shading on FidoNet, MCI Mail, and CompuServe indicates examples of systems that can be reached by DNS addresses, such as *f13.n7.z1.fidonet.org*, *123-4576@mcimail.com,* or *987-6543@compuserve.com,* but which do not use DNS names internally. The WorldNet ellipse indicates the diminishing proportion of these networks that are noncommercial; all of BITNET is still within it, but less of everything else. The Matrix ellipse indicates systems that exchange mail. Most major conferencing systems have moved within it by setting up mail links with the outside world. Prodigy still has not, as of this writing, and thus is shown outside.

A host or network that can only exchange mail is in the Matrix but is not on the Internet. To be on the Internet, a host or network must have direct interactive IP connectivity to the Internet. Put another way, if you can FTP to a host or network known to be on the Internet, such as *is.internic.net, ftp.psi.com,* or *ftp.uu.net,* your host is also **on the Internet.** If you can't do that, but you can send mail to one of those hosts, your host is not on the Internet, but it is still **in the Matrix.**

Some of the other networks in the Matrix are gradually being absorbed by the Internet. All of the following are now carried over the Internet:

- Most USENET news traffic (although much is still carried over UUCP, FidoNet, and BITNET)

- The backbone of BITNET in the U.S.

- Large parts of some other NJE networks, such as EARN

- Some FidoNet traffic across the Atlantic [Barron 1992]

- Most mail traffic to the outside world from some whole national segments of the UUCP network

FidoNet and UUCP have become access networks that reach new countries, regions, and classes of users that cannot yet afford Internet connectivity. The Internet has become the core and main support of the Matrix [MIDS 1993].

2.5   The Internet Now

The Internet has no overall organizational, financial, political, or operational authority. Instead, the Internet is operated in some loose sense by a federation of organizations, each with its own operational arm.

The policy body for the Internet moved from ARPA to a succession of committees of government agencies. Partly due to its funding for NSFNET, NSF has taken a leading role in setting policy for the Internet in the U.S. since the mid-1980s. Each major federal agency or departmental network has its own usage and other policies set by its sponsoring organizations. ARPA, **DOE (Department of Energy),** NASA, **NIH (National Institutes of Health),** and NSF participate in the **Federal Networking Council (FNC),** which is the coordinating body for Internet-related issues in the federal government.

NSFNET is the most prominent of the backbones with policies set by the U.S. government. Approximately a dozen regional networks connect to it, while thousands more local networks at companies, universities, and agencies connect to the regionals. There also are several other national backbones, such as PSINet, Alter-Net, and ANSnet. Most of these are not run by the government. In addition, other backbones, such as **EBONE (European Backbone)** in Europe or **WIDE (Widely Integrated Distributed Environment)** in Japan, are not controlled by the U.S. government, although some of them might be related to governments in other countries.

Although much of the early technical and organization work in the Internet and its predecessor, the ARPANET, was funded by the U.S. government, the Internet itself has grown far beyond being just a government sponsored entity of the U.S or any other country. It is growing fastest in private companies, and in other countries. Most of it consists of thousands of local, metropolitan, state or provincial, regional, and national networks that are owned and operated by a diverse array of corporations, universities, networking companies, nongovernmental organizations, and governments. In some regions, there are coordinating bodies, such as **Reseaux IP Européens (RIPE)** in Europe. RIPE was at one point part of **Reseaux Associés pour la Recerche Européenne (RARE),** which is itself affiliated with the **European Commission (EC).** In some countries, there is a national governmental lead organization, such as that for the national backbone network CA*net in Canada. But no single organization or group of organizations has overall responsibility for the worldwide Internet.

TCP/IP Specifications

The specifications for TCP/IP are written by the **IETF (Internet Engineering Task Force),** which is overseen by the **IAB (Internet Architecture Board),** that was called the **Internet Activities Board (IAB)** until June 1992. The IAB is in turn affiliated with the **Internet Society (ISOC),** a nonprofit professional society See Fig. 2.5.

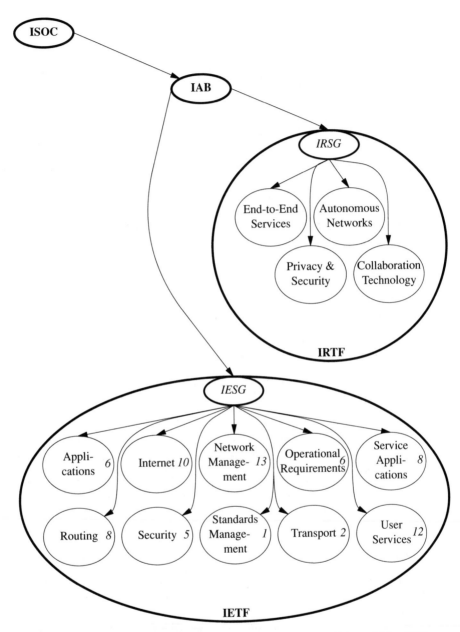

Figure 2.5 Internet working bodies, with working groups per IETF Area, 3 May 1993.
From Quarterman and Wilhelm, UNIX, POSIX, *and Open Systems, The Open Standards Puzzle, Reading, MA: Addison-Wesley Publishing Company, Inc.* © *1993.*
Reprinted with permission.

The IETF produces a set of working documents, each called an **RFC (Request for Comment).** Some RFCs really are just requests for comments or informational documents, but others pass through the **IAB Standards Process** [Chapin 1992; Quarterman & Wilhelm 1993] to become **Internet Standards.** There are Internet Standards for all the basic TCP/IP protocols, and a periodical list of them [Postel 1992].

RFCs are produced, often in conjunction with working protocol implementations, by IETF **WGs (Working Groups).** These Working Groups are grouped into Areas, and the chairs of the Areas, along with a few other people, form the **IESG (Internet Engineering Steering Group).** The IESG also includes the RFC Editor, who publishes RFCs.

There is also an **IRTF (Internet Research Task Force)** that studies subjects more abstract or speculative than would be appropriate for the IETF. The IRTF has an **IRSG (Internet Research Steering Group)** consisting mostly of the chairs of IRSG Areas.

It is important to remember that none of these bodies are responsible for *operating* the Internet. Instead they are concerned with protocols and technical policy.

Research and Educational Usage

The successor to NSFNET, at least for research purposes, will be the **National Research and Education Network (NREN).** Although the NREN was authorized by the U.S. Congress in the **High Performance Computing Act (HPCA)** of December 1991, there has been much discussion about exactly what it should be used for [Kahin 1992]. Researchers want to build a very fast backbone network and were allocated funds to do so. Educators and librarians want much wider access to the existing Internet but were not allocated much money for this purpose. Meanwhile, interest increases in using the Internet in classrooms [Itzkan 1992; McKinney 1993], and in classroom teaching of how to use the Internet itself [Tennant *et al.* 1993]. The Clinton administration has apparently settled on the small research model for NREN, according to the solicitation put out by NSF for it [Carl-Mitchell 1993].

Commercial Use

The Internet reaches many organizations and people beyond its original research and educational base [Malamud 1992]. Perhaps as much as half of the Internet is already owned by commercial companies. If you want access to the Internet, the chances are you will get it from a commercial provider. In this section we discuss historical aspects of some providers. We some of the same providers and others in Chapter 3, *Types of Internet Access*, and a more complete list, with contact information, appears in Appendix A, *Internet Providers*.

Commercial Internet connectivity providers include the following:

- Advanced Network and Services (ANS),
- CO+RE (COmmercial plus Research and Educational) (an ANS for-profit sub-sidiary),
- The members of the Commercial Internet Exchange (CIX).

The original CIX members were:

- UUNET Technologies (UUNET), which runs AlterNet
- Performance Systems International (PSI), which runs PSINet
- California Education and Research Foundation (CERF), which runs CERFnet

Other current U.S. CIX members include the following:

- San Francisco Bay Area Regional Research Network (BARRNet)
- New England Academic and Research network (NEARnet)
- John von Neuman Computer Center Network (JvNCNet)
- NorthWestNet
- Texas Higher Education network (THEnet)
- World dot Net
- SprintLink (run by U.S. Sprint)

Many of the U.S. CIX members have customers outside the United States, and members based in other countries include the following:

- Pipex (run by UniPalm Ltd) in the United Kingdom
- Demon Internet Systems (DIS) in the United Kingdom
- EUnet (European UNIX network), which provides Internet access throughout Europe
- Nordic carriers
- Hong Kong Supernet (HKS)

Many large corporations have become increasingly interested in networking in the past few years, and some have proposed a **National Information Infrastructure (NII)** to be funded by those corporations and others. Many interesting political issues remain to be solved; for example, if local connections to the NII are provided by television cable companies, which are often local monopolies, how is the traditional Internet flexibility of access and usage to be maintained?

CoREN (Corporation for Regional and Enterprise Networking) was formed in 1993 by the eight regional networks BARRNet, CICNet, MIDnet, NEARnet, NorthWestNet, NYSERNet, SURAnet, and WestNet "to provide nationwide TCP/IP data networking services, including connections to the Internet and to the NSFNet national backbone, to the business, higher education and research communities." Their initial method of doing this was to select MCI to provide IP connectivity [CoREN 1993]. It is interesting to note that, while MCI is a primary participant in ANS in providing the NSFNET backbone service, CoREN has no NSF funding. It appears that the regional networks participating in CoREN have taken the initiative in building part of the NII without government support.

Other industry networking projects include **EInet (Enterprise Integration Network)** of **MCC (Microelectronics and Computer Corporation).** EInet is intended to help solve problems above the bare connectivity level, such as exchanging private information across open networks between companies that have deliberately limited access to their internal enterprise networks.

Most of the initiatives mentioned above are from within the United States. On a larger scale, there is the question of how to improve the current situation of most intercontinental traffic going through the U.S., and much of it through the NSFNET backbone, even for traffic that is not destined for the U.S. A **Global Internet Exchange (GIX)** has been discussed, but not yet implemented. Such a GIX would permit exchanging traffic between, for example, Japan and Germany without traversing the United States.

Most of the Internet has no volume charges. Unlike commercial X.25 networks, you do not normally pay per byte or message for Internet traffic. Instead, you pay a local connectivity provider for some sort of local access, and the local provider takes care of interconnections with the rest of the Internet. If you want a big file, you just transfer it, without worrying about a huge bill at the end of the month. Most Internet users and probably most Internet connectivity providers want to preserve this feature of the Internet.

In addition, many traditional Internet services are free of charge. Some of them will continue to be free, since Internet users often become information providers, thus providing a large pool of information of mutual benefit to all Internet participants. Others will begin to require payment, and new commercial services will be added, thus increasing the number and quality of services available over the Internet.

References

Barron 1992.   Barron, Billy, "Tunneling Through the Internet with Gopher," *Matrix News* **2**(2), p. 4, MIDS (February 1992).

Carl-Mitchell 1993.   Carl-Mitchell, Smoot, "NSF NREN Solicitation," *Matrix News* **3**(8), p. 13, MIDS (August 1993).

Cerf 1992a.   Cerf, Vinton G., "A Brief History of the Internet and Related Networks," Internet Society (ISOC), Reston, VA (1992).

Cerf 1992b.   Cerf, Vinton G., Personal communication (March 1992).

Chapin 1992.   Chapin, Lyman, "The Internet Standards Process; RFC1310," *Network Working Group Requests for Comments* (RFC1310), Network Information Systems Center, SRI International (March 1992).

CoREN 1993.   CoREN, "CoREN Selects MCI to Join Forces on National Information Infrastructure Initiatives," CoREN, Washington, D.C. and Ann Arbor, Michigan (1 June 1993).

Itzkan 1992.   Itzkan, Seth J., "How Big is the Global Classroom?," *Matrix News* **2**(10), pp. 1,7-8, MIDS (October 1992).

Kahin 1992.   Kahin, Brian ed., *Building Information Infrastructure: Issues in the Development of the National Research and Education Network,* McGraw-Hill, Inc. (1992).

Malamud 1992.   Malamud, Carl, *Exploring the Internet: A Technical Travelogue,* Prentice-Hall, Englewood Cliffs, NJ (August 1992).

McKinney 1993.   McKinney, Eric, "High School Internetworking," *Matrix News* **3**(7), pp. 1,12-13, MIDS (July 1993).

MIDS 1993.   MIDS, "Matrix Size Estimates for Spring 1993: FidoNet, UUCP, BITNET, and the Internet," *Matrix News* **3**(8), pp. 10-12, MIDS (August 1993).

Partridge 1992.   Partridge, Craig, Personal communication (August–November 1988 and February 1992).

Postel 1992.   Postel, Jon ed., "IAB Official Protocol Standards; STD-1/RFC-1360," *Network Working Group Requests for Comments* (STD-1/RFC-1360), Network Information Systems Center, SRI International (September 1992).

Quarterman 1990.   Quarterman, John S., *The Matrix: Computer Networks and Conferencing Systems Worldwide,* Digital Press, Bedford, MA (1990).

Quarterman 1991.   Quarterman, John S., "Which Network, and Why It Matters," *Matrix News* **1**(5), p. 6–13, Matrix Information and Directory Services, Inc. (MIDS) (August 1991).

Quarterman 1992a.   Quarterman, John S., "Where is BITNET? ," *Matrix News* **2**(10), pp. 3-7, MIDS (October 1992).

Quarterman 1992b.   Quarterman, John S., "Where is FidoNet?," *Matrix News* **2**(6), pp. 7-9, MIDS (June 1992).

Quarterman & Wilhelm 1993.   Quarterman, John S., & Wilhelm, Susanne, *UNIX, POSIX, and Open Systems: The Open Standards Puzzle,* Addison-Wesley, Reading, MA (1993).

Tennant et al. 1993.   Tennant, Roy, Ober, John, Lipow, Anne G., & Lynch, Foreword by Clifford, *Crossing the Internet Threshold: an Instructional Handbook*, 1993.

CHAPTER 3

Types of Internet Access

In this chapter we discuss methods of connecting to the Internet. These access methods are among the basic membership criteria for joining the Internet community. Many of them have not been written down coherently before now.

Types of access to the Internet range from public hosts by modem dialup to direct fiber optic connections at hundreds of megabits per second. These many ways of connecting to the Internet can be confusing, because they involve different organizations, technical methods, pricing methods, and acceptable use policies. Also, some access methods do not actually connect to the Internet, so we need to separate those out.

In this chapter we first give an overview of access types. We categorize them in several ways, including the following:

• As full Internet services (interactive IP connections) or not

• As dialup or not

• By speed

Because types of connections often have to do with network layers, we review network layering. Then we describe advantages and disadvantages of each access type, and kinds of access providers for each type. Finally, we include a note on acceptable use policies.

3.1 Overview of Access Types

Figure 3.1 summarizes the types of access we deal with in this chapter. We emphasize that we have drawn up these categories to clarify the range of choices available to you; real access methods might not fit any of them exactly.

	Matrix Access		Internet Access		
	mailnet[1]	conf[2]	Login Host	Dialup IP	Full IP
Services					
mail:	yes	yes	yes	yes	yes
news:	yes	maybe	yes	yes	yes
FTP:	no	no	yes	yes	yes
interactive:	no	no	yes	yes	yes
Methods					
IP to:	gateway	gateway	login host	your machine	your machine
dialup:	yes	yes	yes	yes	or dedicated
speed:	modem	modem	modem	modem	modem up
cost:	*	*, †	*	*	monthly

mailnet[1]	mail and news only, as in UUCP or FidoNet
conf[2]	conferencing system with mail and news access
*	monthly + connect time charges
†	per message charges

Figure 3.1 Access Types.

Matrix Access

The two categories of Matrix Access in Fig. 3.1, mailnet and conf, put you in the Matrix of systems that exchange mail, but they do not put you on the Internet. You can send and receive electronic mail and often either USENET news or something like it, but you can't use interactive Internet services such as FTP. The mailnet category is for networks like UUCP and FidoNet that provide only mail and news, while the conf category is for conferencing systems such as CompuServe, GEnie, BIX, etc., that provide various conferencing and database services but whose only external network connectivity is mail or news. Once you're in the Matrix, you can participate fully in mail, mailing lists and possibly USENET news. But you can't use or provide any other Internet services directly. Some Internet services (for example, FTP, archie, and WAIS) are accessible indirectly and slowly through electronic mail, but the result is only a shadow of the full service. Even mail service tends to be slower, and sometimes more expensive, if you do not have actual Internet access.

If you already have access to the Matrix through a mail network or conferencing system, you can explore some of what the Internet has to offer by using mail, and you can be at least a peripheral participant in the Internet community. If you don't have any network access now, you might want to try one of these methods of Matrix-only connectivity to start with before joining the Internet.

Internet Access

The three categories of Internet Access in Fig. 3.1 provide, as the name implies, actual Internet access. To have access, you must be able to log in on a host on the Internet, that is, a host that has IP access. Then you can use interactive Internet services such as TELNET, FTP, archie, WAIS, and Gopher. Differences among these types of actual Internet access are based on the following criteria:

• Whether it is your computer or another one you call that has the Internet access

• Speed

• Cost of access

Once you decide to actually connect, you will also need to know technical details about which protocols at which levels are required.

• To use a login host, you need little more than a modem and some common modem file transfer software, such as Kermit.

• To do dialup IP, you will need an IP implementation on your system; this implementation must have dialup capability.

• For full Internet connectivity you may need to set up more software on your system; most of the rest of this book describes how to do this.

A Spectrum of Access

So Fig. 3.1 shows a spectrum of participation in the Internet community, from peripheral participation through Matrix-only access on the left, with types of access that do not put you on the Internet, to full participation on the right, with types of access that do put you on the Internet.

Within the types of Internet access shown, there is a further subspectrum of degrees involving what you can *provide* yourself. With Internet access through a login host, you can sometimes provide some services such as mailing lists. With full Internet connectivity, you can run your own FTP, archie, WAIS, Gopher, or other server, thus becoming a participant in the fullest sense by providing services as well as consuming them.

You can choose a type of access from this spectrum that suits your interests and your financial commitment and needs. You are not limited to one type, either; you can move to another type of access or even use different types depending on where you are or what you are doing at the moment.

3.2   Overview of Internet Protocols

We've tried teaching network services and access methods without mentioning protocol layers, and we're convinced it's not possible. Communications systems are complex collections of cooperating software and hardware. To aid in understanding these systems, network practitioners have developed standard ways to model these systems and break them down into simpler pieces. We present here a very quick refresher on layers and protocols. For more, the reader should refer to [Carl-Mitchell & Quarterman 1993].

Reference Models

A **reference model** is a model that is used to explain how the various components of a system fit together and to explain what the common interface specifications are between the components. For example, a video system has a reference model so that video components like cameras, VCRs, and monitors can work together. Things like video tape formats must be described, so that different manufacturers' equipment can work together.

Figure 3.2 Protocol Models and Layers.
From Quarterman and Wilhelm, UNIX, POSIX, and Open Systems, The Open Standards Puzzle, *Reading, MA: Addison-Wesley Publishing Company, Inc. © 1993.*
Reprinted with permission.

ISO-OSI Model			Internet Model	User Model
7	Application		Process	Network
6	Presentation		/	
5	Session		Applications	Applications
4	Transport		Transport	Network
3	Network	internet	Internet	
		convergence	Network	
		subnet		
2	Data Link		Link	Infrastructure
1	Physical		Physical	

Similarly, in networking there are the TCP/IP and OSI reference models, among others; see Fig. 3.2. The Basic Reference Model for **Open Systems Interconnection (OSI)**, or OSI Model, was specified by the **International Organization for Standardization (ISO)**. ISO also specifies protocols in a protocol suite to fit the model. Several of the OSI protocols were originally specified by **CCITT (International Consultative Committee on Telegraphy and Telephony)**, which also has adopted the OSI Model [Rose 1989].

The Internet Reference Model is described in a few articles [Cerf & Cain 1983; Cerf & Kahn 1974]. Protocols to fit the model are specified in Internet Standards [Postel 1992; Braden & Postel 1987; Braden 1989a; Braden 1989b].

The OSI model is more widely cited in academic journals; however, the TCP/IP protocols are the more widely used. In this book, we discuss only the TCP/IP protocols and the Internet model.

Layers

In an attempt to reduce conceptual complexity, models divide protocols into layers. A protocol in a given layer can be described by the services it provides to the next higher layer and by the services it uses from the next lower layer. Protocols don't have to be implemented in separate program modules for each layer (although they often are); layering is a conceptual aid, not an implementation directive. OSI has seven layers (more or less), while TCP/IP has five (more or less). Yet each protocol model accomplishes similar ends.

The physical layer is essentially the same in both models. It can use anything from twisted-pair cable or fiber optics to point-to-point radio or satellite links. Most wide-area physical links in the Internet are probably copper cable or fiber optic dedicated lines provided by **Inter-Exchange Carriers (IXCs)**, which you may know as long-distance telephone companies. In Europe, such companies were traditionally national monopolies, similar to what AT&T used to be in the United States, but often including other communication services. The usual term for such a company is **Post, Telephone, and Telegraph (PTT)**.

Many machines are connected to networks that use CSMA/CD, token ring, or token bus technology. IEEE 802 standards govern communication at this level. ISO has the corresponding IS 8802 standards. IETF (see Chapter 2, *The Internet and Other Networks*) working groups may produce interface or management specifications for these media-level protocols, but they do not normally specify the latter directly. The one exception so far is the **Point-to-Point Protocol (PPP)**.

We will encounter one OSI protocol several times in the discussion in this chapter: X.25, the CCITT datalink and network layer protocol. It can be used below IP; however, we encounter it most frequently in **Public Data Networks (PDNs)**, which are networks intended to provide host-to-host connectivity for remote login. Such PDNs are provided sometimes by IXCs and sometimes by specialized companies.

Table 3.1 TCP/IP Layers.

Layer	Examples
Process/Applications	TELNET, FTP, SMTP
Transport	TCP
Internet	IP
Network	X.25, Ethernet, FDDI
Physical	various

TCP/IP Layers

The TCP/IP protocols have several traditional layers within the Internet model, as shown in Table 3.1 and described as follows:

Process/Applications   Provides application services to users and programs.

Transport   Handles data consistency functions. TCP and UDP are transport layer protocols. TCP provides a reliable byte stream over a connection between two processes, ensures that data arrives, and ensures it arrives in order and without errors. UDP makes an effort to deliver datagrams but doesn't ensure order or prevent packet loss or duplication. Most TCP/IP applications, such as TELNET and FTP, use TCP. However, some, such as voice and video, use UDP, since for such applications, fast delivery is more important than consistency.

Internet   The key layer. It has one protocol: the Internet Protocol (IP). IP provides many of the same functions as the network layer does, such as addressing and routing. However, it provides them and a common address space across multiple lower-layer network protocols, thus permitting the construction of internets.

Network   Contains whatever IP will run over, such as Ethernet, token ring, FDDI, etc. A network layer protocol routes packets across a network. A link layer is sometimes separated out at the lower end of the network layer.

Physical   The Internet protocol model is really about software, not hardware, so there is no physical layer as such. However, we can call everything under the network layer the physical layer. Standards at this layer describe signal attenuation, voltage levels, physical connectors, and the like.

Protocol Stacks

A protocol model is not much good without actual protocols, no matter how many layers in the model. A **protocol suite** is a set of protocols that fit a protocol model. However, there might be more protocols in a protocol suite than are practical for use with a particular application. Therefore a set of protocols, called a **protocol stack,** is selected from the protocol suite to support an application or a class of applications [Malamud 1992; Lynch & Rose 1992; Padlipsky 1985].

IP Stacks

As you can see in Fig. 3.3, the IP protocol is the key protocol in the TCP/IP protocol model, since all stacks include it. IP provides an internetwork address space, routing, and other services across various underlying networks and network technologies. Above IP, either TCP or UDP may be used, and most application protocols are designed to be used with one of these. For example, TELNET, FTP, and SMTP were designed for use with TCP, while NTP and NFS were designed for UDP. DNS, for example, uses UDP for most purposes, but where 100% reliability is required, it uses TCP. Below IP, a wide variety of network protocols may be used. These might require their own underlying stacks of link and physical layer protocols; however, most TCP/IP application protocols are not concerned with what is underneath IP. A transport layer protocol might need to know the maximum transmission unit of an underlying network protocol in order to facilitate tuning the size of transmitted messages. Or an application might be concerned

---

Figure 3.3 IP Protocol Stacks.

Layer	Protocols					
Process/ Application	TELNET (login)	FTP (files)	SMTP (mail)	DNS (names)	NTP (time)	NFS (files)
Transport	TCP			UDP		
Internet	IP					
Network	Ethernet	ISO 8802-2		X.25	SLIP	PPP
Link		ISO 8802-3 IEEE 802.3 (CSMA/CD)	ISO 8802-5 IEEE 802.5 (token ring)	ISO 7776 X.25 LAPB (HDLC)	(serial)	
Physical	(various)					

with a particular class of service, such as broadcast, and so might need to know whether the network or link layer supports it. But most details below the Internet layer are hidden from the transport and application layers.

Most of this book is about setting up specific Internet application services. However, connecting to the Internet also involves setting up infrastructure services and we discuss those in Chapter 5, *Setting Up IP*.

3.3   Mail Networks

A dialup network like FidoNet or UUCP can provide mail service with other systems, thus giving you access to the Matrix, although not to the Internet. Yet you still can participate in discussions going on in the Internet community by means of mailing lists and newsgroups, which are exchanged among various networks of the Matrix.

FidoNet and UUCP are defined partly by the protocols they use: FidoNet uses the Fido protocols, and the UUCP network uses the UUCP protocols. It is convenient to think of both FidoNet and UUCP as implementing transport and network layers (see Fig. 3.4). The mail and news applications run directly over the Fido or UUCP transport layer. The Fido and UUCP protocols can be used over a variety of modem protocols as well as over other protocols such as X.25. A gateway host may be on both UUCP and the Internet, or on both FidoNet and the Internet, and may transfer mail and news from UUCP or FidoNet protocols to SMTP or NNTP.

To join FidoNet or UUCP, you must have Fido or UUCP software installed; fortunately, this isn't difficult. You can get FidoNet software from someone else who is on FidoNet. UUCP comes packaged with most versions of UNIX, or you can get it from your UNIX vendor, from a commercial UUCP vendor, or as a free implementation off the net. You can even get UUCP software for MS-DOS in a number of implementations, some of them called UUPC. For more information on setting up this software, see [Aboba 1993].

Figure 3.4 Mail and News.

Layer	Access Method	
Process/ Application	Mail	News
Transport	UUCP	Fido
Link	PEP	V.32 bis
Physical	modem	

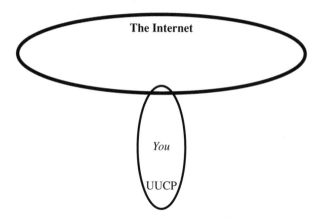

Figure 3.5 UUCP Access to the Matrix.

Mail networks such as UUCP and FidoNet do not use IP. Their advantage is that they are usually less expensive and easier to connect to than the Internet is. On the other hand, they don't carry most of the services that the Internet provides. They do put you in the Matrix, but they leave you outside the Internet, looking in, as shown in Fig. 3.5.

3.4   Conferencing Systems

A conferencing system like CompuServe or GEnie that provides only mail or news access can put you in the Matrix but not on the Internet, although you will have indirect and partial communication with the Internet through an intermediary, as shown in Fig. 3.6. Many such conferencing systems have actual direct IP Internet connectivity, but they don't let their users use it, so from your point of view, its only effect is to speed up your mail. If a conferencing system does permit its users to use a full range of Internet services, as Delphi does, we treat it as a login host. So conferencing systems of the type considered here usually provide only mail access, and sometimes news access.

Technically, connecting to a conferencing system is much like connecting to a login host, which we describe in the next section. Conferencing systems are perhaps more likely to be accessible by X.25 PDNs in addition to telephone modem dialup.

The big advantage of conferencing systems is that they often provide services that the Internet does not yet provide, such as airline reservations, stock market quotes, and specialized databases. So if you are more interested in those services than in current Internet services, your best choice might be to sign up for a conferencing system. In addition, commercial conferencing systems also often have very widespread **points of presence (PoPs),** so one is likely to be only a local telephone call away from you, while Internet PoPs are still mainly in major cities.

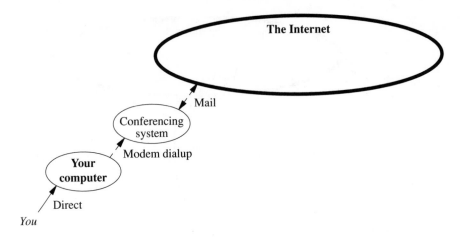

Figure 3.6 Conferencing System Access to the Matrix.

3.5   Public Internet Hosts

A growing number of systems provide Internet access to users by permitting them to dial up the system and log in. This method gives you full Internet access from the login host. Half a hundred of these public Internet hosts are listed in Appendix A, *Internet Providers*. As you can see in Fig. 3.7, there is no actual IP connectivity between the user and the Internet. The login host instead provides Internet connectivity as one of its operating system services. The user has access to Internet services because the login host is on the Internet.

However, as you can see in Fig. 3.8, the machine the user is calling *from* is not on the Internet. For example, the user can FTP a file over the Internet to the login host, but to get the file to the user's own machine, software like Kermit must be used.

Figure 3.7 Login Host.

Layer	Protocol
Operating System	login
Link	PEP V.32 bis
Physical	modem

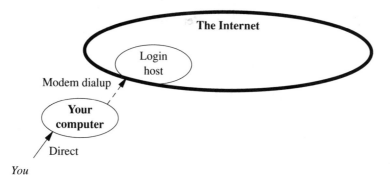

Figure 3.8 Login Host Access to the Internet.

This arrangement has an added advantage because the login host is responsible for setting up Internet service clients, many users get the benefit of the login host's support staff. The login host staff also back up files users leave on the host, answer questions, provide documentation, and in general provide services that each user would otherwise have to find or provide separately.

3.6   Packaged Dialup Software and Services

An intermediate step between mail-only network access and dialup IP is prepackaged software for DOS and Macintosh systems that knows how to dial up a connectivity provider in order to exchange basic services. Following are examples of such software.

PSILink

This package from PSI uses a stripped-down IP implementation to exchange electronic mail and news with PSINet. Unlike UUCP or FidoNet connections, this package doesn't require extensive setup and is expandable to support Internet services. The underlying protocol, however, unlike UUCP or FidoNet, can handle arbitrary IP services.

WorldLink

This package from InterCon is a variation of the PSILink idea, except it applies to the Macintosh. WorldLink currently connects through PSINet and provides FTP access as well as electronic mail and news.

Layer	Protocol	
Process/ Application	various	
Transport	TCP	UDP
Internet	IP	
Network	SLIP	PPP
Link	PEP	V.32 bis
Physical	modem	

Figure 3.9 Dialup IP.

3.7   Dialup IP Connections

You can dial up some IP connectivity services and connect your computer directly to the Internet, thereby giving you full Internet access directly from your machine, as illustrated by Fig. 3.9. Software such as Eudora for the Macintosh or KA9Q for DOS machines can do this. Using this software, you don't need to log in as a user on a login host. You can FTP a file directly across the Internet onto your machine. You are responsible for setting up your own client software for Internet services, although you might get some assistance from your connectivity provider. Much of the basic software you'll need is available off the Internet itself; see Appendix C, *Software and Other Information*. And much of it is the same software you will need for a direct Internet connection, since the only difference on your end is the software to deal with dialing up. We say a bit more about this in Chapter 5, *Setting Up IP*.

3.8   Direct Connections

Direct Internet connections use one of the classical IP stacks shown in Fig. 3.3. In the remaining chapters in this book, we describe how to build the stack, layer by layer, until it has all the layers of Fig. 3.10.

If you have direct IP connectivity to the computer on your desk, as in Fig. 3.11, you don't need to dial up somewhere else even to check your mail. You can easily carry on mail conversations with other people with similar connectivity, since mail delivery usually takes only seconds, and you can set your user interface to notify you when mail comes in. In fact, composing a mail reply is usually the slowest part of such a conversation: the speed of such network service often

Layer	Protocol	
Process/ Application	various	
Transport	TCP	UDP
Internet	IP	
Network	various	
Link	direct	
Physical	direct	

Figure 3.10 Direct IP.

exceeds human speeds. Effective speeds of user services will of course depend on the speed of the underlying Internet link; if too many local users try to use the link at the same time, effective speed for each will decrease, since all their traffic is being multiplexed.

Speeds

You can run IP at 2400bps, but you don't want to; interactive response at that speed is excruciatingly slow. Besides, 14.4Kbps modems only cost a few hundred dollars and their prices are still dropping, so the increased speed is well worth the investment in the modem. Table 3.2 shows some possible speeds for Internet connections. For each speed, the table shows an example of estimated time of transmission of a sixteen megabyte file. These times take into account only eight bits per byte, but they don't account for packet encapsulation, network latency, or other potential sources of drag. The speed given for X.25 is an example of what you often can get in PDNs in the United States; some sources claim speeds of up to 64Kbps for X.25. Regardless of the nominal speed of your Internet connection,

Figure 3.11 Direct Access to the Internet.

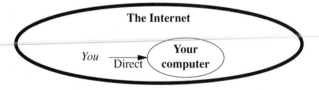

Table 3.2 Speeds.

Speed	Name	Technology	Example Time (16 Megabytes)
1200bps	Bell 212A, V.22	modem	29 hours 38 min
2400bps	V.22bis	modem	14 hours 49 min
4800bps	V.27ter	X.25 PDN	7 hours 25 min
9600bps	V.32	modem	3 hours 42 min
9600bps	V.29	4 wire leased	3 hours 42 min
14.4Kbps	V.32bis, PEP	modem	2 hours 28 min
19.2Kbps	frac. DS-0	copper coax	1 hour 51 min
56Kbps	DS-0	copper coax	38 min 6 sec
64Kbps	E-0	copper coax	33 min 20 sec
1.544Mbps	T-1	fiber optic	1 min 23 sec
10Mbps	Ethernet	various	12.8 sec
45Mbps	T-3	fiber optic	2.84 sec
100Mbps	FDDI	fiber optic	1.28 sec
1Gbps		fiber optic	0.13 sec

your mileage may vary according to hardware, software, and traffic conditions.

14.4K. This is the usual speed for dialup IP connectivity, since it is the current top effective speed of widely available and relatively inexpensive modems.

19.2K. Most IP connectivity providers have a service at this speed, for use through leased lines.

DS-0 (56K). Ordinary voice telephone channels, when used for digital data transmission, can pass about 64Kbps. With the framing commonly used in the United States and some other countries, the remaining bandwidth commonly offered by telephone companies and IXCs to customers is 56Kbps. This speed is called DS-0.

E-0 (64K). In Europe, PTTs normally provide full voice bandwidth for digital use without the extra framing. This end-user speed of 64Kbps is called E-0.

T-1 (1.544M). The IXCs have run so much fiber optic cable that in some regions T-1 is little more expensive than DS-0, even though telephone companies can split 24 DS-0 circuits out of one T-1. Most of the CIX members and NSFNET regionals use T-1 internally. You can buy T-1 readily from your local telephone company to connect to one of them, or you often can get fractional T-1 at a reduced rate.

E-1 (2M). The European equivalent of T-1 is called E-1 and provides 2.048Mbps.

Ethernet (10M). Ethernet is commonly considered a LAN technology, but it can be used with fiber optic or even satellite repeaters to provide metropolitan, regional (for example, NEARNET), or even national (ITESM) or international (NORDUnet) backbone networks.

T-3 (45M). A fast backbone helps in multiplexing traffic from multiple sources. Unless you have a very large organization, you will probably not yet need T-3 directly to your establishment. NSFNET is currently based on T-3, and at least one CIX member is moving to T-3.

Platforms

TCP/IP is implemented for just about every known combination of computer hardware and software, so you can connect directly to the Internet regardless of what you are running. If you use DOS, you can start with a public domain package such as NCSA TELNET. If you want supported commercial software, FTP Software can provide it. Similarly for the Macintosh, there is the Eudora public domain software and InterCon's supported commercial software. If you are connecting a network of machines to the Internet, you will probably have at least one UNIX machine providing services such as mail, news, and DNS. We tell you how to set it up in later chapters.

3.9   Connectivity Providers

It takes two endpoints to make a connection, so you'll need a connectivity provider regardless of whether you're dialing up or using a leased line. We mentioned many of the larger organizations you might want to connect to, in Chapter 2, *The Internet and Other Networks*, and we provide contact information for those and many others, in Appendix A, *Internet Providers*. Here we add a few comments about which of these organizations you might want to approach.

Worldwide

There are doubtless other worldwide Internet providers, but CIX appears to be the largest organized body.

Commercial Internet Exchange (CIX). The Commercial Internet Exchange (CIX) is a cooperative organization of a variety of networks that range from regional to global in extent. CIX itself reaches much of the world. Some of the CIX networks are not very fast (T-1) but are probably fast enough for most organizations.

United States

More than half of the Internet is still in the United States, so we find many providers in that country.

NSFNET and the NSFNET Regionals. The NSFNET backbone service is currently the fastest (T-3) widely used backbone service. However, if your organization is not a major connectivity provider itself, you probably should look elsewhere for connectivity. There probably is an NSFNET regional network in your area, and you should consider connecting to it. The regional networks have varying policies regarding how much they charge and what types of organizations can connect. The regionals also vary in speed, from T-1 (1.544Mbps) to Ethernet (10Mbps), to T-3 (45Mbps) speed.

ANS and CO+RE. ANS is currently the provider of the NSFNET backbone service and also of ANSnet, which is also fast (T-3). ANS is a nonprofit and so has some restrictions on what kinds of services it can provide. But the ANS for-profit subsidiary CO+RE has few such restrictions. If yours is a large organization, you might want to consider ANS CO+RE.

CoREN. The Corporation for Regional and Enterprise Networking (CoREN) is an alliance of eight regional Internet connectivity providers (BARRNet, CICNet, MIDnet, NEARnet, NorthWestNet, NYSERNet, SURAnet, and Westnet). CoREN has let a contract to MCI to interconnect their networks independently of NSFNET. CoREN and CIX are not formally affiliated, but are expected to exchange traffic.

Metropolitan Fiber Systems (MFS). A somewhat unusual provider is Metropolitan Fiber Systems (MFS), which can supply 100mbps wide-area IP service throughout the United States. This is faster than any of the other networks mentioned so far.

Canada

Canada has a national backbone network called CA*net, which has associated regional networks. There are also commercial IP network providers in Canada.

Australia

Australia has a major national backbone network and some local IP providers.

AARNET. The main national backbone network of Australia is called AARNET (Australian Academic and Research Network).

Europe

RIPE. RIPE is an organizational group rather than a network provider. It maintains an electronic mailing list of providers of IP connectivity in Europe that can be reached at *ip-prov@ripe.net*. If your organization is in Europe and you need a provider, send mail to that list and you will very likely get a response.

EBONE. The European Backbone (EBONE) connects national and regional networks in Europe, thereby providing a continental backbone. However, unless your organization is an IP connectivity provider, you probably will not connect directly to EBONE.

EUnet. The European UNIX network (EUnet) started as a UUCP network but has since branched out into providing IP connectivity. It also has spawned many national EUnet providers, all of which work in concert. EUnet and most, if not all, of the national EUnet providers started as nonprofit organizations but are now for profit.

Japan

R&E Backbones. Japan has several R&E backbones: **WIDE (Widely Integrated Distributed Environment), TISN (Todai International Science Network),** and **JAIN (Japan Academic Inter-university Network)**. If your organization is research or academic, you have a good chance of connecting to one of them. If your organization is of some other type, your chances are much less. Another possibility is the **JUNET (Japan UNIX Network),** which is closely associated historically with WIDE. Of all of these networks, WIDE is the most likely to provide IP access to commercial organizations.

AT&T Jens. AT&T's Japanese subsidiary, AT&T Jens, in collaboration with other organizations, is providing commercial Internet access under the name **SPIN.**

IIKK. IIKK (InterCon International, KK) offers IP services in Japan and other countries.

IIJ. WIDE has recently become associated with IIJ (Internet Initiative Japan), which provides commercial Internet access.

3.10 Acceptable Use Policies

If you want to pass traffic through the NSFNET backbone service, you must agree to abide by the NSFNET **Acceptable Use Policy (AUP)**. This policy basically says that all use of the NSFNET backbone service must be for research or educational purposes or in support thereof. That AUP exists because NSFNET is funded partly from taxes; and therefore NSF has to be careful about what it is used for.

Some other networks have AUPs, as well. For example, many NSFNET regional networks were started with seed money from NSF, and some are partly funded by state tax money, so they, too, must be careful about network uses. Even if you connect to the Internet through a commercial provider, such as a CIX member or ANS CO+RE, if you want to route your traffic through the NSFNET backbone service, you must agree that such traffic will abide by the NSFNET AUP.

AUPs might or might not be a problem for you, so next we offer suggestions regarding when they might be. Please remember that we are not responsible for writing or enforcing any AUP and these comments reflect our opinions. When in doubt, consult the author of the AUP in question.

One thing is clear: If all your traffic will be through the commercial parts of the Internet, such as the CIX networks or ANSnet, you have no problem. You don't even need to sign the NSFNET AUP, since you don't need to route through the NSFNET backbone service. But it is hard to predict when you will need to route through a network with an AUP in order to reach any given host or server.

You might have customers who work for or who are universities or government research agencies. Usually, such a case is relatively straightforward. If a researcher or academic wants to buy your service over the network, sale and delivery of that service for that purpose is in support of research or education, and therefore is acceptable under many AUPs. For that matter, if you are simply providing a network service, such as an anonymous FTP server, it's not clear that the contents of such a server must abide by anyone's AUP, since your server is not making connections to anyone else. The user of the service decides whether to connect and use the service, so acceptability according to an AUP is probably their problem, not yours.

The things most likely to cause problems under an AUP are actually things you could do even if you weren't connected to the Internet at all, namely mailing advertisements or invoices.

Because AUPs are usually caused by the use of tax money to fund networks, AUPs will become less important as more of the Internet is privatized. That is, as Internet connectivity and carriage is provided by private companies that derive their income from selling connectivity or services, AUPs will wither away.

3.11 Checklist

At the beginning of this chapter, we compared the services provided by a spectrum of access methods, as shown in Fig. 3.1. Now let's summarize the hardware, communications links, and software you will need on your computer or network to support the same access categories, as shown in Fig. 3.12. We've grouped the necessary items according to Internet protocol layer.

You can use Fig. 3.12 as a checklist for the hardware, software, and communications links we discuss in more detail in the rest of the book. You can see at a glance what you will need to handle each type of access. For a mail network connection, you need UUCP or FidoNet software and a local mail program. If you want news you will also need local news software. You don't need UUCP or FidoNet software for any of the other kinds of access.

Conferencing systems and login hosts are the easiest access methods to use, since you only need a personal login account on the remote computer plus a modem connected to your computer and some personal communication software such as Kermit. Your *software* may need a login account on a remote computer

| Layer | Protocol | Matrix Access | | Internet Access | | |
		mailnet[1]	conf[2]	Login Host	Dialup IP	Full IP
Process / Applications	news	maybe	—	—	yes	yes
	mail	yes	—	—	yes	yes
	FTP	—	—	—	yes	yes
	TELNET	—	—	—	yes	yes
Transport	TCP or UDP	—	—	—	yes	yes
	UUCP or FidoNet	yes	—	—	—	—
Internet	IP	—	—	—	yes	yes
	router	—	—	—	maybe	maybe
Network	SLIP or PPP	—	—	—	yes	maybe
	user login	—	yes	yes	—	—
	Kermit, etc.	—	yes	yes	—	—
	UUCP or FidoNet	yes	—	—	—	—
Link	direct	maybe	—	—	—	probably
	modem	yes	yes	yes	yes	maybe
Physical	leased	maybe	—	—	—	probably
	dialup	yes	yes	yes	yes	—

mailnet[1]   mail and news only, as in UUCP or FidoNet
conf[2]   conferencing system with mail and news access

Figure 3.12 Access Checklist.

for mailnet or dialup IP access, but you do not need a personal account.

You don't need IP software on your computer to use a login host, since you use the remote computer's IP implementation. You do need IP on your computer for dialup IP or direct IP. Many IP connection providers will expect you to have an IP router on your end, especially if you are connecting a network rather than a single host. You will also need TCP, UDP, TELNET, FTP, and mail software. If you want USENET news, you will need news software. You can use many resource discovery services through TELNET, but for best effect you will need local software for those services, too.

We have little more to say in this book about mail network or conferencing system connections. Login hosts are listed in Appendix A, *Internet Providers*, but, as you can see from Fig. 3.12, you do not need to configure much on your computer, so we also say little more about login hosts. The rest of this book is about setting up dialup or direct IP connectivity.

References

Aboba 1993.   Aboba, Bernard, *The Online User's Encyclopedia: Bulletin Boards and Beyond,* Addison-Wesley, Reading, MA (1993). ISBN 0-201-62214-9.

Braden 1989a.   Braden, Robert, "Requirements for Internet Hosts — Communication Layers; RFC1122," *Network Working Group Requests for Comments* (RFC1122), Network Information Systems Center, SRI International (October 1989).

Braden 1989b.   Braden, Robert, "Requirements for Internet Hosts — Application and Support; RFC1123," *Network Working Group Requests for Comments* (RFC1123), Network Information Systems Center, SRI International (October 1989).

Braden & Postel 1987.   Braden, Robert T., & Postel, Jon B., "Requirements for Internet gateways; RFC1009," *Network Working Group Requests for Comments* (RFC1009), Network Information Systems Center, SRI International (June 1987).

Carl-Mitchell & Quarterman 1993.   Carl-Mitchell, Smoot, & Quarterman, John S., *Practical Internetworking with TCP/IP and UNIX,* Addison-Wesley, Reading, MA (1993). ISBN 0-201-58629-0.

Cerf & Cain 1983.   Cerf, Vinton G., & Cain, Edward, "The DoD Internet Architecture Model," *Computer Networks* **7**(5), pp. 307–318 (October 1983).

Cerf & Kahn 1974.   Cerf, Vinton G., & Kahn, Robert, "A Protocol for Packet Network Interconnection," *IEEE Transactions on Communications* **COM-22**(5), pp. 637–648 (May 1974). Also in Partridge, *Innovations in Internetworking,* 1988.

Lynch & Rose 1992.   Lynch, Dan, & Rose, Marshall, *Internet Handbook,* Addison-Wesley, Reading, MA (October 1992).

Malamud 1992.   Malamud, Carl, *Stacks,* Prentice-Hall, Englewood Cliffs, NJ (1992).

Padlipsky 1985.   Padlipsky, M. A., *The Elements of Networking Style,* Prentice-Hall, Englewood Cliffs, NJ (1985).

Postel 1992.   Postel, Jon ed., "IAB Official Protocol Standards; STD-1/RFC-1360," *Network Working Group Requests for Comments* (STD-1/RFC-1360), Network Information Systems Center, SRI International (September 1992).

Rose 1989.   Rose, Marshall, *The Open Book: A Practical Perspective on Open Systems Interconnection,* Prentice-Hall, Englewood Cliffs, NJ (1989).

CHAPTER 4

Registering Domain Names and IP Numbers

To join the Internet, you must tell other Internet participants what to call your computers, and how to address them. That is, you must register an IP network number and a DNS domain name. An IP network number permits routing protocols to find a path to your network. Registering an IP network number registers the network. A domain name applies to your organization (your administrative domain), and can be subdivided to supply a name for each of your computers, so that programs and users can call your computers by names they can remember. Registering a domain name registers the domain. Here's why you need to register both an IP network number and a DNS domain name.

If you don't register your network, others will see your IP packets arriving at their systems over the Internet from an unknown network. Because the source of such packets isn't known to be anywhere in the registered world, they are called **Martian packets.** Martian packets are annoying to the recipient, since they cause error messages and can easily be mistaken for cracking attempts.

More importantly, IP packets can't be routed to an unregistered network, so you won't get any useful service out of the Internet. So, no Martian packets, please. Be sure to register your IP network number. By doing so you also register your IP network, and make it known to the Internet.

When you want to TELNET, FTP, archie, Gopher, WAIS, or otherwise connect across the Internet, you will find typing a domain name like *ws.bigco.com* much easier than typing an IP address like 192.143.7.42. It's easier to remember, too. In addition, computers sometimes move between offices or buildings within organizations, and change IP addresses in the process. If you were using the host's IP address to reach it, that address won't work anymore, but if you were using the host's domain name, you can continue to do so.

Some Internet services check your host's domain name against your IP address as a security precaution. Such services don't permit connections from a **nameless host.** You need a domain name even if all you plan to do is send electronic mail, especially if you expect to get any responses, since many mail systems strongly discourage sending mail to IP addresses. So, no nameless hosts, please. Be sure to register your DNS domain name. By doing so you also register your administrative domain, and make it known to the Internet and to the rest of the Matrix.

In this chapter, we discuss how you to register your IP network number and your DNS domain name.

4.1   What, Where, and How to Register

Before you connect to the Internet, you must register the following items, which are shown in Table 4.1:

- A domain name for your administrative domain, that is, for your organization. You can register more than one domain name, but you probably have only one organization, so you will need only one administrative domain for it.

- An IP network number for each of your IP networks. If you only have one IP network, you will need only one network number; otherwise you will need more than one.

- A **reverse domain** for each network number you register, mapping that network number to a normal **forward domain.**

These registrations are intertwined. For example, you need to specify two DNS servers for your domain. If one of those servers is on your network, you must wait until the network registration is completed before the domain registration can be completed. If you register several network numbers, you must register a reverse domain for each of them.

You do not need to register subdomains. For example, if you're registering *bigco.com,* you do not need to register *eng.bigco.com.* Your *eng* subdomain cannot conflict with some other domain's subdomain *eng,* such as *eng.stateu.edu.* Avoiding name conflicts this way is one of the main reasons for the hierarchical structure of the domain name system. You can set up your own subdomains yourself, without permission of any outside authority, and you can make them known

Table 4.1 What to Register.

What	Example	Template
domain	bigco.com	domain-template.txt
IP network number	192.143.13	internet-number-template.txt
reverse domain	13.143.192.in-addr.arpa	in-addr-template.txt

to the outside world through your domain servers, if you choose to do so. You can even delegate authority to suborganizations within your organization to set up their own subdomains. You could delegate *eng.bigco.com* to your engineering department, for example, so that they could create their own host names, such as *waldo.eng.bigco.com.* Control over Engineering's host names would then reside with Engineering, as it should, instead of with some more distant organization. You do not have to worry about their name *waldo* conflicting with some other *waldo,* such as *waldo.bigco.com* or *waldo.stateu.com.* Engineering does not have to register *waldo.eng.bigco.com* with you or with anyone else, and you do not have to register *eng.bigco.com* or *waldo.bigco.com* with anyone else. You only have to register your main domain name, *bigco.com.*

    You do not need to register subnets, either. For example, if you are registering 128.77 as your IP network number you do not need to register 128.77.1. Subnets permit you to have subnet addresses for each internal network in your organization's internet, while the Internet at large only needs to know about your main IP network number. Using subnets instead of several IP network numbers reduces the size of the routing tables in the routers on Internet backbone networks. Once you have registered your main IP network number, you can assign subnets to your networks as appropriate, without needing to get any of them approved by any outside authority. You can assign an IP host address to each of your hosts without any need to register any host address with an outside authority. If you want your host's IP addresses to be known to the world outside your domain, you can use your domain servers to make them known, but you do not need to do any further registration with an outside authority for this, either.

Registering and Connecting

You can register either a domain or an IP network number without actually connecting to the Internet. You should do this, regardless of whether you now plan to connect to the Internet or not.

    The relations of registered domains and IP numbers to the Internet are shown in Fig. 4.1, which is a Venn diagram. The heavy ellipses indicate networks: the Internet, enterprise networks using IP, and the UUCP network. There is some overlap among these networks.

    We hope all networks on the Internet are registered, since you can't route IP packets to them if they're not. The figure illustrates the fact that many enterprise networks have registered IP network numbers without being connected to the Internet. Unfortunately, some enterprise IP network numbers are not registered, but you can make sure yours is not one of them.

    The DNS domain system covers most of the Internet and most enterprise IP networks, plus parts of other networks, some of which, such as UUCP, may not even use IP at all. There are still some hosts on the Internet that do not have domain names, but you don't want yours to be among them.

    Hosts often migrate from an access network such as UUCP to the Internet without changing domain names [Schwartz & Quarterman 1993]. For example, *tic.com* was a registered domain for years before TIC had direct Internet

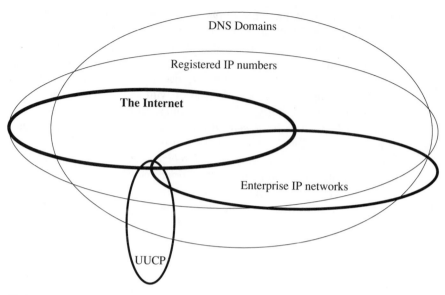

Figure 4.1 DNS Domains and IP Network Numbers.

connectivity. Instead, we exchanged mail through the UUCP network. When we connected to the Internet, most of our mail correspondents didn't know anything had changed.

Similarly, you can register an IP network number and use it internally in your organization without connecting that network to the Internet. In fact, if you are using IP internally, you do want to register an IP network number for it as early as possible, even if you aren't planning on connecting to the Internet any time soon. When you *do* connect, you will *not* want to have to go back and change the IP address of every host on your network. Going ahead and registering your network now will avoid that problem.

Where to Register

If you are paying for Internet access through a commercial connectivity provider, that provider will usually handle most details of registering a domain and an IP network number for you. Some non-commercial Internet connectivity providers will also do this for you. Such a connectivity provider is sometimes called a **service provider.**

If you do not have a connectivity provider, or yours will not assist you in registering, you can then go to your national registry, if you have one, or to a regional registry, if there is one, or to the international top level registry, which is called InterNIC. Such a registry is sometimes called a **non-service provider.** There is a non-service provider for European country.

Although the terms service provider and non-service provider are usually applied to IP network number registries, the same principle also applies to domain registries. Domain and IP network number registration is actually done separately, and there may be separate registries for each in your country or region. However, if you have an Internet connectivity provider, you can usually handle registration for both a domain and an IP network number through that provider.

Getting Templates

To register, you must fill out some forms, called **templates.** You can get them from your IP connectivity provider, if you have one, but you may want to get them yourself. Authoritative copies of all necessary registration templates are available by anonymous FTP from *rs.internic.net,* in the directory *templates.* Completed templates should be sent to *hostmaster@internic.net,* or to your service provider, or to your regional or national registry. You can also get the templates by electronic mail, through the *rs.internic.net* mail server. We discuss anonymous FTP and mail servers and InterNIC in the next two major sections in this chapter. If you have no access to either FTP or electronic mail, you can get the templates by paper mail from the InterNIC registration services, and you can also return completed templates by paper mail.

Registering a Domain

If the domain you are registering is under one of the top level domains EDU, COM, MIL, GOV, NET, or ORG, use the default domain registration templates provided in Appendix B, *Registration Templates.* If you are registering under some other domain, it must be a national top level domain, such as NL for Netherlands or AU for Australia, and you will need to contact your national domain registry, which can also be found through the WHOIS service, or by asking *hostmaster@internic.net.* If you are in Europe, ask *hostmaster@ripe.net* instead.

Getting Two Domain Servers

As mentioned earlier in this section, you must have two independent domain servers before you can register a domain. These two servers should be as independent as possible. They should at least have different connections to the Internet, and preferably should have independent power supplies, administrations, geographical locations, etc.

If you are registering your domain through an IP connectivity provider, you can ask that provider for help in finding two domain servers. Most such providers have at least one server on one of their own machines that they use for this purpose. You may want to run your own primary domain server on one of your own machines. Or you may want to let your connectivity provider do that for you, and let them find you a second domain server, as well.

If you do not have an IP connectivity provider, or yours cannot provide domain service, you need to find at least one outside organization to run a domain server for you. Even if you run your own primary domain server, you still need a secondary server somewhere else. The Internet community is friendly, and finding two servers is usually not difficult.

Registering an IP Network Number

All IP network number registrations were previously centralized, in a single **Internet Registry (IR)**. But the global registry, currently InterNIC, now delegates registration for regions to regional IRs, which may then delegate subregions, such as countries, to local IRs. In addition, you can either register directly with an appropriate IR for your region, or through an Internet service provider, if you have one. If you are in North America or don't know where to go, try InterNIC.

For example, the regional IR for Europe is the RIPE (see Chapter 2, *The Internet and Other Networks*) **Network Coordination Center (NCC),** which has been delegated blocks of IP numbers. The RIPE NCC has in turn delegated blocks of IP numbers to local IRs, usually one non-service provider IR per country, plus service provider IRs.

If you are registering an IP number for use in Europe, use *european-ip-template.txt* instead of *internet-number-template.txt*, and send the completed template to *hostmaster@ripe.net,* rather than to *hostmaster@internic.net*.

Registration Procedures

Registration procedures and information for domains and for network numbers are similar. Registration depends on identifying key administrative and technical people for each domain and network number registered. Each key person must have an electronic mailbox and a **handle,** which is a unique identifier used in NIC databases. If you have a handle already, you can find it using the WHOIS service. For each key person who does not have one, where the handle would go in the template, instead fill in the person's name, paper mailing address, telephone number, organization, and electronic mail address. That person will then be assigned a handle on registration.

The registration templates themselves are included in Appendix B, *Registration Templates*. Here are descriptions of the information needed to fill out each template.

domain-template.txt. For a domain, you'll need to name the top level domain you're registering under, such as COM, NL, or AU. Then you need to supply the full domain name you're registering, such as bigco.com, as well as your organization name and postal address, plus the date you expect the domain to be operational.

Two specific contact persons are wanted: the administrative contact and the technical contact. For each person you need to supply either a handle or enough information (name, postal address, etc.) for a handle to be assigned. You must also supply an electronic mail address for each of the two contacts.

DNS must know where to find information about your domain, so you must supply information about two domain servers for your domain. For each server you must provide its hostname, IP network address, and a brief description of the hardware and software. You can list any hosts that were previously registered under another domain that you want to rename into your new domain.

Finally, you should provide a brief description of your organization's activities, e.g., "Very Big, Inc. makes quite large widgets and uses a TCP/IP network to coordinate worldwide distribution."

internet-number-template.txt. The form for registering an IP network number requests information on a governmental sponsoring organization. This is archaic, since if you're connecting through a commercial Internet connectivity provider such as a CIX member, you don't need governmental authorization. It is probably sufficient to use information about your access provider in that place.

You do need to supply a network name, such as BIGNET, and the name and postal address of your organization's main office.

You are asked to estimate the number of hosts on your network now, and in one, two, and five years from now (guessing is permitted). Those estimates were once used to determine whether you could get a Class B or Class A network number. You can still argue for one of those, but unless you have a very good reason (such as tens of thousands of hosts spread all over the world), you will probably get a Class C number.

You must classify your network as one of the four types Research, Defense, Government - Non Defense, or Commercial, and you must give a purpose for your network.

in-addr.arpa.txt. The reverse domain template is quite short. You must provide the reverse domain, such as *13.143.192.in-addr.arpa,* the name of the network, and the DNS names of two servers for the domain. The servers are usually the same servers you are using for your forward domain, e.g., *bigco.com.* For each server, you must supply the domain name, the IP network address, and the CPU type and operating system type.

european-ip-template.txt. The European IP network number registration template is a bit more concerned with national country codes, but is otherwise quite similar to the InterNIC form.

4.2   Anonymous FTP

Using anonymous FTP is just like using FTP for any other purpose, except that you log in as user *anonymous,* often with password *guest.*

The exact commands to use for anonymous FTP (or any kind of FTP) will depend on your local operating system. Figure 4.2 shows an example of how you can use the 4.3BSD FTP client for anonymous FTP to *ds.internic.net.* In this figure, the text in italics is what you, as user, type (see lines 1, 4, 6, 8, 10, 12, 14, and 15). Everything else is output by the FTP client program. The figure shows the user doing the following:

```
 1  % ftp ds.internic.net
 2  Connected to ds.internic.net.
 3  220 ds FTP server (SunOS 4.1) ready.
 4  Name (ds.internic.net:jsq): anonymous
 5  331 Guest login ok, send ident as password.
 6  Password: guest
 7  230 Guest login ok, access restrictions apply.
 8  ftp> cd rfc
 9  250 CWD command successful.
10  ftp> verbose
11  Verbose mode off.
12  ftp> dir rfc-index.txt
13  -rw-r--r-- 1 101  1  170812 Mar 8 01:50 rfc-index.txt
14  ftp> get rfc-index.txt
15  ftp> quit
16  %
```

Figure 4.2 Anonymous FTP.

- Connecting to the server *ds.internic.net* (line 1)

- Logging in as user *anonymous* (line 4)

- Giving *guest* as the password (line 6); the password does not actually echo, for security reasons, but we show it here anyway

- Changing to the subdirectory *rfc* (line 8)

- Turning off verbose mode (line 10)

- Obtaining a long directory listing of the RFC index (line 12), which is file *rfc-index.txt*

- Retrieving the file (line 14)

- Quitting the FTP session (line 15)

Many hosts also accept the username *ftp* in *anonymous;* most UNIX hosts accept this alternate convention.

The "anonymous" adjective is a historical relic when applied to FTP. Years ago, most users used timesharing systems and were anonymous in the crowd. Today, workstations and PCs are common on the Internet so that now it is usually easy to guess who a user is even on a timesharing system. However, large systems are still sufficiently anonymous that some people abuse them by transferring spurious files from them to anonymous FTP servers. For this reason, some anonymous FTP servers now require an electronic mail address as a password.

4.3 The InterNIC

The InterNIC is a **Network Information Center (NIC)** service sponsored by the U.S. National Science Foundation (NSF) to provide and coordinate services for the NSFNET community. InterNIC also provides services to the Internet at large. Its services are provided by the following three companies. The servers listed here each support anonymous FTP service and sometimes other services as well.

- *is.internic.net*
  InterNIC information services, provided by General Atomics/**California Education and Research Foundation Network (CERFnet).** The same host also supports a Gopher server and a WAIS server. If you don't have a Gopher client, TELNET to *is.internic.net* and log in as the user *gopher.* General Atomics provides a general referral service as well.

info@internic.net	InterNIC Information Services
800-444-4345	General Atomics
+1-619-455-4600	P.O. Box 85608
fax: +1-619-455-3990	San Diego, CA 92186-9784

- *ds.internic.net*
  InterNIC directory and database services, including RFCs and Internet Standards [Postel 1992], provided by **American Telephone and Telegraph (AT&T).** The same host supports a WAIS server, which can be accessed by TELNET either with the username *wais* or via other WAIS clients. The host also supports various other services, such as archie and netfind.

  admin@ds.internic.net
  +1-908-668-6587
  fax: +1-908-668-3763

- *rs.internic.net*
  InterNIC registration services, including DNS domain and IP network registration templates and WHOIS service, all provided by **Network Solutions, Inc. (NSI).**

hostmaster@rs.internic.net	Network Solutions
+1-703-742-4777	Attn: InterNIC Registration Services
7AM through 7PM EST	505 Huntmar Park Drive
	Herndon, VA 22070

- *nic.ddn.mil*
  This server is *not* part of InterNIC. Rather, it provides MILNET information,

that is, public information related to U.S. military IP networks. For general Internet information, do not use *nic.ddn.mil;* use instead one of *is.internic.net, ds.internic.net,* or *rs.internic.net.*

• *ftp.ripe.net*
This server also is not part of the InterNIC, but it is the regional IR for Europe. This is the server to use for European registration templates, although copies of those templates also can be found on *rs.internic.net.*

hostmaster@ripe.net	RIPE NCC
+31-20-592-5065	Kruislaan 409
fax: +31-20-592-5090	1098 SJ Amsterdam
	The Netherlands

4.4   Mail Document Servers

Many hosts on the Internet, and some on other networks, such as BITNET, support mail document servers. These facilities allow remote users to retrieve information by electronic mail and are usable even by people who are not on the Internet, provided they can send mail to the Internet. Following are examples of mail servers at the InterNIC and at ISI.

InterNIC. Each of the InterNIC providers supports a mail server. To get details on InterNIC information services, send a HELP command like the following:

```
To: mailserv@is.internic.net

HELP
```

For directory and database services, send the following command:

```
To: mailserv@ds.internic.net

HELP
```

Most of the servers in these examples expect commands to be in the body of the message; they ignore the Subject: header. The exception is the InterNIC registration server, *rs.internic.net,* which expects commands in the Subject: header, not in the message body. For example, you can get any RFC from that server by sending a message with a header like the following:

```
To: mailserv@rs.internic.net
Subject: RFC 791
```

In this case, the Subject: header line contains the keyword RFC, a space, and then the RFC number. The RFC will be returned by mail to the address in the From: header of your message. The rest of the message is ignored.

To get an index of RFCs, use

```
To: mailserv@rs.internic.net
Subject: RFC Index
```

ISI. ISI supports a mail server that expects queries in the body of the message; the contents of the Subject: are ignored. The ISI server permits searches by organization or date and keyword searches with wildcards. To obtain details on other commands, send the server the following request for help:

```
To: RFC-INFO@ISI.EDU
Subject: anything

HELP
```

RFCs on Paper

To obtain paper copies of RFCs, contact ISOC as follows:

isoc@nri.reston.va.us   The Internet Society
                               1895 Preston White Drive, Suite 100
                               Reston, VA 22091

RFCs on Disks

At least two companies distribute RFCs on disks.

SRI's *TCP/IP CD-ROM*. This CD offers a variety of information that is otherwise scattered across many Internet sites, making the data accessible without consuming network bandwidth. It includes RFCs, FYIs, registration templates, and other network documentation. Several online mailing list archives also are included, such as the technical mailing list *tcp-ip,* which discusses the implementation issues around TCP/IP.

All of this information is accessible as ASCII files, and in some cases PostScript documents are also included. The CD-ROM also has a convenient line-oriented *ifind* program for searching some of the documentation for keywords; this facility is particularly useful for looking at the voluminous RFC set. Because the CD-ROM can be on DOS and Macintosh, as well as UNIX systems (the disk itself is in High Sierra format), the documentation has files with all three styles of line termination, as follows:

• line feed for UNIX

• carriage return for the Macintosh

• carriage return and line feed for DOS

In addition to the documentation, this CD-ROM has an extensive collection of network source code for UNIX, MS-DOS, and MacOS, including several entire TCP/IP implementations. For further information, contact the SRI at the following address:

TCP/IP CD-ROM   SRI International, Room EJ291
$195 in the United States   333 Ravenswood Avenue
$198 outside the United States   Menlo Park, CA 94025
                                       +1-415-859-3695
                                       +1-415-859-6387
                                       fax: +1-415-859-6028
                                       nisc@nisc.sri.com

InfoMagic's *RFCs in Hypertext.* These floppies provide RFCs in an indexed hypertext format accessible using the MicroSoft Multimedia Viewer, under Windows 3.0. Along with this software, the user gets a search engine built around the RFCs that aids access to and speeds searches for specific information.

Organization of the RFCs follows the host (RFC1122 and 1123) [Braden 1989a; Braden 1989b] and gateway (RFC 1009) [Braden & Postel 1987] requirements. The user is initially presented with a window showing a general outline organized by topic area. The user then selects one of the topic areas and a submenu appears for each topic area. Within this submenu, specific topics can be selected and the relevant RFC is then displayed. The user also can search for RFCs using a keyword index or can run full text searches using an alternate menu. Also included is a numeric list of all the RFCs from which the user can select the one of interest. For more information, contact Infomagic, Inc., as follows:

RFCs in HyperText   InfoMagic, Inc.
$99.00 US   P.O. Box 338
                                       Pennington, NJ 08534-0338
                                       info@infomagic.com
                                       800-800-6631

References

Braden 1989a.   Braden, Robert, "Requirements for Internet Hosts — Communication Layers; RFC1122," *Network Working Group Requests for Comments* (RFC1122), Network Information Systems Center, SRI International (October 1989).

Braden 1989b.   Braden, Robert, "Requirements for Internet Hosts — Application and Support; RFC1123," *Network Working Group Requests for*

Comments (RFC1123), Network Information Systems Center, SRI International (October 1989).

Braden & Postel 1987.   Braden, Robert T., & Postel, Jon B., "Requirements for Internet gateways; RFC1009," *Network Working Group Requests for Comments* (RFC1009), Network Information Systems Center, SRI International (June 1987).

Postel 1992.   Postel, Jon ed., "IAB Official Protocol Standards; STD-1/RFC-1360," *Network Working Group Requests for Comments* (STD-1/RFC-1360), Network Information Systems Center, SRI International (September 1992).

Schwartz & Quarterman 1993.   Schwartz, Michael F., & Quarterman, John S., "A Measurement Study of Changes in Service-Level Reachability in the Global Internet," University of Colorado, Boulder, CO (May 1993).

CHAPTER 5

Setting Up IP

Most computer and software vendors provide useful instructions on how to set up basic IP connectivity. Consequently, our discussion in this chapter is brief. We begin by describing some general IP routing issues common to Internet connected sites. Then we discuss the two major connectivity options — direct IP and dialup IP — which of the access methods described in Chapter 3, *Types of Internet Access* are the only ones that require IP configuration on your host.

5.1 Connectivity Options

Figure 5.1 shows the basics of how to connect a site to the Internet. Here, all local machines at the site are connected to a LAN using a single network interface. A router, also connected to the LAN, has in addition a serial line interface to an Internet provider's **point of presence (PoP).** The provider's PoP is usually another router that is interconnected with other routers that make up the Internet network cloud. All machines shown below the dashed line are part of the local network, while those above the dashed line in the figure are other routers and hosts that make up the rest of the Internet. LANs at other sites are attached to other routers at some Internet provider's PoP. All IP packets bound for a remote network pass through the local router; those from a remote network to a local host also pass through this local router.

The router shown in the diagram may be either a specialized machine that only does IP routing or a host system that supports IP routing. Most network-capable versions of UNIX support routing of IP packets. The serial interface shown may be a high-speed dedicated connection running at speeds varying from 19.2 kbps to 45 mbps per second. Or it may be a dialup connection using high-speed dialup modem; today, the typical high-speed modem runs at speeds up to 14.4 kilobits per second. We say more about the differences between dedicated connectivity and dialup connectivity after we discuss basic routing issues.

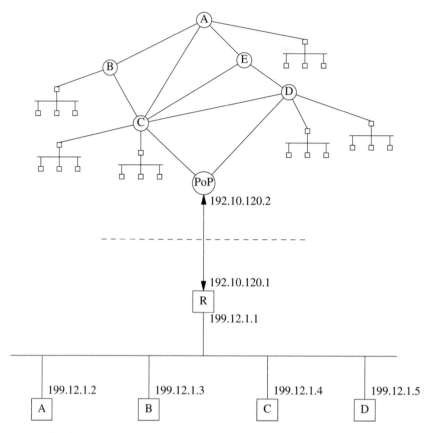

Figure 5.1 Internet Connectivity.

5.2   Packet Routing

Regardless of whether your connection to the Internet is dedicated or switched, the router that provides the connectivity must know how to correctly forward the packets it receives. Figure 5.1 shows the interface addresses of all the local systems. Note that the router in this figure has two interface addresses: The IP address 199.12.1.1 is the interface address of the LAN connection; the network part of the address (199.12.1.0) is identical to that of all other hosts attached to the LAN. Having these addresses set properly is very important for ensuring that IP routing works properly.

The address 192.10.120.1 is that of the point-to-point interface. The network part of the address differs from the LAN network address. The remote end of the point-to-point link also is given an unique address (199.10.120.2), one that usually has the same network address as does the local serial interface, although this is not required.

For routing to work properly, the router must use the IP destination address found in each packet header to learn on which interface to forward packets. The router does this by using a routing table. A routing table consists of entries with the following format:

<destination, gateway, interface, flags, metric>

where the fields mean the following:

• *destination*
 The destination address. This is normally an IP network number. However, on point-to-point links, it is a host IP address.

• *gateway*
 The IP address of the packet's next destination. This address is of a host on one of the directly connected networks. For a route to a directly connected network, it is the address of a local interface. For a point-to-point link, it is the IP address of the remote end of the link.

• *interface*
 The name of the interface on which the packet will be transmitted

• *flags*
 Flags that alter the forwarding process

• *metric*
 A number that indicates the relative value of a route compared to another route to the same destination. This field comes into play only when there are two or more routes to the same destination.

For the configuration shown, the router should have the following routing table entries:

```
destination        gateway          flags    interface metric
199.12.1.0         199.12.1.1       U        le0       0
192.10.120.2       192.10.120.1     UH       sl0       0
0.0.0.0            192.10.120.2     UG       sl0       1
```

The first two routing table entries are installed when the LAN and the serial interfaces are configured. If a UNIX system is used as a router, the interfaces are configured with the following *ifconfig* commands:

```
ifconfig sl0 192.10.120.1 192.10.120.2 netmask 255.255.255.0
ifconfig le0 199.12.1.1 broadcast 199.12.1.255\
                    netmask 255.255.255.0
```

For a dedicated router, the commands differ but essentially the same information is supplied. For a broadcast interface, such as Ethernet, a broadcast address is supplied. In the case of a point-to-point interface, you set the address of the remote end of the point-to-point link and the network mask. There is no broadcast address, since there is but a single remote address.

Line 1 in the example routing table is the LAN interface on the router. In this case, only a "U" flag is set. This tells the router that the *destination* field is a network address and the route is "up." So an IP packet bound for a host on that network will be sent out on the given interface and encapsulated in a datalink frame with a datalink destination address of the IP destination. On a LAN like Ethernet, the datalink address is discovered by using the **Address Resolution Protocol (ARP),** which maps an IP address to its corresponding datalink address. For example, an IP packet inbound for host A (199.12.1.2) will be examined and encapsulated in a datalink frame with a datalink destination address of host A's interface.

Line 2 in the routing table is the entry for the serial interface. In this case, the flags field is set to "UH." This flag indicates the route is to a host rather than to a network. An IP packet bound for that remote host is simply sent over the point-to-point link to the remote host.

Line 3 in the table is the default route. IP packets not bound for the local network are sent by default to the remote router over the point-to-point interface. By convention, a *destination* field of all 0's means a route to any IP address not found in a previous routing table entry is sent to the indicated gateway. In this case, the *flags* field is set to "UG" and the next destination for the packet is an intermediate gateway, not the final destination. Note that the *gateway* field is the IP address of the remote end of the point-to-point interface. So, for example, an IP packet bound for the address 123.12.3.4, when received by the router, will be sent out on the point-to-point interface to the remote router at the PoP. The remote router then uses the same method to forward the packet on the next hop towards its final destination.

Once your router is set up with proper routing, it is a simple matter to set up a default route for all your internal hosts so they can communicate successfully with remote hosts. Host A's routing table has the following entries:

```
destination        gateway           flags    interface metric
199.12.1.0         199.12.1.2        U        1e0       0
127.0.0.1          127.0.0.1         UH       1o0       0
0.0.0.0            199.12.1.1        UG       1e0       1
```

Line 1 indicates the locally attached network. Line 2 details a route to the software loopback interface found on some systems (notably UNIX). This interface loops packets back to the sending host. Line 3 shows the default route. In this case, a packet with an IP destination address that does not match the previous two entries gets sent to the host indicated in the *gateway* field. Note the "UG" flags. The packet is encapsulated in a datalink frame with a datalink destination address of the LAN interface of the router. When the packet is received, the router forwards it on to the next hop towards its final destination.

Setting up default routing is easy and is a good approach for this simple topology. On a UNIX system, a default route can be added manually by using the following *route* command:

```
route add net 0.0.0.0 199.12.1.1 1
```

This command, which is usually added to the system startup script, adds a route with a destination of 0.0.0.0 (the default network). The gateway is 199.12.1.1 and the metric is 1. If there are several routes to the same destination, the one with the smallest metric will be picked.

More complex topologies usually require use of a dynamic routing update protocol. Discussion of very complex routing topologies is beyond the scope of this book. Suffice it to say that the general idea shown here remains the same: Packets to nonlocal networks should be directed to your Internet gateway and packets to your network should be directed to the correct internal destination.

5.3   Dedicated Connectivity

Dedicated connectivity requires a leased line to your Internet provider. This is usually what is called a local-loop and is leased from your local telephone company. The line can be any of a variety of technologies. The most common today is a point-to-point circuit. The line goes to the local PoP of the Internet provider.

Most sites with dedicated connectivity use a specialized router. Doing this is usually advisable, since a router can typically handle more traffic than can a host configured as a router. Also, because the router does not have any other purpose, user accounts can be eliminated or severely restricted. This enables you to better isolate the router from attacks by potential intruders. See Chapter 9, *Security Issues* for a discussion about firewalling your system.

5.4   Dialup Connectivity

With the advent of low-cost, high-speed modems capable of speeds of up to 56kbps (with compression), the cost of Internet connectivity at usable speeds has dramatically decreased. Dialup connectivity uses a standard switched voice telephone line instead of a dedicated line to connect a site to an Internet provider. This method differs in several ways from using a dedicated line:

1. A dedicated router is no longer required because the software that provides dialup connectivity can be configured on almost any host with IP networking support. Some dedicated routers do have dialup capability, however, and might be a better option, depending on your budget. There also are small relatively inexpensive routers with dialup support available. In addition many terminal servers support dialup connectivity and can serve as an inexpensive router.

2. With a dialup connection, the connection to the Internet is intermittent. To obtain Internet connectivity, the Internet provider must be dialed up. Hence the phone dialing functionality must be part of the software.

3. The cost of connectivity might be less than that of a dedicated line, since a leased data line is no longer required and dialup rates from Internet providers are typically less than rates for a dedicated connection. However, you should be aware that factors such as dialup rate metering from the local telephone company and how long you stay connected all play a part in whether dialup connectivity is in fact cheaper than a dedicated connection.

Dialup connectivity uses a standard serial RS-232 connection that can be found on virtually any computer system. A modem is connected to the serial port. For best results, use a high-speed V.32 or V.32bis modem with V.42 error correction and V.42bis compression. Then, set up one of two possible communication protocols on this serial line: **SLIP (Serial Line IP)** or **PPP (Point-to-Point Protocol)**. Both SLIP and PPP are datalink protocols. They determine how IP packets are encapsulated and framed for transmission over the serial line. PPP is much more elaborate than SLIP in that it potentially allows multiple network protocols to be sent over the same serial line. SLIP on the other hand allows only IP packets to be encapsulated. Note also that both SLIP and PPP can be used over a dedicated serial line, although their use is much more common over dialup lines.

Software for SLIP and PPP is available both commercially and as freeware. See Appendix C, *Software and Other Information* for a description of some of the available packages. Most of the software is UNIX-based and can be added on to provide the required functionality. Some UNIX systems come with SLIP or PPP support built in. (Check your vendor documentation.) See also Chapter 10, *Setting Up Resource Discovery Services* for some comments on FTP security and dialup IP.

Using SLIP or PPP in a Dialup Environment

Both SLIP and PPP have been modified to work in a dialup environment. Next, we discuss generally how these packages are integrated into a UNIX system without the dialin or dialout functionality.

A UNIX network interface consists of a device driver to control the actual network device. For an Ethernet interface, the device driver comes as a part of the operating system kernel. A network device is given a name; for example, an Ethernet interface might be called *le0*. This name is known to the operating system and can be used in commands like *ifconfig* to identify the internal network device.

RS-232 serial interfaces are normally used to connect terminals to a host system. These terminal devices are usually named something like *tty01, tty02* , etc. To use a serial line as a SLIP or PPP device requires an operating system modification that adds some pseudo-devices to serve as network interfaces. For SLIP, these devices might be called *slip0* or *slip1;* for PPP, they might be called *ppp0* or *ppp1*.

For both SLIP and PPP, an auxiliary program is run to configure a specific RS-232 serial port as a network device. Usually this program specifies the name of the serial device (for example, *tty1*) and the necessary IP parameters for the serial network interface. In some cases, this auxiliary program does all the work to configure the pseudo-device. In others, it might simply map the serial device to the specific pseudo-network device and allow you to use the *ifconfig* utility to do the rest. Once the serial interface is mapped and configured, it can be used just like any other network interface.

IP packets sent out on the serial interface are encapsulated in a SLIP or PPP frame and sent as a serial bitstream using the standard RS-232 serial driver. When a SLIP or PPP frame is received, the frame header and trailer are stripped and the IP packet is sent to the IP input routine. Using this basic paradigm, you will find it relatively easy to configure a serial interface for use either by PPP or SLIP.

Dialup connectivity requires the SLIP and PPP software to handle both dialin and dialout connections. Establishing a dialin connection is relatively easy. It is usually handled by having the remote network user dialin with a special user account. The shell for the account is a special login program that maps the serial line on which the user dialed in as a network interface and configures it. Once this is done, the serial line dynamically becomes another network interface. Normally the IP address used on the interface is handled by a configuration file that maps from the special user name to a specific IP address. Alternatively, pseudo-network interfaces can be preconfigured, and then the user name is mapped to a specific pseudo-device.

Dialout connecting is only a little more difficult. In this case, a configuration file maps one of the network pseudo-devices to a phone number. Associated with the phone number is a login script used to actually login to the remote system. A dialout program is used to dial the remote system. Once a connection is established on a serial port and a successful login is made, the dialout program maps the serial port to the network's pseudo-device.

It's a little more difficult to do a dynamic dialout on demand. A dynamic dialout means that when the kernel has a packet to send to a SLIP or PPP interface, the kernel itself invokes the dialout program to establish the connection. For this to occur requires some judicious kernel hooks and a means of communicating between the kernel and the dialout program. This is generally accomplished by using an interprocess communications mechanism to a dialout daemon process that waits for dialout requests. from the kernel.

Common Modem and Data Communications Issues

By far the biggest problem when configuring SLIP or PPP in a dialup environment is getting the modems configured properly. The first step is to obtain a high-quality modem that has proven reliability. Usually your Internet provider has an approved list of modems. Next, ensure your modem is configured correctly. This is easier said than done, however, since modem manuals are notoriously difficult to understand and there are a myriad of ways to configure any modem. The best bet is to configure it in accordance with specifications from your Internet provider.

Following are some of the more common configuration problems you might encounter when using SLIP or PPP:

• Phone line problems
One of the more common problem with dialup connectivity is phone line prob-lems. Noisy phone lines can cause modems to drop or lose the carrier signal. They also can cause high-speed modems to renegotiate the connection at a lower speed, thus causing a loss of throughput. Further, some high-speed modems work better with noisy lines than do other high-speed modems. Problems caused by line noise can be very subtle and extremely difficult to track down.

• Flow control
Be sure you use hardware (RTS/CTS) flow control or no flow control. SLIP and PPP generally require and operate more reliably with it. Do not use software flow control that uses the ASCII DC1 and DC3 characters; if these characters are included in the data stream, they will be interpreted as flow control characters and not as data.

• Hardware overruns
Be sure your serial hardware can support the data rates you configure. If charac-ters are consistently lost when received, the network connection will seem very slow or even seem to stop. This results from many frames being truncated and dropped before they are processed by the IP input module.

• Header compression problems
Many versions of SLIP and PPP support header compression. With header com-pression, slow-speed SLIP or PPP links operate with less overhead. This style of compression is different from V.42bis or MNP data compression found in some modems. Header compression is handled in software on the hosts. There are several methods available. Just ensure both ends of the SLIP or PPP link sup-port the same method. If you experience problems with your SLIP or PPP link, turn off compression and see if the link works.

CHAPTER 6

Setting Up the Domain Name System

The **Domain Name System (DNS)** is the official distributed naming system for the Internet community. Any site with Internet connectivity must use DNS for mapping domain names to various resources. If you have direct Internet connectivity, you must have at least two DNS servers for your domain. However, you don't have to maintain a DNS server yourself; your Internet connectivity provider can do this for you. If you have taken this route, you don't need to read this chapter, although you might find the information useful.

In this chapter, we discuss the basics of setting up an authoritative DNS server for your registered domain. Our coverage is by no means exhaustive. Although flexible, DNS is a complex system. Good references that go into greater depth on the subject include [Carl-Mitchell & Quarterman 1993] and [Ablitz & Liu 1992].

6.1 DNS Basics

DNS defines a hierarchical, distributed naming system. A DNS name is called a **domain name,** also known as a **fully qualified domain name (FQDN).** The domain name uniquely identifies a single node in the DNS naming tree and consists of alphanumeric tokens separated by periods. Each token in the name is associated with a node of the naming tree. The tokens are not case sensitive, so the node name *EDU* is the same as the node names *edu* and *eDu*.

A node is uniquely named by traversing the tree from the node of interest to the root of the tree. Figure 6.1 shows a small subset of the total DNS tree; the full tree has millions of nodes. A node may have any number of child nodes, but only one parent. This arrangement guarantees that any node can be uniquely identified as long as all its sibling nodes have different names. Nodes with different parents may have the same node name but will still have unique FQDNs.

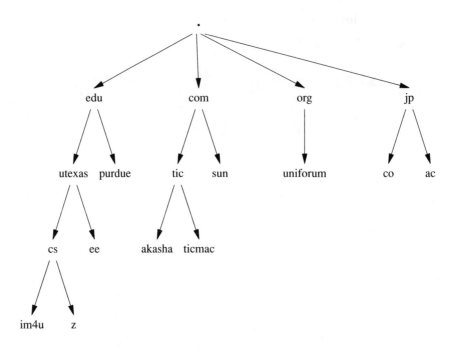

Figure 6.1 Part of the DNS Naming Tree.

The single node at the root of the tree is identified with a period and is called the **root node** of the DNS tree. The children of the root node are called **top-level domains.** These domains divide the tree both by type of organization and geographically by country. A U.S. organization that wants to connect to the Internet picks a new domain name under one of the top-level domains. For example, a commercial company will register under the top-level domain *com,* while an educational institution will register under the top-level domain *edu.* An organization outside the U.S. usually registers under the top-level domain that consists of the two-letter code for the pertinent country. Usually, each country domain is also subdivided organizationally, resulting in an extra level added to domain names outside the U.S. For example, an educational institution in the U.S. would register a domain *bigu.edu,* while an educational institution in Japan would register a domain *jbigu.ac.jp.* The exact registration procedure varies and depends on the naming registrar's procedures.

Registration adds a new child under the registrar's domain. For example, *tic.com* is the domain name for Texas Internet Consulting. Once a site registers a new domain, that site is given sole authority to add new nodes under its domain, that is, the site is *authoritative* for that domain. These new domains are called **subdomains** and that portion of the naming tree that an organization is authoritative for is called a **zone.** Each zone has a **zone database** associated with it that holds the name mapping information for the zone.

The first zone in the DNS hierarchy is the root node itself, while each top-level domain is another single node zone. A site can delegate any of its subdomains to a new naming authority. In this case, the delegated subdomain is the start of a new zone. The organizational top-level domains are usually grouped under the same naming authority, while the geographic top-level domains are in most cases distributed to a naming authority within a country. See Chapter 4, *Registering Domain Names and IP Numbers* for information about how to contact a naming authority to get a new domain name.

6.2   Zone Databases

Each DNS zone, as we stated in the last section, has an associated database. The database consists of one or more resource records. A **resource record** defines the type and value of a domain name resource found in the zone. Each resource record has the following format:

<domain, class, type, ttl, value>

The fields are defined as follows:

• *domain*
The FQDN this resource is associated with

• class
The class of the resource. This is generally the IN (Internet) class.

• *type*
The type of the resource. While there are many resource types, only a few are heavily used by most DNS servers.

• *ttl*
An optional field that is the maximum time in seconds the resource record may be cached on another server. In almost all cases, this field is omitted and takes on a default value, usually in the range of a few days to a week.

• *value*
The value of the resource. A resource value may be a single value or a set of values, depending on the resource type.

Typically, a site has four zones for which it needs to maintain databases:

• forward

• reverse (sometimes called *inverse*)

• localhost

• reverse localhost

```
(1)   ; forward zone database
(2)   $ORIGIN tic.com.
(3)   @ IN SOA akasha.tic.com. hostmaster.tic.com. (
(4)             930521   ; serial
(5)             86400    ; refresh
(6)             3600     ; retry
(7)             360000   ; expire
(8)             604800 ) ; minimum

(9)       IN NS akasha
(10)      IN NS ns2.psi.net.

(11)      IN MX 10 xfrsparc
(12)      IN MX 5 akasha

(13) akasha IN A 192.135.128.129
(14) ticmac IN A 192.135.128.131
(15) xfrsparc IN A 192.135.128.132

(16) src IN CNAME xfrsparc
(17) printserver IN CNAME akasha
(18) ftp IN CNAME akasha
(19) gopher IN CNAME akasha
```

Figure 6.2 Forward Zone Database File.

Forward Zone Database

A forward zone database contains resource records that map a domain name to a specific resource. Figure 6.2 shows an example zone database for the domain *tic.com.* This file is set out in the standard zone database format. It is read by a nameserver and a copy of the database is kept in server memory for fast access. Several meta-commands that are part of this standard format allow domain names to be abbreviated. Also, leading whitespace may be used to avoid repetition of domain names. Each line of this file is explained as follows:

• Line 1

Introduces a comment. The commenting convention provides that anything after a ";" in a line is commentary and not part of the database.

• Line 2

A meta-command. All meta-commands are introduced with a "$." In this case, the ORIGIN meta-command sets the default domain, which is appended to every non-fully qualified domain name found in the database file.

• Lines 3–8

The **Start of Authority (SOA)** record for this zone. This is always the first record in any zone database. The "@" as the first character substitutes for the name of the default domain defined by the last ORIGIN meta-command. The value of the SOA record is a series of parameters. The first parameter is the name of the host where the authoritative copy of the database was found; the second is a mailing address of the naming authority for this zone. Replacing the first period in the parameter with an "@" gives the real mail address, which you can use to contact a naming authority when problems arise. The mailing address should be an alias for a real system administrator. The final 5 parameters, enclosed in parentheses, define various operational characteristics of the zone database. We explain these in more detail in Section 6.6. Note the continuation convention used by this record, as follows: An open-parenthesis starts a list of parameters and the close-parenthesis ends the list, regardless of the number of lines the parameters take. The SOA record is one of the very few resource records that uses this convention. Most resource records easily fit on a single line.

• Lines 9 and 10

Names of the two **Nameserver (NS)** records that give the domain names of each authoritative nameserver for the zone. The leading whitespace is significant in that it indicates that the domain name for each record should be the same as that of the previous record. In this case, the domain name for both records will be *tic.com*. In line 9, the domain name of the nameserver is a single token, *akasha*. Because there is no trailing dot on the name, the default domain name is appended to the name. So this is a shorthand for the FQDN *akasha.tic.com*. In line 10, the name is an FQDN with a trailing dot, so the default name is not appended. When you type an FQDN in a zone database file, be sure to include the trailing dot; otherwise the default domain name will be appended, which is usually not what is intended. Without the trailing dot, line 10 would be inter-preted as

```
tic.com. IN NS ns2.psi.net.tic.com.
```

• Lines 11 and 12

Define **Mail Exchanger (MX)** records for the default domain. These are the names of hosts that act as mail exchangers for mail directed to the domain. In this case, two machines, *xfrsparc.tic.com* and *akasha.tic.com,* act as mail exchangers. We say more about the use of MX records in Chapter 7, *Setting Up Internet Electronic Mail*. Suffice it to say that every zone should have at least one MX record defined for it. Note again the leading whitespace, which indi-cates that the domain associated with this record is *tic.com*.

• Lines 13–15

Address (A) records that define the IP address for a given host. In this case, the IP address of the host *akasha.tic.com, ticmac.tic.com* and *xfrsparc.tic.com* are, respectively, 192.135.128.129, 192.135.128.131, and 192.135.128.132. A host with multiple interfaces may have multiple IP address. This situation is handled by simply adding additional address records for the host's domain name.

• Lines 16–19
   Alias (Cname) records that define alternate names for a given domain name. In the first record, the domain name *src.tic.com* is another name for *xfrsparc.tic.com*. Note again that a non-fully qualified domain name has the default domain name appended.

Reverse Zone Database

A reverse zone database contains special resource records that map IP addresses back to their associated domain names. These zones are found under the special domain *in-addr.arpa*. The subdomain *in-addr* is short for "Internet address." the top-level domain *arpa* is a historical artifact and no longer has anything to do with the old ARPANET or ARPA. The format of the reverse domain database is identical to that of the forward domain database. Figure 6.3 shows an example of a reverse zone database file. The pertinent lines are described as follows:

• Line 2
   The ORIGIN meta-command for the reverse zone. Note that it is the network number written backwards in dotted-decimal notation with the domain *in-addr.arpa* appended.

Figure 6.3 Reverse Zone Database File.

```
(1)   ; reverse zone database
(2)   $ORIGIN 128.135.192.in-addr.arpa.
(3)   @ IN SOA akasha.tic.com. hostmaster.tic.com. (
(4)           930521    ; serial
(5)           86400     ; refresh
(6)           3600      ; retry
(7)           360000    ; expire
(8)           604800 )  ; minimum

(9)      IN NS akasha.tic.com.
(10)     IN NS ns2.psi.net.

(11) 129 IN PTR akasha.tic.com.
(12) 131 ticmac IN PTR ticmac.tic.com.
(13) 132 IN PTR xfrsparc.tic.com.
```

• Lines 3–8

The SOA record for this zone. This record is almost identical to that for the forward zone. Note the careful use of trailing dots on the domain name parameters. Without them the default domain would be appended.

• Lines 9 and 10

The nameservers for this domain. In this case, they are the same as those for the forward domain. Different nameservers could be used. However, using the same servers as for the forward domain is conventionally done for ease of maintenance.

• Lines 11–13

The **PTR (Pointer)** records that map the reverse domain back to a forward domain name. A PTR record points back to the domain name that is the name of a host with the given IP address. Note that only the last digit of the IP address is listed, since the default domain will be appended. Line 11 could have been written as

```
129.128.135.192.in-addr.arpa. IN PTR akasha.tic.com.
```

Although this notation looks peculiar, since the IP address is written backwards, it allows delegation of network numbers. Also notice that the target forward domain is written as a FQDN with a trailing dot. A common error is to leave the trailing dot off, in which case the default domain would be appended. Another common mistake in a reverse zone file is to treat the components of the reverse IP address as *numbers*. These numbers are treated by DNS as *strings;* do not place leading zeros in these numbers. Doing so is incorrect and refers to an illegal domain.

Under most circumstances, all hosts within a particular domain use the same IP network number. So for each address record in the forward domain database, an associated pointer record must exist in the reverse domain database. There are tools that do this automatically to avoid common typing errors.

Some programs use the reverse domain to map an IP address into its corresponding domain name. IP addresses are 32-bit integer numbers and a reverse domain is a reversed dotted-decimal string representation of the number, so the client uses the following algorithm:

1. Take the IP address and convert it to dotted decimal notation without leading zeros.

2. Reverse the dotted-decimal number.

3. Append the string *in-addr.arpa,* with a leading and trailing dot, to the reversed dotted-decimal IP address.

4. Make a query to a DNS server for a PTR record using the above domain name.

```
; localhost zone database
$ORIGIN localhost.
@ SOA localhost. hostmaster.tic.com. (
       930518
       86400
       3600
       3600000
       604800 )
  IN NS localhost.
  IN A 127.0.0.1

; reverse localhost zone database
$ORIGIN 127.in-addr.arpa.
@ SOA localhost. hostmaster.tic.com. (
       930518
       86400
       3600
       3600000
       604800 )
  IN NS localhost.
localhost. IN A 127.0.0.1
1.0.0       IN PTR localhost.
```

Figure 6.4 Localhost and Reverse Localhost Zone Database Files.

Localhost and the Reverse Localhost Zone Databases

Every nameserver also must maintain a zone file for the loopback interface and its associated network. Network 127.0.0.0 is reserved as the address of the software loopback interface and every machine that supports a software loopback network interface is assigned the address 127.0.0.1. As a result of this convention, both a forward and a reverse zone file for this interface must be maintained by every nameserver. Figure 6.4 shows examples of these special zone database files.

6.3   Nameserver Cache

In addition to the four zone databases, each nameserver also reads in a cache of the names and addresses of the root nameservers. Figure 6.5 shows an example cache database. Note that it contains NS and A resource records but does not start with an SOA record, since the information contained in the cache is nonauthoritative. All the NS records are the names of servers authoritative for the root domain. Note the single period that stands for the root domain in the first column of the second line.

```
; Full cache of all known root domain servers
.           99999999       IN      NS          C.NYSER.NET.
            99999999       IN      NS          TERP.UMD.EDU.
            99999999       IN      NS          NS.NASA.GOV.
            99999999       IN      NS          NIC.DDN.MIL.
            99999999       IN      NS          A.ISI.EDU.
            99999999       IN      NS          GUNTER-ADAM.AF.MIL.
            99999999       IN      NS          AOS.BRL.MIL.
;
NS.NIC.DDN.MIL.     99999999      IN      A       192.112.36.4
A.ISI.EDU.          99999999      IN      A       26.3.0.103
A.ISI.EDU.          99999999      IN      A       128.9.0.107
AOS.BRL.MIL.        99999999      IN      A       128.20.1.2
AOS.BRL.MIL.        99999999      IN      A       192.5.25.82
C.NYSER.NET.        99999999      IN      A       192.33.4.12
GUNTER-ADAM.AF.MIL. 99999999      IN      A       26.1.0.13
NS.NASA.GOV.        99999999      IN      A       128.102.16.10
NS.NASA.GOV.        99999999      IN      A       192.52.195.10
TERP.UMD.EDU.       99999999      IN      A       128.8.10.90
```

Figure 6.5 DNS Cache Database.

The cache "hot-wires" the nameserver when it starts up and allows it to find the root servers so it can answer queries for nonlocal domains. Without the cache, a nameserver has no way of answering these queries. The design of DNS allows a server to answer any query, provided the server knows the IP address of one or more of the rootservers. The time-to-live field also is explicitly filled in for each resource record in the cache database and is set to a large value, thus keeping these important resource records from timing out. The current root nameserver cache file can be obtained by anonymous FTP from *ftp.rs.internic.net* in the file */domain/named.root*.

6.4 Bootstrap File

The most common DNS implementation is the **Berkeley Internet Name Daemon (BIND).** Implementations of BIND run on most UNIX variants. Almost without exception, a site's nameservice will employ a BIND server. BIND uses a boot-strap file to initialize itself. This file tells the nameserver where BIND's various zone and cache database files are located. It also defines which zones the server is authoritative for and is used by nonauthoritative servers to locate where authoritative data can be found. The bootstrap file is usually located, by default, in the pathname */etc/named.boot*.

```
(1) directory    /etc/named
(2) primary      tic.com                    tic.com
(3) primary      128.135.192.in-addr.arpa   f.192.135.128
(4) primary      localhost                  localhost
(5) primary      127.IN-ADDR.ARPA           f.127
(6) cache        .                          cache
```

Figure 6.6 Bootstrap File.

An example bootstrap file is shown in Fig. 6.6 and explained as follows:

• Line 1

Sets the directory in which all relative file references are found.

• Lines 2–5

Tells the nameserver that it is a primary server for the domain given as the second argument. The third argument is the name of the file in which the zone database resides. The file name can be any arbitrary name. The convention we use is as follows:

  • For a forward domain, give the file the same name as for the domain.

  • For a reverse domain, give the file the same name as the network number, prefixed with an "f."

• Line 6

Tells the nameserver the location of the cache file. The second field sets the domain for this file as the root of the DNS tree.

6.5   Typical Internet Server Arrangement

Operationally, DNS is a distributed database system. While it would be possible to keep all the zone databases on a single server, such an arrangement would be impractical. Instead zone databases are distributed on many hosts around the Internet. The nameserver on each host answers DNS queries that are generated by host applications requesting naming information.

The most typical query is generated when a client program needs the address of a remote host. The client program uses a set of routines found in a **resolver** library. These routines generate a query that is sent to a nearby nameserver, which then attempts to answer it. If a nameserver can't answer a query (that is, the query is for a domain for which it doesn't have information), then the nameserver forwards the query to another nameserver with better information. The servers of last resort are the root nameservers, since they know how to get to each top-level server, which in turn knows how to get to nameservers serving zones at lower levels in the naming tree. That is why every nameserver needs to keep a list of the root nameservers in their caches.

To reduce the amount of network traffic generated by queries, every name-server may cache responses to a query. Then when the nameserver gets a request for the same information, it can use the cached information rather than forwarding the query as it did the first time. After a while, caching enables a nameserver to answer most queries locally. A nameserver also can copy another server's zone files. That server then becomes a authoritative server for that zone. Such a server is called a **secondary nameserver.** The secondary nameserver periodically checks with the server it copied the zone file from to see if the file has been updated. By caching and using secondary nameservers, DNS improves its own performance and reliability.

A typical nameserver configuration is shown in Fig. 6.7. Note that in the fig-ure, a nameserver does not run on all machines. The site has a single authoritative server located on a host within the site and another authoritative server located at a remote site. The remote server, which is typically maintained by the site's Internet connectivity provider, is usually set up as a secondary server for the site's zone. Then when updates are applied to the zone databases, the remote secondary is automatically updated. The internal server fields all domain requests from all local hosts. The easiest way to arrange this is to point all the internal hosts at the authoritative server for all name requests. This is done on a UNIX system by cre-ating the file *letc/resolv.conf* on each host with the following information:

```
domain tic.com
nameserver 192.135.128.129
```

Figure 6.7 Typical Nameserver Configuration.

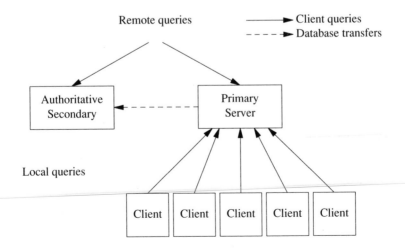

Each line is a keyword value. The *domain* line directs the resolver to append the domain name onto simple names. This convention lets you refer to a local host by its simple name rather than its FQDN. The *nameserver* line contains the IP address (not name) of a host that is running a nameserver. The naming request is sent to the server that answers the query and then returns the answer to the client. For non-UNIX systems, the method is similar, although the configuration file name and format may vary. The primary server also is configured with the same */etc/resolv.conf* file for fielding queries that originate on the server.

A larger site might have several secondary servers, all of which copy the zone database from the primary server. This procedure adds reliability to the overall system. We explain how to set up a secondary server in Section 6.7.

6.6   SOA Record Parameters

The most important set of parameters in a zone database file are kept in the SOA record for the zone. The first two parameters were described in Section 6.2. Each of the last five parameters is an integer number and is described as follows:

- *version*

The version number of the zone database. This number should be incremented each time the database is updated. A secondary nameserver uses this number to determine if it has a stale copy of the database.

- *refresh*

The zone refresh interval in seconds for a secondary server that copies this zone database. After retrieving the initial copy, the secondary nameserver contacts the primary only after the *refresh* interval and checks whether the *version* field has been updated. If so, the secondary retrieves the new zone file.

- *retry*

When an initial refresh attempt fails, the interval in seconds after which a secondary nameserver can attempt again to contact a primary nameserver. This number should always be smaller than the *refresh* interval.

- *expire*

The interval in seconds that a secondary nameserver's copy of a zone database is considered authoritative. After this interval, the copy of the database is no longer considered to be up-to-date. In this case, queries can still be fielded against the database, but the results are not flagged as being authoritative. Note that client programs can set a query bit to specify that only authoritative answers should be returned; however, this is rarely done.

- *minimum*

The default expiration time in seconds for a resource record. Future queries for the same resource record by that nameserver will use the cached record. After the expiration time is reached, the cached record is discarded and a fresh copy retrieved from an authoritative server. This procedure prevents stale information from being maintained indefinitely on remote servers. Most resource records use this default expiration value. For records that change more frequently, you might want to set a smaller value.

The values of these parameters shown in the examples are fairly reasonable. You must be sure to update the *version* number each time the zone file is updated. Otherwise any secondary nameservers will not copy the updated information.

6.7   Complete Examples of DNS Database Files

The following example files show a typical DNS configuration for a site. The site is relatively small, as shown in Fig. 6.8. It uses a single Class C network, 192.160.1.0, connected to the Internet by a router. The domain name for this site is *smallsite.com*. You would maintain four zone database files for this site:

• *smallsite.com*

• *1.160.192.in-addr.arpa*

• *localhost*

• *127.in-addr.arpa*

The *localhost* and *127.in-addr.arpa* zone database files are identical to the previous examples, except that the mailing address in the SOA record should be changed. In this example, the host *alpha.smallsite.com* is the primary nameserver for each zone database. All other machines use only the resolver routines and all queries are directed to *alpha.smallsite.com*. The *smallsite.com* and the *1.160.192.in-addr.arpa* zone database files and the nameserver bootstrap file are shown in Fig. 6.9. Note that the nameserver records in the *smallsite.com* and the *1.160.192.in-addr.arpa* zone databases include an NS record for the remote primary nameserver required for redundancy. The bootstrap file tells how the server is configured.

Figure 6.8 Network Configuration for smallsite.com.

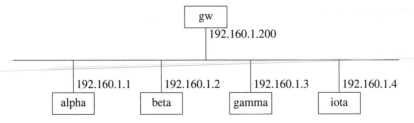

smallsite.com forward zone file
```
$ORIGIN smallsite.com.
@ IN SOA alpha.smallsite.com. hostmaster.smallsite.com. (
            1            ; serial
            86400        ; refresh - 1 day
            3600         ; retry - 1 hour
            345600       ; expire - 4 days
            604800 )     ; minimum - 7 days
   IN NS alpha
   IN NS ns.ipnet.net.

   IN MX 10 alpha
   IN MX 20 gamma

alpha     IN A 192.160.1.1
beta      IN A 192.160.1.2
gamma     IN A 192.160.1.3
iota      IN A 192.160.1.4
gw        IN A 192.160.1.200
```

smallsite.com reverse zone file
```
$ORIGIN 1.160.192.in-addr.arpa.
@ IN SOA alpha.smallsite.com. hostmaster.smallsite.com. (
            1            ; serial
            86400        ; refresh - 1 day
            3600         ; retry - 1 hour
            345600       ; expire - 4 days
            604800 )     ; minimum - 7 days

   IN NS alpha.smallsite.com.
   IN NS ns.ipnet.net.

1    IN PTR alpha.smallsite.com.
2    IN PTR beta.smallsite.com.
3    IN PTR gamma.smallsite.com.
4    IN PTR iota.smallsite.com.
200 IN PTR gw.smallsite.com.
```

bootstrap file for alpha.smallsite.com
```
directory     /etc/named
primary       smallsite.com              smallsite.com
primary       1.160.192.in-addr.arpa     f.192.160.1
primary       localhost                  localhost
primary       127.in-addr.arpa           f.127
```

Figure 6.9 Smallsite.com Configuration Files.

On each of the other local hosts, you would create the file */etc/resolv.conf* with the following entries:

```
domain smallsite.com
nameserver 192.160.1.1
nameserver 111.1.1.1
```

where 111.1.1.1 is the address of the remote secondary server *ns.ipnet.net.* If the local primary server is down, queries are directed to the remote secondary server.

A slight variation on the above configuration lets you add a local secondary server for redundancy. Suppose you want the machine *beta.smallsite.com* to act as a secondary server. Simply copy the zone databases for the *loopback* and the *127.in-addr.arpa* domains to the machine *beta.smallsite.com* and create the bootstrap file shown in Fig. 6.10. This file is identical to the primary nameserver bootstrap file, except that the zone databases for the domains *smallsite.com* and *1.160.192.in-addr.arpa* are copied automatically from *alpha.smallsite.com.* You accomplish this by placing two "secondary" lines in the bootstrap file. Note that these lines closely resemble the "primary" lines in *alpha's* bootstrap file, except the arguments are slightly different. You would specify the IP address (not name) of *alpha.smallsite.com* rather than the file from which to read the zone database file. This address is followed by the name of a local file to which to save a copy of the zone database after it is retrieved from the primary server. This file is read as a backup in case the primary server is unavailable.

Note that you don't need to add the new secondary server as a registered server for each of the zones; doing this would require you to register it with the higher-level naming authority. The new secondary server is used solely for local redundancy. To get hosts to use the new secondary, you simply append the following line to each host's */etc/resolv.conf* file:

```
nameserver 192.160.1.2
```

If you want to provide a degree of load balancing by having some machines query the new secondary first, put the above line before the other nameserver lines in the file. Each server is then tried in turn in a round-robin fashion until a response is received.

Figure 6.10 Secondary Bootstrap File.

```
; bootstrap file for beta.smallsite.com
directory    /etc/named
secondary    smallsite.com             192.160.1.1 smallsite.com
secondary    1.160.192.in-addr.arpa    192.160.1.1 f.192.160.1
primary      localhost                 localhost
primary      127.in-addr.arpa          f.127
```

For a large site with many physical networks, it's a good idea to set up one or more local secondary servers on each physical network. As your site grows, you might also wish to create subdomains. (Discussion of subdomains is beyond the scope of this book.)

6.8   Hints and Tidbits

Many host systems, especially workstations, don't come packaged with DNS as the default nameservice. Many use instead static tables or Sun's NIS (Network Information Service). If you have just a few machines or an isolated network, these latter methods can be quite adequate. However, as we have stressed in this book, when you are connected to the Internet, you must use DNS. DNS is particularly important when you want to connect to a remote host using its domain name. Without DNS, you must use an IP address, which is harder to remember than a domain name.

To get your client services to use DNS rather than one of the other naming services, you might need to do some local configuration and read your vendor documentation. Some machines allow you to switch from one service to another or allow you to specify the order of services in a configuration file. Others require you to replace the front-end library routines used to direct the name lookup functions. For example, SunOS 4.1.x by default has a very kludgy way of directing DNS lookups through a NIS server. To do DNS correctly on a Sun requires replacing the standard C library routines that do host name lookups with the ones that use DNS. Doing this is not difficult.

You also can set up MS-DOS PCs and Apple Macintosh computers to use DNS. Typically, these systems will run just the resolver code and access a remote DNS server. Most of the TCP/IP-based software that runs on them supports DNS lookups. Note that the standard Apple TCP/IP driver, MacTCP, has a DNS resolver built into it. In the MS-DOS world, however, things are more complex and DNS must be supported by the application programs themselves. Also some MS-DOS implementations of TCP/IP don't support DNS and rely instead on static host tables maintained on the MS-DOS machines.

The name of the server program and where it is kept varies by vendor. You also should check your vendor manuals for its directions on getting DNS set up. In addition, be sure the DNS well-known ports are entered in the port mapping database (the file /etc/services on UNIX systems). The entries should look like the following:

```
domain          53/udp      # Domain Name System
domain          53/tcp      # Domain Name System
```

Note that DNS uses both a TCP and a UDP port for proper operation.

Several tools for debugging DNS are available. One called *nslookup* is usually shipped as an integral part of most UNIX OSs. The other, *dig*, is available from public FTP archive sites. Also the latest BIND release is publicly available from Internet archive sites. You can install this version if you are interested in the latest BIND bells and whistles and bug fixes. Most OS vendors ship versions of BIND based on earlier releases. See Appendix C, *Software and Other Information* for the location of these resources.

6.9   Checking It Out

Once you have set up your DNS server, you can verify its operation by doing the following:

1. Start up the DNS server daemon and ensure it has properly loaded the local DNS database. To verify this, initially run the server with the command

   ```
   named -d 1
   ```

   which leaves the server in the foreground but creates a debugging file called */usr/tmp/named.run*. Terminate the server and look in this file for any error messages. If there are errors there, correct the database error.

2. Start the server with no options. Doing this will put the server in the background.

3. Try to TELNET to the machine *is.internic.net*. You should see the following on a UNIX host:

   ```
   csh> telnet is.internic.net
   Trying 192.153.156.15 ...
   Connected to is.internic.net.
   Escape character is '^]'.
   SunOS UNIX (is)
   login:
   ```

   If you at least get the line starting with *Trying,* then your nameserver is configured properly.

4. Try using TELNET or FTP to get to other known hosts on the Internet. You can, for example, use FTP to get to the machine *ftp.tic.com*. Log in as the anonymous user and retrieve some useful DNS support scripts from the file */pub/dns.tar.Z*. You also can try FTPing to *ftp.rs.internic.net* and getting an up-to-date copy of the root server cache file found in the file */domain/named.root*.

5. To see if your nameserver is accessible from another Internet site, use TELNET to log in to machine *tic.com* with a login name of *dns-test*. This login account runs a simple test on your nameserver from the remote location.

If the above quick test fails, then check for some of these more obvious errors:

1. Be sure hostname lookups are using DNS. You can verify this by starting the server with debugging on and issuing a query against the server. The debugging output in */usr/tmp/named.run* will show whether the server got the query. If it did not, then recheck your configuration.

2. Ensure at least one of the root servers is accessible. You can do this easily by using the *ping* program and trying each of the root server IP addresses found in the DNS root cache file.

References

Ablitz & Liu 1992.   Ablitz, Paul, & Liu, Cricket, *DNS and BIND,* O'Reilly & Associates, Sebastapol, CA (1992).

Carl-Mitchell & Quarterman 1993.   Carl-Mitchell, Smoot, & Quarterman, John S., *Practical Internetworking with TCP/IP and UNIX,* Addison-Wesley, Reading, MA (1993). ISBN 0-201-58629-0.

CHAPTER 7

Setting Up Internet Electronic Mail

Electronic mail is the most widely used Internet service. With it, you can reach more than 25,000,000 people on the worldwide Matrix of networks that exchange mail, including more than 12,000,000 people on the Internet. These networks include the UUCP Mail network, BITNET, and FidoNet, plus commercial conferencing systems such as CompuServe and BIX and mail services such as MCI Mail and America Online. Because the Internet is the hub of the worldwide electronic mail community, it is important that your mail system be robust and reliable.

In this chapter, we explain how to establish reliable Internet mail service. We discuss configuring *sendmail*, the most common UNIX mail transport agent used in the Internet community, and review some of the common mail user agents used on networked UNIX systems. We talk primarily about configuring UNIX systems, since they are by far the most widely used systems with Internet access. However, after you have reliably connected your UNIX hosts to the Internet, you can use them as a foundation for extending mail services to your organization's other computer systems, such as PC or Macintosh systems.

7.1 Mail Architecture

Figure 7.1 shows the general architecture of a mail system. Such a system has two major parts: MTAs and UAs. A **message transfer agent (MTA)** routes a mail message towards its final destination by sending the message to another MTA. A **user agent (UA)** interacts with an end-user and allows the user to send and receive mail messages. The arrows in the figure show the path a message might take when sent from a user using UA1 to a user using UA3.

The interaction between an MTA and a UA is not defined in this general architecture. However, the usual paradigm is for the MTA to deposit a mail message in a user's mailbox. A **mailbox** is a file that stores mail messages deposited by the local MTA that the user can then read. When transmitting a message

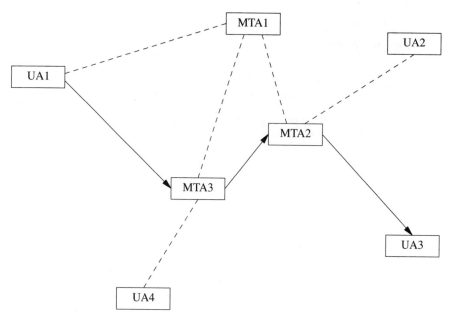

Figure 7.1 Mail System Architecture.

composed by a user, the UA sends the outbound message to the local MTA, usually through some kind of interprocess communications facility. On a UNIX system, the outbound message is normally passed to the MTA via a pipe. On the Internet, MTAs communicate with each other using the **Simple Mail Transfer Protocol (SMTP)** [Postel 1982]. This protocol, as its name suggests, is very simple. An example SMTP dialogue is shown in Fig. 7.2. SMTP follows the client/server model of computing. The SMTP client initiates the dialogue with an SMTP server by sending a message to the remote server. This message includes the following three pieces of information:

• The sender address (line 4)
  The argument (in angle brackets) to the MAIL FROM: command.

• The recipient address (line 6)
  The argument (in angle brackets) to the RCPT TO: command. There may be more than a single recipient address, each of which appears as an argument to additional RCPT TO: commands. This convention enables you to send the same message to multiple recipients on the same server.

• The message itself (line 10)
  Sent by the client after the response to the DATA command from the server (line 8). The client signals the end of the message by sending a line with a single period (line 11). The client then can send another message or use the QUIT command (line 13) to the session with the server.

```
(1)   220 cs.utexas.edu Sendmail 5.64/1.129 ready \
          at Thu, 7 May 92 16:08:02 -0500
(2)   HELO akasha.tic.com
(3)   250 cs.utexas.edu Hello akasha.tic.com
(4)   MAIL FROM:<sally@tic.com>
(5)   250 <sally@tic.com>... Sender ok
(6)   RCPT TO:<fred@cs.utexas.edu>
(7)   250 <fred@cs.utexas.edu>... Recipient ok
(8)   DATA
(9)   354 Enter mail, end with "." on a line by itself
(10)  { message header }
          .

          .

          .
      { message body }
(11)  .
(12)  250 Mail accepted
(13)  QUIT
(14)  221 cs.utexas.edu closing connection
```

Figure 7.2 SMTP Dialogue.

7.2 Mail Envelopes and Contents

Each mail message comprises two parts: the mail envelope and the envelope contents.

Analogous to the recipient and return addresses found on a paper mail envelope, the mail envelope supplies the addressing information. It is the only part of the message an MTA examines. Using SMTP, an MTA sends the envelope information to another MTA in the SMTP dialogue.

The mail envelope contents consists of two parts: a header and a body [Crocker 1982]. An example of an envelope's contents is shown in Fig. 7.3. Headers always start with keywords followed by a colon; for example, *To:*, *From:*, and *Subject:*. The message body is separated from the header lines by a blank line.

The header lines are not used to route the message to its destination. Rather they serve as information to the user receiving the message. The envelope addresses are used to route the message. However, because the user never sees the envelope as part of the message, the header lines include the addressing information in the *From:* and *To:* lines enabling the user to reply to the message by simply using the information contained in the received message. This is a very powerful feature of mail, and all modern UAs perform this function automatically for the user.

```
Date: Wed, 13 Oct 93 08:49:54 -0500
From: sally@tic.com
To: fred@cs.utexas.edu
Subject: Party Invitation
Cc: jane@tic.com

Hi,

You are invited to a party at 5:00 PM after work
at the office.  Bring a friend.

Sally

P.S.  Rememeber this is also a surprise party
for Stan, so don't let him know.
```

Figure 7.3 Example Message.

7.3 Internet Mail Addresses

An Internet mail address comprises two parts separated by an "at" sign (@) as follows:

local_part@domain_part

The *domain_part* is any legal domain address, such as *tic.com* or *cs.utexas.edu.* This part of the address indicates the location of an MTA where the *local_part* of the address will be further processed. In some cases, it is an actual host address. More often it is simply the domain name of the organization to which the mail will be forwarded. The specific server to send the message to is derived from the domain name. We explain how this is accomplished when we discuss MX records in Section 7.4.

The *local_part,* which is any printable string of ASCII characters, designates the final destination of the mail message. There are conventions for escaping characters with special meaning, such as the "at" sign (@), however, these conventions are seldom needed, since most *local_part* addresses are composed of letters and numbers. When the mail reaches the MTA designated in the *domain_part* of the address, an MTA processes only the *local_part*. This part may be the login name of a user or, possibly, a local alias that points either to a list of recipients or the actual destination mailbox of the message. The *local_part* also may incorporate other mail addressing standards, such as UUCP Mail addresses, etc. The important point to remember is this part is processed only when the message reaches the destination specified in the *domain_part* of the address.

7.4   Internet Mail and DNS MX Records

In the early days of the Internet, the *domain_part* of a mail address had to be the name of a specific host system. This convention proved to be limiting, so a form of indirection called a **Mail Exchanger (MX)** record was developed as part of DNS to support mail delivery.

An MX record is a DNS resource of the general form

domain IN MX *priority host*

The *domain* is any legal domain; the *priority* is a numeric priority; and the *host* is the domain address of a host system that runs an MTA for the domain.

When an MTA looks at the *domain_part* of a mail address, it first attempts to find all the MX records associated with that domain. Next, it tries to forward the message to the hosts in the list in ascending priority order. The first host available receives the message and does any further processing necessary for final delivery. This system accomplishes several goals:

1. Mail addresses are decoupled from any specific host address. Doing this allows an organization to use mail addresses that use a *domain_part* that references the organization; for example, *sally@tic.com,* where the *domain_part* of the address need not necessarily refer to a real hostname. Here, the MX indirection allows *tic.com* to point to the address of a real mail gateway.

2. MX records allow redundant mail gateways to be created. If one gateway is down, other gateways can pick up the slack. Multiple MX records can even support a limited form of load balancing. An MTA with MX support selects at random two or more mail gateways that have equal priority.

3. Perhaps most important, MX records let you use Internet mail addressing to forward mail to recipients who are not on the Internet but are connected via a smart mail gateway that is on the Internet. For example, our address *tic@tic.com* is a domain mail address, but until about two years ago, our computer systems were not on the Internet. In that case, mail to that address was sent to a smart gateway on the Internet that knew how to forward the mail to us using UUCP over a dialup connection. The details of this routing were completely hidden by the use of an MX record that pointed at the smart gateway.

Many commercial mail systems use MX records in a similar way. For example, with Internet connectivity, you can send a message to the MCI Mail system by using an address like *3304.23455@mcimail.com.* However, there is no machine *mcimail.com* on the Internet. Rather an MX record for that domain points to the MCI Mail gateway on the Internet. Compuserve works the same way using the MXed domain *compuserve.com.*

All MTAs that exchange mail with the Internet must understand MX records and must know how to route mail using them. Unfortunately, all MTAs do not use MX records but instead incorrectly assume the *domain_part* of an mail address is a hostname. When configuring your Internet mail gateway, be sure the MTA you are using understands how to use MX records. Consult your vendor's documentation to be sure such support exists and to determine how to enable MX record processing.

7.5 Example Mail System

The ability to transfer messages between hosts using SMTP gives you a great deal of flexibility when configuring your mail system. That flexibility lets you construct very robust mail configurations. To simplify matters, we show you next how to build the mail system for the site shown in Fig. 7.4. In this example, a single UNIX host running *sendmail*, *mailgw.smallsite.com*, acts as a mail gateway for all the other hosts at the site. All mail to and from the Internet is funneled through this machine. Note that the figure shows the flow of mail messages to be from one host to another. The actual physical architecture of the system, however, can be quite different from this flow. For example, the mail gateway may be connected to a LAN that is interconnected to the Internet via a dedicated router. Or the client machines may be on separate subnets. The important point is that regardless of the physical configuration, all mail flows through the mail gateway on its way to its final destination. This lets the mail gateway make all the more complex routing decisions about a message's destination.

sendmail Basics

sendmail uses a configuration file to set various parameters about its operation. Typically the configuration file is called *sendmail.cf* and is found in the directory */etc*, */usr/lib*, or */usr/ucblib*. In this section, we show replacements for the standard configuration file shipped with most systems. You should move the original configuration file to an alternate filename and replace it with the configuration file in this example.

Figure 7.4 Example Site Configuration.

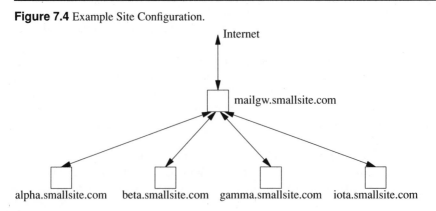

Once the new configuration file is installed, be sure to terminate the running *sendmail* daemon process. The daemon process is run at startup and listens for inbound SMTP connections. Before starting it, freeze the new configuration file with the following command:

```
/usr/lib/sendmail -bz
```

This command compiles the configuration file into a more compact format for speedier startup of *sendmail*. Be sure it runs without any errors. If a *sendmail* daemon is already running on your system, be sure to terminate it and restart it after freezing the configuration file. If a daemon is not running on your system, be sure to add the appropriate commands to your system's startup scripts. The usual *sendmail* startup command is like the following:

```
/usr/lib/sendmail -bd -q1h
```

This command runs *sendmail* as a daemon and transmits queued mail once an hour. Note that both of the above commands must be run as the superuser. You can check the operation of *sendmail* using the test mode with the following command:

```
/usr/lib/sendmail -bt
```

The output from the test mode is cryptic at best. Refer to your system's documentation for further details. Good *sendmail* references are found in [Allman 1983a], [Allman 1983b], [Carl-Mitchell & Quarterman 1993], and [Costales *et al.* 1994].

   sendmail performs three complementary functions: mail routing, header address rewriting, and address aliasing.

Mail Routing. *sendmail* routes a message based on the syntax of the recipient envelope address. *sendmail* takes the recipient address from the SMTP envelope dialogue or as an argument passed to it by a UA. The examination of this address results in a triple of the form

<mailer, host, user>

The parts of the triple are explained as follows:

• *mailer*
  The name of a mailer used to transport the message. Mailers are defined as part of the configuration, so this name is a placeholder for a method used to deliver a mail message. A *sendmail* mailer specifies a program for the MTA to invoke to deliver the message. It also defines a set of header rewriting rules through which all addresses in the message header are processed. The most common method on the Internet is to use the *tcp* mailer, which in turn uses SMTP to deliver the message. Use of SMTP, which is built in to *sendmail*, is a special case in the *sendmail* code. Local mail is delivered using the *local* mailer. This mailer uses

a simple program to lock the recipient's mailbox, appends the message to the end of the mailbox, and unlocks the mailbox to allow other programs access to its contents. The actual program used as the mailer depends on the implementation.

• *host*
The domain name to which the message will be sent. This name is used to look up MX records, which in turn are used to look up the IP address of an MTA.

• *user*
The recipient address used as the argument to the RCPT TO: command in the SMTP dialogue.

Header Address Rewriting. *sendmail* also ensures the correctness of header addresses in the *From:, To:,* and other header lines having addresses. For example, a message sent from a local UA usually will have a sender address as just a simple name without a *domain_part. sendmail* ensures the *domain_part* is added to all occurrences of this address in both the envelope and message header.

Unfortunately, *sendmail* uses a rather cryptic language to perform these two vital functions. Although that language is flexible and relatively simple, it's not very easy to read. Fortunately, much of the information required in a *sendmail* configuration file is the same from one configuration to the next, so with judicious configuration organization, much of the information from one configuration file can be reused in the next. Most of the constant information is derived from "boilerplate" files and pieced together with the *m4* macro program found on UNIX systems. We don't show the boilerplate files here, but a list of these files and instructions on retrieving copies of them are in Appendix C, *Software and Other Information*.

Aliasing. *sendmail* also does address aliasing by looking up addresses in a global alias database. The alias database location is specified in the configuration, but it is usually kept in the file */etc/aliases* or */usr/lib/aliases*. An alias entry looks like the following:

```
joe: joseph@tic.com
```

In this example, mail addressed to *joe* is sent to the address *joe@tic.com*. The target of an alias may be several addresses. For example the alias

```
tic: smoot, jsq
```

sends mail addressed to *tic* to both *smoot* and *jsq*.

The alias database is kept in a hashed file format for speedy lookups. Each time the alias file is updated, the following command should be run:

```
/usr/lib/sendmail -bi
```

which will create a hashed database from the alias file.

Site Mail Addressing

The mail addressing used in this example assumes all mail addresses are of the form *user@smallsite.com* regardless of the internal machine to which the mail is finally delivered. This is accomplished in part by adding a single MX record to the DNS database for the *smallsite.com* domain. This MX record looks as follows:

```
smallsite.com. IN MX 10 mailgw.smallsite.com.
```

Next, we show you how the *sendmail* configuration on *mailgw.smallsite.com* supports this type of addressing.

Gatewaying Mail

Figure 7.5 shows the flow of mail for a message from another domain, detailed as follows:

1. A mail message is addressed to *jill@smallsite.com.*

2. The MTA on the remote system looks up the MX records for the domain *smallsite.com.*

3. The MTA forwards the message to *mailgw.smallsite.com.*

Figure 7.5 Mail Routing from another Domain.

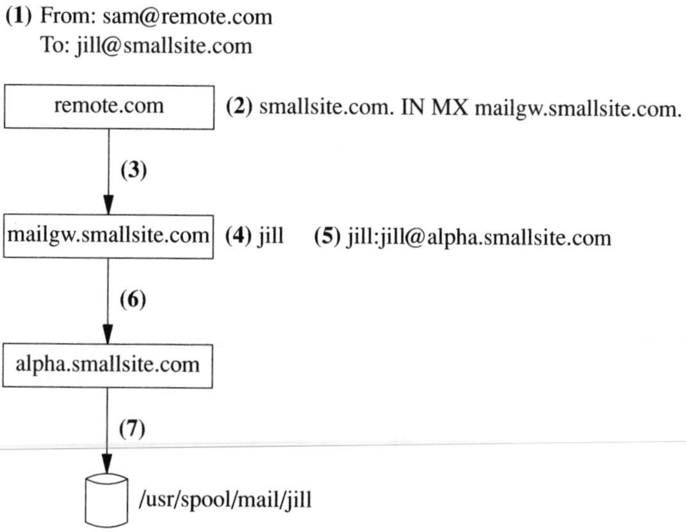

(**1**) From: sam@remote.com
       To: jill@smallsite.com

remote.com   (**2**) smallsite.com. IN MX mailgw.smallsite.com.

(**3**)

mailgw.smallsite.com (**4**) jill   (**5**) jill:jill@alpha.smallsite.com

(**6**)

alpha.smallsite.com

(**7**)

/usr/spool/mail/jill

4. The MTA on *mailgw.smallsite.com* receives the message and looks at the *local_part* of the address.

5. The address is checked against the *sendmail* alias database and a matching entry is found that maps the address to *jill@alpha.smallsite.com*. The alias entry for jill in the alias database looks as follows:

```
jill: jill@alpha.smallsite.com
```

This entry acts essentially as a redirector for mail destined for Jill's mailbox, which is located on the machine *alpha.smallsite.com*. This is a powerful alias feature. Also, note that only the envelope recipient address is aliased. The address in the *To:* line in the message header is still just *jill@smallsite.com*.

6. The message is forwarded to the machine *alpha.smallsite.com*.

7. The MTA on *alpha.smallsite.com* determines that *jill* is a local user and appends the message to the appropriate mailbox.

Figure 7.6 shows the flow of a message from one of the local hosts to a recipient outside the local system, detailed as follows:

1. A user on *alpha.smallsite.com* composes a message to *jsq@tic.com*. The UA forwards the message to the local MTA.

2. The local MTA forwards the message to the MTA on *mailgw.smallsite.com*.

3. The MTA on *mailgw.smallsite.com* looks up the MX records for *tic.com*.

Figure 7.6 Mail Routing to Another Domain.

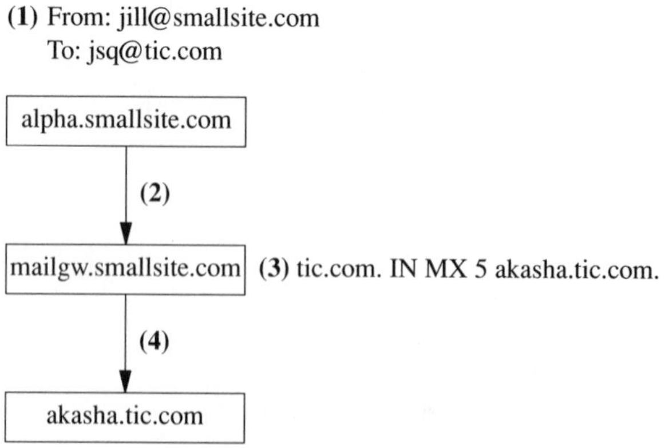

(**1**) From: jill@smallsite.com
To: jsq@tic.com

(**3**) tic.com. IN MX 5 akasha.tic.com.

4. The message is forwarded to one of the mail gateways for the *tic.com* domain. The header addresses in the message are standardized to always have a *domain_part* of *smallsite.com,* so that the reply address in the *From:* header reads *jill@smallsite.com.*

Finally, the route taken for a mail message from *jill@alpha.smallsite.com* to *jack@beta.smallsite.com* is shown in Fig. 7.7 and explained as follows:

1. Jill composes a mail message on *alpha.smallsite.com* addressed to simply *jack.*

2. The local MTA on *alpha.smallsite.com* sees that *jack* is not a local user and forwards the message to the MTA on *mailgw.smallsite.com.* This MTA also appends the domain *smallsite.com* to every header and envelope address that doesn't have a *domain_part.* So the simple address *jack* becomes *jack@smallsite.com.* The sender address *jill,* which is derived from the userid of the sender, also is appended with the *domain_part smallsite.com.*

3. The MTA on *mailgw.smallsite.com* checks its alias database and sees an alias that maps the address *jack* to *jack@beta.smallsite.com.*

4. The message is sent to the MTA on *beta.smallsite.com.*

5. The message is placed in Jack's mailbox on *beta.smallsite.com.*

Figure 7.7 Mail Routing within the Local Domain.

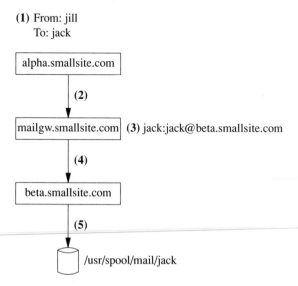

(1) From: jill
    To: jack

alpha.smallsite.com

(2)

mailgw.smallsite.com (3) jack:jack@beta.smallsite.com

(4)

beta.smallsite.com

(5)

/usr/spool/mail/jack

This architecture funnels all mail through a common gateway machine, where the MTA does all the address aliasing. This setup greatly simplifies the overall mail system management, since all MTAs except for the mail gateway are configured identically. Also the gateway machine is the only one that needs to maintain the alias database, a useful simplification in a heterogeneous host environment.

Gateway Configuration

Figure 7.8 shows the *sendmail* configuration file for the gateway machine. Each line of the configuration file is explained as follows:

• Line 1
The version number of this configuration. This is the "V" macro. A macro definition always starts with a "D" in column 1, followed by the single letter name of the macro and then the value of the macro, which is any arbitrary string of characters. This particular macro appears in the SMTP server banner message.

• Line 2
The macro definition for the domain name of the site: *smallsite.com*. All addresses without a *domain_part* have this domain appended to them. This means any locally generated mail will have addresses of the form *local_user@smallsite.com*. Also, any incoming mail with this *domain_part* is considered local by the MTA.

• Line 3
The official name of this host. This is the "j" macro. Note that it is the interpolation of the "w" macro, which gets its value from the name of the host when

---

Figure 7.8 Gateway Configuration.

```
(1)   DVgw.1.0
(2)   DDsmallsite.com
(3)   Dj$w
(4)   DMtcp

(5)   include(general.m4)
(6)   include(rules.m4)
(7)   include(local.m4)
(8)   include(tcp.m4)
(9)   include(zeropre.m4)

(10)  R$*<@$-.$D>$*        $#$M $@$2.$D $:$1<@$2.$D>$3
(11)  R$*<@$+>$*           $#$M $@$2 $:$1<@$2>$3
(12)  R$+%$+               $@$>29$1@$2
(13)  R$+                  $#local $:$1
```

sendmail starts up. A macro value is interpolated into a string by prefixing the macro name with a dollar sign. This configuration depends on the hostname being a FQDN. So be sure to set the hostname correctly.

• Line 4

The name of the major relay mailer. Messages are sent between machines using this mailer. In this case the name of the mailer is *tcp*.

• Lines 5–9

The *include* files that contain the invariant parts of the configuration. These files include general information, various rulesets used by all configurations, and the definitions for mailers. The definition for the *local* mailer is found in the file *local.m4*, while the definition for the *tcp* mailer is found in the file *tcp.m4*.

• Line 10

A *sendmail* rule that sends all mail with an envelope recipient address, such as *user@alpha.smallsite.com,* to the MTA for that specific host.

• Line 11

A rule that sends all mail for domains the local domain to the mail gateway for that specific domain.

• Line 12

A rule that takes care of addresses that use the internal routing syntax of *user%domain@site_domain*. This is an ad hoc convention. If the MTA on *mailgw.smallsite.com* receives a message with a recipient address of *user%domain@smallsite.com,* the *local_part* of the address is examined and the "%" is replaced with an "at" sign (@). The address is then reprocessed. If you don't want to support this convention, you can remove this line from the configuration file.

• Line 13

A rule that handles all other addresses. These addresses are considered local addresses. Any recipient address that matches this rule is aliased and then each address in the alias expansion is reprocessed by the configuration file rules. If no alias is found for an address, the address is considered local and is sent to a local user's mailbox.

Subordinate Configuration File

Figure 7.9 shows the configuration file for all nongateway machines. It is built from the same *include* files as the gateway configuration but differs from that configuration as follows:

• Line 3

The name of a file that lists all local users. A user found in this list receives mail on this machine. For workstations, this file usually contains the name of the user of the workstation.

```
(1)    DVsub.1.1
(2)    DDacme.com
(3)    FL/etc/local_names
(4)    Dj$w
(5)    DMtcp
(6)    DRmail_relay.$D


(7)    include(general.m4)
(8)    include(rules.m4)
(9)    include(local.m4)
(10)   include(tcp.m4)
(11)   include(zeropre.m4)


(12)  R$=L      $#local $:$1
(13)  R$+       $#$M $@$R $:$1
```

Figure 7.9 Subordinate Configuration.

• Line 6

An alias for the mail gateway machine. In this example, a CNAME record of the form

```
mail_relay.smallsite.com. IN CNAME mailgw.smallsite.com.
```

should be added to the DNS nameserver. Using an alias here keeps you from having to change all the configuration files if the mail gateway changes from one machine to another.

• Line 12

A rule that locally delivers messages wth a simple address without a domain part found in the file */etc/local_names*. A mail message to the recipient address *jack@beta.smallsite.com* will be delivered to Jack's mailbox, provided the name "jack" appears in the file. The *domain_part* of the address is matched against the local machine name and it, along with the "at" sign (@), is stripped from the address before being evaluated by this rule. This address is the *envelope* address, not the address found in the message header, which will be *jack@smallsite.com*. The header address is not used for routing.

• Line 13

A rule that handles all other addresses. These addresses are sent to the mail gateway.

7.6   The Post Office Protocol

Another useful mail protocol is the **Post Office Protocol (POP).** POP lets you set up a machine as a mail drop point, analogous to a postal box at a post office [Butler *et al.* 1985] and [Rose 1991]. Just as the leasee of a postal box must go to the post office to pick up mail, POP performs the same function for electronic mail. POP lets a user's mailbox reside on a remote host, but allows the user to retrieve the messages from the remote mailbox on demand. As such, POP is user driven, since mail is not transferred until the user requests that be done. After the transfer, the user can read mail on the local system whenever it's convenient. Replies are relayed to the POP server using SMTP. This facility is very useful when the user's primary machine is a PC or Macintosh computer that either doesn't have the capacity to run an SMTP server or may be switched off at the time a reply is sent, rendering it unable to receive the reply. It also is useful when connecting a home computer to a remote network using SLIP or PPP. Several freeware mailers are available that offer POP support for both Macintoshes and PCs. See Appendix C, *Software and Other Information* for how to obtain this software.

Using POP is not an essential part of Internet mail connectivity, but it is a useful addition, especially if you have a Macintosh or PC with network connectivity. Setting up a POP server is relatively straightforward. Several UNIX server implementations also are available (see Appendix C.)

Incorporating POP into your *sendmail* configuration is relatively straightforward and depends on the specific server implementation. Follow the instructions found with the server software for how this is done. We offer here some general guidelines:

- There are two versions of POP—POP2 and POP3. Be sure the clients and servers use the same version. Most newer POP clients use POP3. Note that POP3 and POP2 use different well-known ports (POP2 uses 109 and POP3 uses 110).

- Some POP servers use the same mailbox directory for storing mailboxes as is used by a local UA for reading mail. In this case, the mail configuration requires no changes other than adding local user accounts to the system for use by remote POP clients. Logins can be disallowed on the server machine by setting the UNIX password file shell field to either something illegal or to a harmless program like */bin/date*.

- Other POP clients allow you to specify a separate POP password file. In this case, some special provisions must be made to identify which users use POP. This is done easily by having an alias for a POP user similar to the following:

```
james: james@pop.smallsite.com
```

Then add a line to the gateway configuration providing for mail with this form of recipient address to be sent to a special POP mailer, which then will send the

POP mailer definition (in the file pop.m4)

```
Mpop, P=/usr/local/lib/mh/spop, F=nsmFDM, S=17, R=27,
     A=spop $u
S17

S27
```

Gateway with POP Server

```
(1)   DVgw.1.0
(2)   DDsmallsite.com
(3)   Dj$w
(4)   DMtcp

(5)   include(general.m4)
(6)   include(rules.m4)
(7)   include(local.m4)
(8)   include(tcp.m4)
(9)   include(pop.m4)
(10)  include(zeropre.m4)

(11)  R$*<@pop.$D>           $#pop $@pop $:$1
(12)  R$*<@$-.$D>$*          $#$M $@$2.$D $:$1<@$2.$D>$3
(13)  R$*<@$+>$*             $#$M $@$2 $:$1<@$2>$3
(14)  R$+%$+                 $@$>29$1@$2
(15)  R$+                    $#local $:$1
```

Figure 7.10 POP Mailer and Configuration.

message to the right POP mailbox. Figure 7.10 shows such a mailer definition and the modified gateway configuration file that uses it. Line 9 of the file adds the POP mailer definition found in the file, while line 11 provides that any mail with a *domain_part* of *pop.smallsite.com* gets directed to the POP mailer. The mailer then appends the message to the appropriate POP mailbox, *pop.m4*.

7.7   MIME: Multipurpose Internet Mail Extensions

The SMTP protocol suffers from one significant defect: It understands only 7-bit ASCII characters. Consequently, you can't use SMTP to send binary data such as graphics or programs. To correct this, several ad hoc and nonstandard methods exist for encoding binary data into 7-bit ASCII. For these conventions to work successfully in a large community, however, some kind of standard is needed for the encoding rules. MIME (Multipurpose Internet Mail Extensions) provides this standard by specifying a set of encoding rules and header extensions to the Internet standard mail message specification [Borenstein & Freed 1992]. These rules let a UA encode messages with text, graphics, and even sound into 7-bit ASCII. If the receiving UA understands the MIME standard, then it can decode the message. Thus multimedia messages can be sent over the Internet using SMTP without modifying the transport structure.

Some UAs understand MIME already. An optional extension to the standard mail system, MIME can be added to an existing 7-bit-only system of UAs as the need arises. You can in fact run MIME-capable UAs alongside nonMIME-capable UAs. A nonMIME compliant UA simply displays the encoded parts of the message as text.

In Fig. 7.11, we show an example multimedia message that contains some ASCII text and a PostScript document. The message is shown as it appears in straight ASCII text as encapsulated within a conventional mail message. A UA

Figure 7.11 MIME Example.

```
To: smoot@tic.com
Subject: MIME example
Mime-Version: 1.0
Content-Type: multipart/mixed; boundary="----- =_aaaaaaaaaa0"
Date: Tue, 14 Sep 93 15:34:20 -0500
From: jack@tic.com


------- =_aaaaaaaaaa0
Content-Type: text/plain; charset="us-ascii"

This is an example of a MIME message.

------- =_aaaaaaaaaa0
Content-Type: application/postscript
Content-Transfer-Encoding: quoted-printable

%!PS-Adobe-3.0
%%Creator: groff version 1.03
%%DocumentNeededResources: font Times-Roman
%%DocumentSuppliedResources: procset grops 1.03 0
            .
          .
          .
```

without MIME support would display the message as shown. A UA with MIME support would interpret the *Content-Type:* fields imbedded in the message body and invoke an appropriate display program. In the example, the second body part is a PostScript program. The UA upon interpreting the *Content-Type:* field would invoke a program that knows how to display PostScript.

7.8   Mail User Agents

Mail user agents (UAs) that support sending and receiving Internet mail are supported on virtually every type of computer in use. Many of the more popular UAs are found on UNIX systems; however, UAs exist for both PCs and Macintoshes, which are found in many LAN environments. Next, we briefly describe some of the more popular UNIX UAs. You may run more than one UA on your system. The only requirement is that every UA adopt the same protocol for accessing a user's mailbox and share that protocol with the local MTA. Usually this involves being sure the UAs adopt the same file locking protocol used by the local MTA and all other UAs.

Berkeley Mail

The Berkeley mail UA is sometimes called "big" mail, since on earlier UNIX systems it was distinguished from the original UNIX UA, **mail,** by being spelled as *Mail.* Although very capable, it is a line-oriented MTA. A variation of Berkeley is the **mailx** program found on System V UNIX systems. Berkeley mail comes packaged with virtually every UNIX system.

MUSH

The Mail User's Shell (MUSH) is an enhanced version of Berkeley mail with character-mapped, full-screen terminal support. It attempts (with some success) to put a simplifying veneer on a line-oriented UA. MUSH is in the public domain and is available from many Internet archive sites.

elm

elm is a screen-oriented UA that many users find very simple to use. It also is available from Internet archive sites.

Pine

Another screen-oriented UA, Pine also is available from Internet archive sites. is useful because it has MIME capability as part of its standard configuration.

MH

MH is an older, generally line-oriented UA. Users familiar with the UNIX shell usually like it because it uses the shell itself as its command environment. This setup makes it easy for you to build some very powerful tools using the existing MH. The latest version of MH also supports MIME. There also is a variation of MH called XMH, which runs under the X Window System.

7.9   Checking It Out

To isolate delivery problems, check your mail system configuration in stages. Start by seeing if mail is delivered locally. This is very important, since if mail cannot be delivered locally, any error messages generated by the system cannot be delivered.

If mail can be delivered locally, determine whether mail can be delivered correctly to a remote location. We have set up a mail echo server for this purpose. Sending a message to the address *connect@tic.com* will echo your original message back to you. This will let you determine if mail is delivered to the remote location correctly and also lets you check if your mail header addresses are correctly rewritten.

References

Allman 1983a.   Allman, Eric, *Sendmail — An Internetwork Mail Router*, 1983.

Allman 1983b.   Allman, Eric, *Sendmail Installation and Operations Guide*, 1983.

Borenstein & Freed 1992.   Borenstein, N., & Freed, N., *MIME (Multipurpose Internet Mail Extensions) Mechanisms for Specifying and Describing the Format of Internet Message Bodies (RFC1341)*, June 1992.

Butler et al. 1985.   Butler, M., Postel, John B., Chase, D., Goldberger, J., & Reynolds, Joyce, *Post Office Protocol: Version 2 (RFC937)*, February 1985.

Carl-Mitchell & Quarterman 1993.   Carl-Mitchell, Smoot, & Quarterman, John S., *Practical Internetworking with TCP/IP and UNIX*, Addison-Wesley, Reading, MA (1993). ISBN 0-201-58629-0.

Costales et al. 1994.   Costales, Bryan, Allman, Eric, & Rickert, Neil, *Sendmail*, O'Reilly & Associates, Inc., Sebastopol, CA (1994).

Crocker 1982.   Crocker, David, *Standard for the format of ARPA Internet text messages (RFC822)*, August 1982.

Postel 1982.   Postel, John B., *Simple Mail Transfer Protocol (RFC821)*, August 1982.

Rose 1991.   Rose, Marshall T., *Post Office Protocol: Version 3 (RFC1225)*, May 1991.

CHAPTER 8

Setting Up USENET News

By recent estimates, approximately 2.7 million people read USENET news on 93,000 hosts, and 59 megabytes of news are transferred daily, in 27,000 messages [Reid 1993]. News is organized into more than 4,000 newsgroups, however, it's not like television with 4,000 channels. Anyone may choose to respond to any article, or to post a new article. Tens of thousands of people do so in a typical month. In this chapter, we explain how to join them.

USENET once was a store and forward dialup network. A posting could take a day or two to reach all participating hosts, and sometimes even a week. But USENET now isn't really a network at all. It has become a service carried over many networks, starting with UUCP, and now including the Internet. USENET news articles carried over the Internet often propagate in seconds.

We begin this chapter with an overview of news from the user's viewpoint, followed by an overview of the major pieces of news software. Then we discuss getting a news feed and the amount of space news will require on your machine. We keep this early material brief so we can use the bulk of the chapter to describe how to set up news software: the basic news package; news transfer software; and news user agents. You have many choices for each of these, but in the interests of clarity, we have chosen to describe in detail only one for each, as follows:

- INN
  For the basic news package

- *nntplink*
  For the news transfer software

- *trn*
  for a news user agent

The chapter ends with a discussion of basic news system administration.

Installing a news system will probably take you about two days work time and a week or two of elapsed time (just as with automobiles, your mileage may vary, and we can only give rough estimates). Every implementation of news we know of was intended to be installed by experts, but they're also fairly well documented. The basic software will compile and run on many hardware and software platforms. If your platform is one of them, news is not hard to install. Follow the basic concepts spelled out in this chapter and you should not have too many difficulties.

8.1   Overview of USENET News

The following are the major features of the USENET news service from the user's viewpoint.

Figure 8.1 An Example News Article.

```
Path: tic.com!...!haven.umd.edu!purdue!not-for-mail
From: spaf@cs.purdue.edu (Gene Spafford)
Newsgroups: news.announce.newusers,news.answers
Subject: Introduction to news.announce
Supersedes: <spaf-intro_726770470@cs.purdue.edu>
Followup-To: news.newusers.questions
Date: 11 Jan 1993 11:54:20 -0500
Organization: Dept. of Computer Sciences, Purdue Univ.
Lines: 74
Approved: spaf@cs.purdue.edu
Expires: 13 Mar 93 04:54:19 GMT
Message-ID: <spaf-intro_726771259@cs.purdue.edu>
NNTP-Posting-Host: ector.cs.purdue.edu

Archive-name: news-announce-intro/part1
Original-author: mark@stargate.com (Mark Horton)
Last-change: 23 Sept 1992 by spaf@cs.purdue.edu (Gene Spafford)

The news.announce hierarchy contains the four moderated
newsgroups news.announce.important, news.announce.newgroups,
news.announce.newusers, and news.announce.conferences.

[etc.]
```

USENET Articles

A news article looks much like an electronic mail message, see Fig. 8.1. In fact, the news article format specification, RFC 1036 [Horton & Adams 1987], is based on the Internet mail format specification, RFC 822 [Crocker 1982]. Many of the headers are identical, although a few have slightly restricted formats, and some new ones have been added.

All the news headers you're likely to use are shown in Table 8.1. *Subject:*, *From:*, and *Date:* are as in RFC 822, although *From:* has a slightly more restricted format. A mail message never has a *Path:* header, which records the news systems traversed by the article from its posting to the local machine. This header is used to determine where *not* to send an article because it's already been there.

USENET Delivery. News looks like electronic mail and people sometimes have trouble telling the difference. The first time an article gets responses from all over the world, the difference becomes clearer: it's not the format; it's the style of delivery. While a mail message is addressed to specific people, a news article goes to many machines, and anyone on those machines can read the article. Anyone who reads it also can post a followup. So mail is one-to-one and news is many-to-many. In between are mailing lists, which go to a preset lists of mailboxes.

An ordinary electronic mail message is similar to a paper letter delivered by the post office; it reaches a few people. A mailing list is like a newsletter or a magazine; it reaches thousands of people. A newsgroup is like a newspaper consisting entirely of letters to the editor, being printed in tens of thousands of locations around the world, and with perhaps hundreds of thousands of people

---

Table 8.1 News Article Headers.

Header	Description	Header	Description
by the user:		*added by news:*	
Newsgroups:	newsgroups for the article	Path:	eliminates duplicate copies
Followup-To:	redirects future postings	From:†	who's posting
Distribution:	where to send the article	Date:†	date and time posted
Organization:	your posting organization	Lines:	number of lines in the body
Subject:†	brief article description	*administrative:*	
Keywords:	to help find the article	Expires:	for administrative articles
Summary:	what's in the article	Supersedes:	a previous article to expire
References:†	previous articles	Approved:	for moderated articles

† In RFC 822.

Table 8.2 Comparision of Communication Methods.

Type		Paper	Electronic	CMC
1–1	person-to-person	post	fax	mail
1–n	broadcast	newspapers	radio	lists
		magazines	TV	BBSes
n–n	many-to-many	—	—	news
				conferencing

participating, not just reading. For paper media, freedom of the press applies to those who own a press. With USENET news, anyone can own a "press." Some of these analogies are illustrated by Table 8.2.

USENET Addresses. You'll often hear people talk about a USENET mail address. They usually mean a UUCP mail address, that is, something like *uupsi!foobar!user*. USENET news used to be carried almost exclusively over the same UUCP transport protocol that supports the UUCP mail network, so the confusion is not surprising. But, today most of USENET news is carried over the Internet, using TCP/IP. So an address for a user at a host that participates in USENET could just as easily be a DNS address like *user@foobar.edu*. In this book, we simply refer to a DNS address when that's what we mean; we never refer to a USENET address.

USENET Newsgroups

As might be expected, the freedom for anyone to post anything as news results in a lot of repetitive and generally useless stuff appearing on USENET. To alleviate this problem, posting topics are organized into thousands of newsgroups, so you can pick the articles you want to read by topic. Some newsgroups are **moderated,** which means a **moderator** reads submissions, selects some to approve, inserts an *Approved:* header in each, and posts it to the newsgroup. Sophisticated news software user agents also can help sift out articles you don't want. This is done according to keywords and posters' addresses, even in unmoderated newsgroups.

Many newsgroups are on quite technical topics. Some are discussion groups, where people are trying to solve a practical or theoretical problem. Others are for distribution of software, either in source or binary form. There's enough variety that some newsgroup is likely to be useful for any given organization or person.

Newsgroups are organized into a hierarchy. A newsgroup name reflects the hierarchical organization. For example, the newsgroup *comp.unix* is a newsgroup in the top level newsgroup *comp* (short for "computer") with a specific subtopic about the UNIX operating system. The newsgroup hierarchy can extend to any depth, but usually doesn't go deeper than about five levels.

Table 8.3 Top Level Newsgroups.

Distribution	Geography
comp	Computer science, software source, hardware and software systems
sci	Technical discussions about sciences
soc	Social issues and socializing
misc	Topics that don't fit elsewhere
rec	Hobbies and recreational activities
news	The news network and its software
talk	Debates and lengthy discussions
alt	Most anything
bionet	Biology
biz	ClariNet
gnu	GNU (GNU's not UNIX)
bit	Gatewayed BITNET LISTSERV lists

Table 8.3 lists generally distributed top level newsgroups, plus a few more local ones. A recent USENET traffic survey showed 188 top level newsgroups that carried at least one article a day each, and more than 6,000 total newsgroups [Adams 1993]. The top ten in that survey were, in order from the busiest: *alt, rec, comp, soc, sci, talk, misc, news, clari,* for the **ClariNet** newsgroups, which provide information for pay, and *bit,* for gatewayed BITNET LISTSERV lists.

These newsgroup categories have varying levels of seriousness and verbosity, as do the newsgroups within them. For example, the *talk* category was intended to separate those subjects that usually produced more heat than light. Among the others, it is hard to say which include more serious discussions. While *comp* has technical material related to computers, *rec* is just as likely to have technical material related to the motion picture or book publishing industries. The *alt* top level newsgroup was set up to carry topics that some institutions found too controversial, too ephemeral, too silly, or otherwise not acceptable as newsgroups. Ironically, it now carries more traffic than any other top level newsgroup.

Other top level newsgroups include *bionet* for biology, *biz* for business, and *gnu* for **GNU (GNU's Not UNIX)** software from the **FSF (Free Software Foundation).**

New newsgroups are created all the time, some via a voting system involving the newsgroup *news.newsgroups,* others unilaterally by individuals.

Table 8.4 Some USENET Distributions.

Distribution	Geography	Distribution	Geography
world	Everywhere	ca	California
inet	over the Internet	ba	San Francisco Bay Area
eunet	EUnet (Europe)	ga	Georgia
can	Canada	ne	New England
na	North America	tx	Texas
usa	United States	austin	Austin, Texas

USENET Distributions

In keeping with the totally decentralized philosophy of USENET, a site can chose to subscribe or not subscribe to any newsgroup. Further, in addition to being divided into general categories, newsgroups can be distributed locally, within a group of related machines, within a defined geographic boundary, and worldwide. Basic distributions include all the top level newsgroups, plus some specialized distributions, plus whatever two communicating news systems agree is a distribution. The most common news distributions are listed in Table 8.4. Many are geographical, but notice the *inet* distribution, which is used to explicitly carry articles over the Internet.

8.2   News Software

USENET news on the Internet is implemented as a client/server protocol, so you need the protocol, a server, and clients. Sources for all the software mentioned in this chapter are listed in Appendix C, *Software and Other Information.*

NNTP: Network News Transport Protocol

The key to transport of news over the Internet is the Network News Transfer Protocol (NNTP), which can carry news over TCP [Kantor & Lapsley 1986]. It is the preferred method for moving news from one system to another when both systems support TCP/IP. Before NNTP, news systems sometimes used UUCP on top of TCP/IP to transfer news across the Internet; few sites do that anymore. Instead, most sites use NNTP, thus permitting peer-to-peer NNTP/TCP/IP interchange of news among USENET hosts on the Internet. For example, one news system acts as an NNTP client and sends the command IHAVE to another news system's NNTP server. This command takes an article's message-ID as an argument and asks the server whether it has a specific article. The server then determines whether it has received the article; if not, it asks the client to send the article.

Several implementations of NNTP exist, including one that contains a server daemon, *nntpd,* that can feed incoming news into the news database software. However, because INN implements the NNTP server directly, we don't need *nntpd* for the setup described in this chapter. INN still needs an NNTP implementation to send news to a foreign news system. It comes with one, *innxmit,* for transmission of batched articles. However, we choose to describe a different one, *nntplink,* because it permits fast and continuous news article transmission.

NNRP: Network News Reading Protocol

NNTP also can interactively retrieve selected news articles for use by a news reader. This use of NNTP is sometimes called Network News Reading Protocol (NNRP). Traditionally, reading news required the news article of interest to be on the same system as the user. To read news from a workstation, all news articles had to be either stored locally or remotely mounted from the news server. The first alternative meant adding much more disk storage to the workstation; the second meant the workstation needed NFS support, which was not always available.

NNTP solves this problem by letting a user on a remote system query a server on the system on which the news articles resides and then retrieve interactively the specific articles of interest. For example, a client can use the NEWNEWS command to ask a server if it has new news in a specific newsgroup since a certain date and time.

INN implements the NNRP part of NNTP directly (as a separate *nnrpd* server), so no additional server software is needed. Any news reader must implement the NNRP client to work with INND, but NNRP is currently just another name for a subset of NNTP, and most news readers implement that.

Basic News Software

The basic news server software is more complicated than servers for many other network services, both because it has to maintain a database of many megabytes of news articles, organized by newsgroups, and because the servers talk to each other, not just to news reading clients.

News Software Functions. Software is needed to place each incoming news article in a file according to its newsgroups and retrieve it later when someone wants to read it. Each article contains a unique message-ID that the news software records in a file named *history.* Suppose your news feed does not find your machine named in the *Path:* header of an article and sends the article to your machine. If your machine has seen that article before (perhaps it got it from a different news feed), your news software detects the article's Message-ID in the history file and rejects it as a **duplicate.**

As each article comes in, the news software puts it in a directory whose name is made by replacing dots in the newsgroup name with slashes, within a subtree that traditionally starts under */usr/spool/news*. The news system gives the article a sequence number per newsgroup and puts the article in a file whose name is the sequence number. In other words, an incoming article for newsgroup *comp.unix* might get the local sequence number 233 for that newsgroup, and would be placed in the file */usr/spool/news/comp/unix/233*. The same article may have been posted to several newsgroups at once, in which case the local news system will file it under each newsgroup. On UNIX systems, these files are not copies, however; to save space they are hard links.

The news system records the highest sequence number so far used for each newsgroup in a file named *active*. To save space, old articles have to be thrown away; a program called *expire* does that. Later in the day, the news software records the lowest remaining sequence number per newsgroup in the active file. Articles are usually expired according to a default time interval that is set on the local machine; separate intervals can be set for groups of newsgroups or specific newsgroups. An article also may have *Expires:* or *Supersedes:* headers that affect expiration of specific articles. The news reading software can use the low and high numbers from the active file to determine what range of numbers is valid for a newsgroup.

News Implementations. Several implementations of this sort of specialized database software are available. The original news package was called **A news,** and was a collection of shell scripts. After that came many versions of **B news,** which was mostly written in C, plus a few shell scripts. The late 1980s saw a complete rewrite of the news system as **C news,** which was quite a bit faster than its predecessor [Spencer & Collyer 1987].

The early 1990s saw yet another reimplementation, called **INN (InterNet News).** All previous implementations of news were designed before the exponential growth of the Internet had reached its stride, and were built based on the assumption that news was primarily carried over UUCP. Although INN can handle UUCP news feeds, it assumes the primary transport mechanism for news is TCP/IP. In addition, previous news implementations were built as collections of programs to be called in various ad hoc manners whenever news came in by UUCP, a user posted an article, or some other event occurred. There was a master news database manager program, called *inews* in B news and *relaynews* in C news, but even that program was run as needed by other programs; it did not run as a daemon.

INN is triggered by the same kinds of events, but it has a daemon that runs all the time and maintains control of the news article database. Almost all accesses of news articles and related control files, such as the active and history files, are handled by calls to this server daemon, *innd*. Somewhat like *sendmail* acts as an SMTP daemon directly, *innd* acts as an NNTP daemon directly, receiving incoming news through TCP connections.

Both C news and INN have their advantages. Some commercial news providers run both: C news on one machine to feed their dialup UUCP news customers and INN on another machine to feed their TCP/IP news customers. We discussed C news briefly in a previous book, *Practical Internetworking with TCP/IP and UNIX* [Carl-Mitchell & Quarterman 1993]. Because the current book is about Internet connections, we discuss INN.

News User Agents

You need a way to read news, once you've got it and to post it, once you compose it. News user agents, commonly called news readers, do this. There are far too many news readers to describe all of them in this chapter. So we give a quick overview and then describe one of them, *trn* in more detail.

At least half a dozen USENET news readers are in common use. The oldest still in use is called *readnews,* is line-oriented and rather painful to use. All the others mentioned are screen-oriented, some through the use of the **curses** package that is intended for ASCII character-cell terminals, and others through the **X Window System** that is intended for bitmapped terminals, or through other means. The earliest was *vnews,* which was the first to work on most character-cell terminals or terminal emulations, using curses.

Next was *rn,* which has so many features no one can remember them all, although perhaps the most popular is the "K" command, which tells rn to never show anything with a particular subject again. Using this command, you can construct rn kill files that filter out messages by subject, author, keywords, or logical combinations. A variant of *rn* called *xrn* is adapted to use a mouse with the X Window System. An update to rn, *trn,* or threaded *rn,* gives the user a menu of threads of conversation, which it deduces from *References:, Keywords:,* and *Subject:* headers.

The biggest problem with news is that there is so much of it; you go to get a drink of water and you get knocked down by a firehose of information. A more radical way to drink from the news firehose is *nn,* for no news, as in good news. You can tell it characteristics of articles you *do* want to see, even across newsgroup boundaries; it will ignore everything else. Other interfaces include *vn, tin,* and *gnus,* which works within *Emacs,* the well-known text editor.

Most of these news readers can co-exist without any problems. You can have as many on your machine as you care to maintain. Unlike mail readers, which often use slightly different mail storage formats and locking protocols, news readers all use the same article format. With INN locking is done by *innd.*

Any choice among this superfluity of possible news readers must be to some extent arbitrary, since different people have different styles of reading news and will pick a news reader to match.

8.3   News Feeds and News Costs

USENET is not the same as the Internet, but they are alike in at least one way: Neither has any organized overall administration. There's no single USENET, Inc. to go to for news. However, many Internet connectivity providers are also news feed providers, so ask yours if they will give or sell you a feed. Otherwise, try asking a neighbor, colleague, vendor, client, or university for a news feed. Traditionally, any new organization on USENET agrees to feed news to at least one other organization. Commercial news providers fill in the remaining gaps.

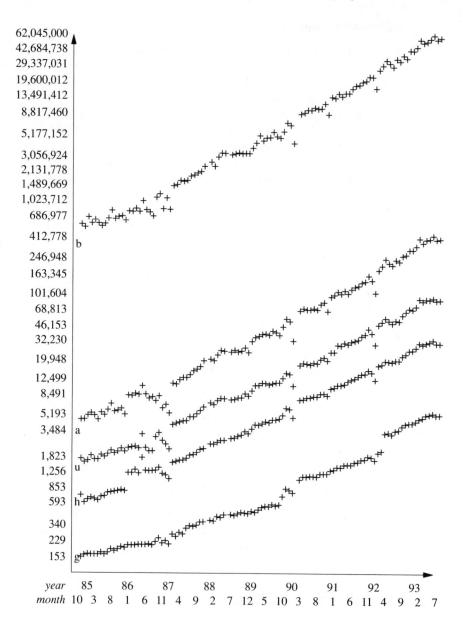

Figure 8.2 USENET News Growth.

Adapted from Quarterman, "USENET Growth," Matrix News, *Vol. 3, No. 9,*
MIDS, Austin, mids@tic.com, September 1993. Copyright © 1993 MIDS.

Reprinted with permission.

USENET has grown exponentially for years by both methods, as shown in Fig. 8.2. So you should have no problem finding a feed by either a commercial or noncommercial route.

If you want to set up a news feed by UUCP before you set up an Internet connection, the you may find it easiest to get a feed from one of the same companies that provide IP connectivity. Both PSI and UUNET, for example, made names for themselves as UUCP and USENET providers before they were known as IP connectivity providers. If you can't or don't want to get news from a commercial provider, try looking around as suggested for an Internet feed; the main difference is that you will get news by UUCP instead of TCP/IP. Some providers also charge for connect time for picking up news by UUCP dialup.

News also requires disk space. A full news feed for only a thousand or so newsgroups runs about 50 megabytes a day. The old traditional expiration interval was 14 days; any article that was posted more than 14 days ago would get expired today. So a feed kept for the full traditional expiration interval would need about 700 megabytes just for the news article themselves. The true amount of needed disk space is larger, because of active, history, and log files, and the various files associated with news user agents. A gigabyte of disk would probably not overflow. Disks are inexpensive, and you may choose to do it this way. Or you can pick some combination of a smaller set of newsgroups and shorter expiration intervals for selected newsgroups. You can squeeze a full news feed into around 150 megabytes of disk space if you expire almost everything every two days. You can use as little as 80 megabytes of disk space if you get fewer newsgroups, perhaps keeping some of them around longer.

Once you have a feed selected and your news software set up, get your feed to send you a small set of newsgroups as a test for a few days, and then have them turn on a full feed.

8.4   INN: InterNet News

There are too many differences among UNIX systems and too many news parameters for us to describe every step for installing INN; besides, the INN installation documentation covers the details. In this section we present an overview of news installation, emphasizing some important points. See Appendix C for where to get the software itself.

INN Architecture

First let's look at the pieces of INN and how they interact, as shown in Fig. 8.3. Almost everything revolves around the server daemon, *innd*. Incoming news may be spooled in */usr/spool/news/in.coming* and outgoing news may be spooled in */usr/spool/news/out.going*, but it all passes through *innd*. This daemon updates *active* and *history* and is controlled by parameter files such as *newsfeeds*. It handles NNTP connections from other USENET hosts on the Internet, while a separate daemon, *nnrpd,* handles the news reading parts of NNTP, which, as we have seen, are sometimes referred to as NNRP.

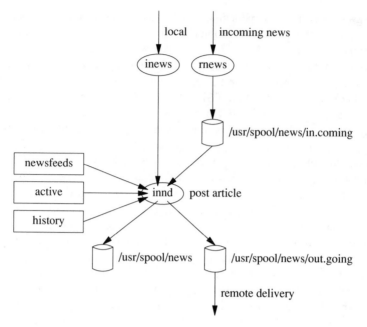

Figure 8.3 INN Architecture.

UNIX Parameters for News

USENET news expects to use various UNIX (or other) system parameters. In this section we describe UNIX user, group, mail alias, and filesystem parameters that are used in a similar way by the common news implementations, including INN.

The News User and Group. A good thing to do first when installing news is to make a UNIX system group *news* and put yourself in it, so you don't have to be root for most news installation and administration. You probably already have such a group in your */etc/group* file; if not, the following line will do:

```
news:*:6:you
```

You'll also need a user named *news* to own news article database and administrative files. Its home directory should be the news administrative directory, not the news database spool directory. The example */etc/passwd* file entry that follows will do:

```
news:*:6:6::/usr/lib/news:/bin/csh
```

If you're distributing the group or passwd files with NIS, don't forget to push them. Also, with NIS the passwd file entry may really need to go in */etc/passwd.nis*.

The usenet Mail Alias. The news system also needs to send mail about error conditions, newsgroup creation requests, etc. The usual mail address for this purpose is *usenet,* usually set up as an alias in */usr/lib/aliases,* like this:

```
usenet:you,sysadm
```

Using an alias allows you to change who receives such mail without recompiling the news system.

Alternatively, you can make an actual user named *usenet* and put a *.forward* file in its home directory, with contents like this:

```
you,sysadm
```

If you choose this alternative, remember to make the file owned by the *usenet* user and not writable by anyone else.

The News Spool Directory (/usr/spool/news). You will need considerable disk space, probably a whole partition, for the news articles. Traditionally, these go under */usr/spool/news,* so if you've got the partition mounted somewhere else, such as */export/news/spool,* soft link the former to the latter. On many systems, you also may want to link */var/spool/news* to the news spool directory.

It is best *not* to mount the news spool directory with NFS. News implementations tend to use specific UNIX semantics, and NFS is just enough different from UNIX that problems can occur. For example, NFS can send a duplicate *symlink* (symbolic link) request if the NFS reply to the first request is lost; this duplication can confuse *innd.*

News Parameter Files (/usr/local/news). Traditionally, news parameter files go in */usr/lib/news,* and some news readers may look there for them. However, INN likes to keep them in */usr/local/news.* We avoid a potential problem by making the former a symlink to the latter. Some news parameter files, such as *history,* can get quite large, so you may want to put the parameter files on the big disk with the news articles, for example, in */export/news/lib,* with a symlink from */usr/local/news.* However, if you have space elsewhere, put */usr/local/news* on a different disk than the news articles to prevent excessive incoming news from filling up the disk with the parameter files.

UNIX Parameters for INN

Most of the configuration just described applies to any news system. In this section we describe configuration of UNIX system parameters for INN.

News System Startup. Because *innd* runs as a daemon, it needs to be started when the system boots. It comes with a shell script to handle cleaning up lock files and startup parameters. You want to put this script in */usr/local/etc/rc.news.* If you don't have a */usr/local/etc* directory, we recommend creating one. Then edit your */etc/rc.local* file (or equivalent) to call *rc.news* on system startup.

```
news.err        /var/log/news/news.err

news.crit       /var/log/news/news.crit

news.notice     /var/log/news/news.notice

news.debug      /var/log/news/news.debug

news.*          /var/log/news/news
```

Figure 8.4 News syslog.conf Entries.

News System Locking. INN needs some lock files and can also support some security parameter files for newsfeeds. We recommend putting these in a directory */usr/local/etc/news*, which can be made writable by group *news,* unlike */usr/local/etc*, which should of course be writable only by *root*.

News System Logging. INN uses **syslog** to log a spectrum of events. You want these news log entries separate from other system logs, so you need to edit your */etc/syslog.conf* to put them in a convenient place, as shown in Fig. 8.4. You also will need to make the directory */var/log/news*, that is owned and writable by user and group *news*.

News Manual Pages. Finally, if your system supports */usr/local/man*, we recommend putting the news manual pages there.

Compiling INN

In addition to setting various UNIX system parameters, you also must set parameters in the INN software itself. You must set the appropriate INN parameters for the user, group, alias, and pathnames we have discussed in this section, so that INN will know what choices you have made. Many of them are are in the Makefile, and others are in */usr/local/src/inn/config/config.data*, as shown in Fig. 8.5.

Figure 8.5 Example Parameters in config.data.

```
# Put lock files outside of spool partition:
_PATH_LOCKS             /usr/local/etc/news
# Put NNTP and NNRP access files outside of spool partition:
_PATH_NNTPPASS
_PATH_NNRPACCESS        /usr/local/etc/news/nnrp.access
```

8.5   Outgoing News (nntplink)

If you want your news to go out quickly, you need a program to take a list of news articles, act as an NNTP client, establish a connection to a destination news system's NNTP server, and send the articles. Several programs can do this. The one we choose is *nntplink*. This program keeps a TCP connection open to a target machine most of the time, and sends news articles over it as they come in. See Appendix C for where to get this software.

One reason we chose INN rather than C news for this book is that INN can use *nntplink* to better effect. With C news, *nntplink* can be set up to monitor the C news log file to find out what news has come in so it then can send that news back out to a different news system. INN can be configured so that *innd* will pipe lists of articles directly to *nntplink* without any need for indirect monitoring. Also, with C news you need a separate *nntpd* daemon (available in a separate software package; see Appendix C) to collect incoming news via NNTP. You must configure this daemon for various parameters and then edit */etc/inetd.conf* to run it. With INN, *innd* acts as the NNTP server directly; once you've configured INN, you've configured incoming NNTP.

No special compilation configuration is needed to use *nntplink* with NNTP. Just compile *nntplink* and install it. Then arrange to call it by putting appropriate lines in *newsfeeds*, like the following:

```
# A real-time nntplink feed
bigu\
    :/!foo\
    :Tc,Wnm:/news/bin/nntplink -i stdin news.bigu.edu
```

Don't forget to tell *innd* about it afterwards, as follows:

```
ctlinnd reload newsfeeds nntplink to bigu.edu
```

8.6   A News User Agent (trn)

If you expect to read news only on the machine with the news articles, you can install almost any news reader with no trouble. In this case, you can configure the news reader to read the *active* file directly from */usr/local/news* and the news articles directly from */usr/spool/news*. However, because you're connecting to the Internet, you'll probably also be using TCP/IP internally, and will probably want to read news from several machines on your own internal network. To read news across the network you need news readers that understand NNTP. For where to get them, see Appendix C.

NNTP as NNRP

You'll almost certainly never want to read news directly with NNTP. However, you may want to use NNTP directly for occasionally debugging. Typical NNRP (NNTP news reading) commands include the following:

help   List the NNTP commands supported by this server.

group   Display the article range for this newsgroup.

article Retrieve an article.

next   Increment the article number and name that article.

UNIX System Parameters for News Readers

We recommend putting the *trn* programs and libraries in separate subdirectories, such as */usr/local/bin/trn* and */usr/local/lib/trn*, respectively, so that you can export them easily with NFS. Users on client machines then will have to put */usr/local/bin/trn* in their search path in the UNIX environment variable PATH, but this is a small price to pay for being sure you have all the *trn* programs on the client machines.

   You also must ensure the news user and group are recognized on all the client machines. You can export them with NIS or copy the appropriate entries into */etc/passwd* and */etc/group* on each of the client machines.

   On each client, you'll also need the news user's login directory so that you can have ˜*news/nntp.server* (where ˜*news* refers to that user's login directory) hold the domain name of the NNTP server used by *trn*.

Compiling trn

The *trn* news user agent uses Larry Wall's famous chatty *Configure* script which deduces what kind of system it's running on and does most configuration automatically. Some say it even washes the dishes and takes out the trash. We can't confirm that, but it does work well.

   The main thing to watch out for about *trn* software for use with INN is version mismatch, since the two packages are maintained by different people. Use *trn3.0* or a newer version, since earlier versions of *trn* expected to look inside a separate NNTP software package to find NNTP parameters. A separate NNTP package isn't otherwise needed with INN, so INN comes with patches to alter the *trn* configuration scripts to use parameters from the INN software. If you use *trn3.0* or a newer version, you won't need these patches. However, you may need other patches for *trn*. The *patch* program that applies them is one of the most useful programs you will find and we recommend installing that program as well (see Appendix C).

News Overview (nov)

An ability to follow threads of conversation is a major feature of *trn*. Having each running instance of *trn* computing these on the fly would be slow and redundant, so instead *trn* uses the **nov (news overview)** database. INN comes with a version of nov, which has a tool, *overchan,* to enter articles in the overview database and a tool, *expireover,* to expire old articles from it. News readers can access the news overview database through an extension to NNTP, using the added command *xover,* which retrieves overview information about a range of articles. INN supports the *xover* command.

Old versions of *trn* used a program called *mthreads* to compute threads and build a binary database; unfortunately, other news readers did not use the same format. Although *trn* supports an XTHREADS extension to NNTP that permits retrieving thread information through NNTP, other news readers do not support XTHREADS at all. While INN for the moment supports XTHREADS, the INN documentation indicates that XTHREADS may not be supported in future INN versions. So XTHREADS was useful, but incompatible with other news readers, and probably will not work with INN much longer. Fortunately, all modern news-readers, including *trn,* now support nov, so that the compatibility problem has vanished.

Posting with trn

Posting with trn is done through *Pnews,* which is called either indirectly by *trn* when you do a followup or directly when you post a new article. Before users can post, you need to configure distributions and moderators. The *Configure* script walks you easily through a set of distributions; just remember to pick a local distribution name for your organization, such as *bigco* for Big, Inc.

When a user posts to a moderated newsgroup, the article is not actually posted directly; instead it is mailed to the moderator. So your news system has to know where to find the moderator. This information is kept in the file *moderators* in the news home (library) directory. Unless you are a moderator, we recommend you set up this file to forward all moderator mail to a system that does have a current list, as follows:

```
*:%s@uunet.uu.net
```

8.7   News Administration

If you have too much time on your hands, news administration can easily eat all of it. However, news can be run without much effort. Next, we discuss the main things to pay attention to.

Table 8.5 Important News Parameter Files.

Filename	Description
active	Current status of each newsgroup
history	History of all articles received
inn.conf	Basic INN configuration
newsfeeds	Incoming and outgoing newsgroup specs
hosts.nntp	Permissions for incoming newsfeeds
expire.ctl	Expiration intervals
moderators	Mail addresses of newsgroup moderators
nntp.server	Domain name clients will use for NNTP server

Except where otherwise specified, all parameter files named in this section are in the news *lib* directory, which INN sets by default to */usr/local/news*, which we have recommended making a symlink to as */usr/lib/news*. A list the most important parameter files is shown in Table 8.5. These are not all of them; INN offers you 43 different parameter files and shell scripts to tune. Fortunately, you can leave most of them alone. For those you do update, you usually need to tell *innd* about by using the *ctlinnd* command.

Basic News Database Files

You will need *active* and *history* files. To create the *active* file, start with a copy of your news feed's *active* file; you can get it by using the NNTP *list* command. Then rewrite the numbers in it to be zero.

INN comes with a *makehistory* command that makes a blank *history* file, together with its associated *history.dir* and *history.pag* **dbm** database files.

Basic INN Configuration

The most basic INN configuration is done in *inn.conf*, which can supply defaults for various purposes. For example, you can use this file to supply an organization name to go in *Organization:* headers of local postings. You also can supply your news server's domain name and a domain name to put in the *From:* line of posted articles. These two domain names often need to be different. For example, if your news server's domain name is *news.bigco.com,* you might want all your news postings to go out as follows:

```
From: you@bigco.com
```

Mail sent from outside in response to news postings from your organization can then be handled by a single mail daemon that you configure for that purpose. In

```
##   Format:
## site[/exclude,exclude...]\
##     :pattern,pattern...[/distrib,distrib...]\
##     :flag,flag...\
##     :param

##   The local site.
##   The "pattern" field gives the initial subscription list for
##   what to feed all other sites.
##   The "distrib" subfield limits incoming articles.

ME\
    :*,!control,!junk,!bigco*\
    ::

# A real-time nntplink feed
tic.com\
    :/ut,austin,dfw,houston,tx,info,to,news\
    :Tc,Wnm:/usr/lib/news/bin/nntplink -i stdin tic.com
```

Figure 8.6 Example newsfeeds file.

---

addition, people at other organizations will not be confused by irrelevant details of your internal domain configuration, and any system crackers who might try to break in will be given one less piece of information with which to work.

News Feeds

Incoming and outgoing news feeds are controlled primarily by the *newsfeeds* file. Each line in that file that is not a blank or comment has four fields separated by commas (see Fig. 8.6.) The four fields contain a news site name, newsgroups and distributions, flags, and other parameters, respectively. The parameter field may contain a filename or a program name, depending on the flags. The example in Fig. 8.6 shows the two kinds of possible *newsfeeds* entries: the local site (ME), and all others.

The Local News Site Entry. The local site entry controls both incoming and outgoing news. Its *distrib* field limits what comes in to the local site, and its *pattern* field sets defaults for what goes out to other sites.

The example ME entry in Fig. 8.6 permits everything to come in, since it sets no limits. You also must list each incoming news feed in *hosts.nntp*. An incoming connection from any host not listed in that file will be handed to *nnrpd*, since only news readers should be connecting from such a host.

This entry also sets a default of sending all newsgroups out, except the *control, junk,* and *bigco* newsgroup hierarchies. An entry for a site can further specify which newsgroups go to that site.

Outgoing News Site Entries. The other *newsfeeds* entries control only outgoing news, and only to the named site. The figure shows an outgoing feed to *tic.com* that uses *nntplink* to send some relatively local newsgroup distributions, plus *to, info,* and *news*. If you want to use nntplink to send news to a system whose USENET name is different than its domain name, you may need to use the *nntplink −s* option.

The patterns used to specify newsgroups for outgoing feeds can include shell-like wild card characters, such as asterisk (*). The old-style news wildcard words, such as "all," are no longer used. But *distrib* words contain no wildcards; they are literal words.

This *newsfeeds* file has important functions but an obscure format, so it is one parameter file for which you really need to read the manual page in detail.

News Expiration

News expiration is handled by the *expire* program, which is usually called by *cron* out of a *crontab* entry. However, expiration is not the only daily news function that should be automatic. You really want *cron* to call the *news.daily* script, which calls *expire* and also does various administrativia. For example, *news.daily* updates the low numbers per newsgroup in the *active* file, by doing:

```
ctlinnd renumber
```

Running *news.daily* once a day is usually enough and is best run when few are on the system.

Parameters for *expire* are set in *expire.ctl* (not *explist*, as in C news). This control file has a relatively obvious format. You should have no trouble using it to set expiration intervals for broad categories of newsgroups or single newsgroup. You can set different intervals for the time an article will expire, as follows:

default   Used if no *Expires:* header is present

earliest   Used despite what any *Expires:* header it has might say

latest   Again used despite what *Expires:* might say

The old default was fourteen days for all newsgroups, but expiration intervals as brief as three days are not uncommon now.

New Newsgroups

You may want to create local newsgroups, accept newsgroups created elsewhere in USENET, or even create USENET-wide newsgroups yourself.

Creating a Local Newsgroup. To create a local newsgroup, such as *bigco.announce* , use a control command like this:

```
ctlinnd newgroup bigco.announce x For company announcements.
```

Don't create a newsgroup by sending a *newgroup* control message, unless you are trying to create it for use on other machines in USENET. Instead, use the INN *makegroup* script. Also check parameters in your *control.ctl* file to be sure they allow you to create newsgroups.

Accepting a Newsgroup Creation. If you're in the *usenet* alias, you will frequently receive messages from INN saying that someone is attempting to create a new newsgroup. You then can either create the newsgroup locally, or not. The message from INN will tell you how to create it, which is by using the same kind of command as just described.

Voting on a Newsgroup. If you decide you want to create a USENET-wide newsgroup, you need to learn the voting procedures [Woods & Spafford 1992]; see Appendix C for where to get them. Alternatively, you can try creating an *alt* newsgroup, which may require less consensus with other people.

Logs and Monitoring

We advised putting the news logs in a */var/log/news* directory. Watching those logs will tell you most things you need to know. The *news.daily* script will also mail you a daily summary of news system activity.

Emergencies

The most common news emergency is news filling a disk. You can stop incoming news for a while by commenting out entries in *newsfeeds*. For changes to that file to take effect, use the *ctlinnd* command. Remember to turn the feeds back on again later when the emergency has passed.

You can run *expire* manually to retrieve disk space. Or if you're in a hurry, you can remove some articles manually; newsgroups that distribute binaries are good targets for this, since they absorb a lot of disk space.

Sometimes the problem is a single newsgroup that either is producing too much traffic, has been found objectionable by local management, or is simply not wanted anymore. You could limit incoming news to just distributions listed in the ME entry in the *newsfeeds* file, but that's not what INN is designed to do. In INN, unlike in previous news implementations, the list of acceptable newsgroups is instead simply all newsgroups found in the *active* file. To stop a newsgroup coming in, you should remove it from the *active* file using the *ctlinnd rmgroup* command. Remember to tell your news feed neighbor to stop sending it, so as not to waste their disk space and bandwidth.

Finally, if the news software itself is out of control somehow (not likely), you can kill *innd* itself, thus turning off most news functions.

8.8   Checking It Out

Now that you have news installed, try permitting incoming news from *tic.com*, and send an outgoing news article there. Send us *only* the one newsgroup *alt.internet.connection*, and we will feed you the same newsgroup.

We will need to permit the feed from your system first, so send mail to the special mail alias *newcon@tic.com* first. Then permit an incoming connection from *tic.com* by editing your *host.nntp* file. Permit the outgoing connection to *tic.com* by editing your *newsfeeds* file. Remember you have use *ctlinnd* to tell your *innd* about changes to each of those files. Then create the newsgroup *alt.internet.connection* with the *ctlinnd newgroup* command. Finally, use *trn* to read *alt.internet.connection*, and *Pnews* to post to it.

References

Adams 1993.   Adams, Rick, "Total traffic through uunet for the last 2 weeks," *news.lists*, UUNET Communications (22 August 1993).

Carl-Mitchell & Quarterman 1993.   Carl-Mitchell, Smoot, & Quarterman, John S., *Practical Internetworking with TCP/IP and UNIX*, Addison-Wesley, Reading, MA (1993). ISBN 0-201-58629-0.

Crocker 1982.   Crocker, David, *Standard for the format of ARPA Internet text messages (RFC822)*, August 1982.

Horton & Adams 1987.   Horton, Mark R., & Adams, Rick, *Standard for Interchange of USENET Messages (RFC1036)*, December 1987.

Kantor & Lapsley 1986.   Kantor, B., & Lapsley, P., *Network News Transfer Protocol (RFC977)*, February 1986.

Reid 1993.   Reid, Brian, "USENET Readership Summary Report for Jun 93," DEC Network Systems Laboratory, Palo Alto, CA (3 July 1993).

Spencer & Collyer 1987.   Spencer, Henry, & Collyer, Geoff, "News Need Not Be Slow," *Proceedings of the Winter 1987 USENIX Conference (Washington, D.C., 21–23 January 1987)*, USENIX Association (1987).

Woods & Spafford 1992.   Woods, Greg, & Spafford, Gene, "Guidelines for USENET Group Creation," *news.announce.newusers*, USENET (23 September 1992).

CHAPTER 9

Security Issues

Internet connectivity not only allows you easy access to many useful services and resources; it also allows access to your network from would be intruders and system crackers. Most users on the Internet are trustworthy. However, there are always people who will try to break into your system either for fun or for malice.

Security is never an absolute. Some people argue that connecting to the Internet is inherently insecure. In a sense, they are correct. But dialin modems on your system also are insecure. Your level of concern about security is directly related to what you are trying to protect. You must weigh the risk of a cracker breaking into your system against the benefits of Internet connectivity.

We discuss in this chapter how to deal with many of the security issues surrounding Internet access. Any computer that is accessible from the outside, whether via modem or Internet connectivity, can be attacked, and any security setup can be broken. We make no warranty that this information will prevent your network from being cracked. These techniques have been used successfully by others. But security is not an absolute standard, and you should not become complacent because you feel your system is secure. Real security results from understanding both the real and potential threats to your network, monitoring your network for those threats, and vigilantly combatting those threats.

In this chapter, we explain how to secure each host system that has Internet access and how to configure a router to act as a more general firewall and packet filter. An overview of many of these security issues appears in [Carl-Mitchell & Quarterman 1992].

9.1 Air Gapping

The degree to which you elect to protect your network results from a tradeoff between security and convenience. If you want to be really safe, you can do what some large security and law enforcement agencies do: air-gap your network connections. This means you have a machine on the Internet, but you don't connect it to any other machine or network inside your company. Anybody who wants to transfer information between the Internet and the corporate network must carry it across the air-gap on a printout and type it back in. Slightly less paranoid institutions might permit tape or disk transfers. Even more paranoid organizations might insist on having other corporate machines isolated electromagnetically in order to avoid having outside parties decipher the electromagnetic field typically generated by a computer system. If you consider the information kept on your internal network to be that sensitive, then this is the level of security required. Generally, you probably won't want or need to go this far.

9.2   Passwords

The only way to completely secure a host is to physically secure it and monitor and control physical access. For most sites, this is probably overkill, since the whole purpose of a network is to allow convenient access to information from remote locations.

An alternative security mechanism commonly used is the password. Operating systems that evolved from earlier timesharing systems such as UNIX typically have built-in password control. Individual PCs or Macintoshes typically do not have password mechanisms as a part of the operating system, but many of these systems, when networked, do have some add-on password control for accessing remote resources such as file servers. Also, most specialized network hardware such as routers or terminal servers rely on passwords to restrict access to sensitive configuration information.

However, an easily deciphered password offers little in the way of protection. They are a system cracker's dream come true because a system cracker who can masquerade as an ordinary user can more easily exploit security holes. Good passwords give your site protection in depth. If a system cracker gets through a firewall or through a modem server, the next wall encountered is user passwords on hosts. Many users, left to their own devices, will use passwords that are, for example, their favorite color, their spouse's name, their own name spelled backwards, or the name of the family dog. Worse, many passwords end up written on blackboards in publicly accessible offices.

Encourage your users to use passwords that aren't easily guessed. Don't keep generic accounts that several people use. Don't have accounts without passwords. Don't let sensitive administrator accounts have easily cracked passwords. Software that checks for such easily guessed passwords is freely available. This software disallows use of the person's name, of a short password, or of words contained in one or more dictionaries. See Appendix C, *Software and Other Information* for the Internet archive location of these packages.

9.3   Hiding Information

The less outsiders know about your internal network, the fewer handholds they will have to hang onto if they climb inside. Besides, it's more efficient if outside organizations know only minimal information about your system because their routers, hostname mapping daemons, and other network logistics need fewer resources to communicate with your users.

You can hide your internal network topology by using a single class B network number, with subnets for your internal physical networks. You can hide most hostnames by having all mail to the outside world appear to come from your main domain name, with no host subdomains. And you can hide login names by having, for all users, company-, department-, or office-wide mail aliases that differ from the user's real login ids.

Following is a short list of some potential information sources you might want to plug:

1. DNS

An outsider can get a list of all your host names and IP addresses via DNS. If you are concerned about having the names of specific hosts known, then don't list them in the DNS database.

2. *finger*

The *finger* protocol can provide a wealth of information for a system cracker. It lists the name of the user, that user's login account, and other potentially useful information. If you have users that use easily guessed passwords, the *finger* output might give some definite clues as to what the password is.

3. SMTP

The VRFY/EXPN commands in SMTP allow a remote user to expand a mailbox address that is an alias. To plug this source, you must modify the SMTP server. This usually requires source code. Fortunately, if you use a system as your mail gateway, sources for *sendmail* are available from Internet archive sites.

4. *rlogin* and *rsh*

Both *rlogin* and *rsh* allow a user to put in the user's home directory a file called *.rhosts*, which contains the names of the remote systems that are allowed to access the local system without a password. There are two problems with using this file. If a user allows access from a remote account that the user has on a system with less security, then a system cracker who breaks into the account on the remote system is just one easy step from breaking into the local system. Also, if a user creates a *.rhosts* file on a remote system, the information in the file gives the system name from where the user remotely logs in. Usage of this file should be discouraged. Where it is used, the user should always use a different password on the remote system.

5. *.netrc* file

This UNIX home directory file contains the name and password of remote systems which can be FTPed to. It should be readable only by that user. This file contains an unencrypted password which is also very bad idea; therefore the use of the *.netrc* file should be discouraged.

In some cases, you can eliminate the threat by simply turning off the service. In other cases, you must modify the source program. For example, limiting VRFY/EXPN to local users is an easy change to *sendmail* but doing so requires source code. Preventing users from using *.rhosts* and *.netrc* files is harder. This requires continual education, particularly since these files can reside on remote systems outside your administration.

9.4   Dangerous Services

Several Internet services have potential security holes you should watch out for.

• TFTP

TFTP (Trivial File Transfer Protocol) should never be allowed from outside your own network. TFTP has no password security and, if badly configured, allows anybody to make copies of any files on your network and in some cases replace them. If TFTP is necessary (it is used to bootstrap diskless workstations), then be sure it runs as a user without special privilege and that it allows access only to a well-protected directory that is read-only. If you can, just turn TFTP off.

• *sendmail*

If you are using *sendmail* on your UNIX systems, be sure the *sendmail* version you are using doesn't have the old *sendmail* debug hack, which allows a remote user to become *root*. You can easily check for this by TELNETing to port 25, waiting for the SMTP banner, and typing "wiz." If the program asks for a password, then your version has the bug. Also search your *sendmail.cf* file for the *OW* command. The string following the OW is the wizard encrypted password. If you can't replace your copy of *sendmail*, immediately replace this encrypted password with an asterisk. Also watch out for an alias called *decode* in your alias database. If this alias calls the program *uudecode*, then be sure that *uudecode* is not setuid to *root*; if it is, it can create setuid programs, which you don't want.

• Anonymous FTP

If you need to run anonymous FTP, read the installation instructions carefully and be sure the anonymous FTP server has access only to a restricted portion of your filesystem. For more information, see Chapter 10, *Setting Up Resource Discovery Services*.

• NFS

If you are using Sun's NFS, be sure that exported filesystems are exported only to hosts on your local network. The default action is to export them to any host for read-only access. However, with this default action, any remote host can mount the filesystem and thereby compromise security. Be very careful about security if you export a filesystem read/write and allow remote superuser access to the filesystem. In this case, a remote user with superuser privileges can create setuid programs and easily plant Trojan Horses in your filesystem. Also ensure you use the NFS version that limits who can bind to your domain. On a UNIX system, the file */var/yp/securenets* contains a list of IP addresses that are allowed to do this.

• R* services
The R* services also can potentially cause trouble. Check the */etc/hosts.equiv* and the */.rhosts* files to ensure they don't contain a line with a single "+," which allows any remote user to login without a password. Having this line in the */.rhosts* file is especially dangerous because it allows a remote user to login as the superuser.

9.5   Kerberos

Kerberos is a secure authentication system. A kerberos system consists of a physically secured authentication server. A user wanting to use a service asks the authentication server for a ticket. A **ticket** is an encrypted message that when delivered to a service, authenticates the identity of the client.

Kerberos can be useful in specific environments. In particular, it can be effective in a relatively open environment in which users share public workstations, such as is found in many academic communities. However, kerberos is not a security panacea. For it to be effective, all sensitive services must employ its authentication method and know what to do when presented tickets. Kerberos is ineffective in situations in which a client program accesses a service using other, less secure authentication methods. For example, if you allow incoming TELNET using the standard password authentication, using kerberos internally will not protect your site from outside intruders.

Note that beneath all its sophisticated encryption techniques, kerberos relies on hard-to-guess or hard to decrypt passwords. So if your user's employ bad passwords, kerberos will offer little real protection for your system.

9.6   CERT

The CERT (Computer Emergency Response Team) is an organization whose goal is to aid Internet users with security issues. CERT was formed after the famous Internet Worm episode that occurred over five years ago. A major CERT benefit is a mailing list it provides for obtaining security advisories. These advisories usually comprise reports of operating system bugs and security holes. Very useful for helping you maintain security systems and keep up-to-date about security issues, these advisories are posted to the USENET newsgroup *comp.security.announce* and are also distributed to a mailing list. To get on the CERT mailing list, send a message to *cert-advisory-request@cert.org*. If you have more than one person who is receiving CERT advisories, send the advisory to an alias that expands the recipient list locally. Doing this saves network bandwidth and keeps the advisory list down to a reasonable size.

CERT also maintains an anonymous FTP site, *cert.org*, with archived copies of past advisories as well as papers on a variety of Internet security issues. A good file to read initially is *cert_faq*, which contains the answers to frequently asked questions about CERT and explains what is available on *cert.org*. Source code for several security related systems can also be found at *cert.org*. These include *cops*, a set of programs for scanning a UNIX system for potential security threats; *crack*, a program for checking passwords; and *tcpd*, which we will discuss in detail in the next section.

9.7   Host Connection Protection: tcpd

Attacks on a host often target specific services and usually come from specific places, so it is useful to be able to protect a host against connections to specific services from other hosts, domains, or networks. You can provide such protection for an individual host by using a software package called variously *tcpd*, *tcp_wrappers*, or *log_tcp*. You do this by installing and administering *tcpd* on the host you want to protect [Carl-Mitchell & Quarterman 1993a; Carl-Mitchell & Quarterman 1993b]. If you have a router, you can implement more general network access protection schemes for your network. Whether you have a router or not, *tcpd* lets you control access to your own host from your host.

With *tcpd*, you can turn off TELNET access from a host that shows suspicious login attempts, while leaving TELNET access on for use from other hosts so that your legitimate colleagues can reach your machine and you can log in while traveling. If a remote mail system breaks and floods your machine with repeated spurious messages, you can preserve your incoming mail service and reduce your machine's load by turning off SMTP for just that one remote host.

You also can control access to classes of hosts. For example, you can make finger available to everyone inside your organization but not to anyone elsewhere on the Internet, except for a few selected organizations. You can turn off a whole university, network, or even country if you're tired of trying to localize break-ins from there and you see no legitimate traffic from there.

The most basic function of *tcpd* is logging incoming connections and attempts. In addition, you can set traps to spring on selected connection attempts. These traps can call arbitrary shell scripts, so essentially anything you can program, you can make *tcpd* do on a trap (although not everything that is possible is advisable).

inetd: the Server's Server

Because *tcpd* depends on it, we first must describe inetd, the server's server.

The simplest way to support a network service is to have a process act as a daemon and that wait for connection attempts for the service's protocol. When a connection is established, the daemon process can fork a server process to handle the service, thus freeing the daemon to wait for another connection. A host wanting to support many services could require a daemon process for each service. But there are many Internet services, and even on UNIX systems the number of idle server processes could easily grow large, absorbing inconvenient amounts of system resources. Instead, the *inetd* server accepts connections for a range of protocols, invoking appropriate servers when needed. This method reduces the number of processes, since a separate server process is needed only when a client has actually requested service. It also simplifies servers, since *inetd* can handle much of the complexity of setting up TCP or UDP communications.

tcpd Architecture

The *tcpd* facility works by using *inetd* to give the *tcpd* program control of an incoming connection as if it were the real server for the intended service (see Fig. 9.1). If *tcpd* decides to accept the connection, it executes the real server, which never knows anything unusual happened. If *tcpd* decides *not* to accept a connection, it closes the connection and exits without executing the real server. In either case, *tcpd* logs the connection attempt and calls any appropriate traps.

By default, *tcpd* will permit (almost) everything. You can tell it what to accept by creating and editing the files /etc/hosts.allow, which is searched first, and /etc/hosts.deny, which is searched only if no match has already been found in /etc/hosts.allow.

Figure 9.1 tcpd Architecture.

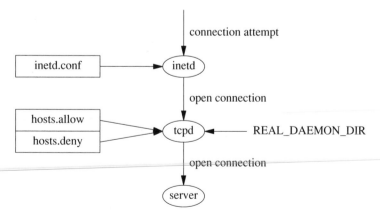

Allowing and Denying Connections

The same format applies to both *tcpd* permission files. Comment lines start with
an octothorpe (#). Anything else is a control line. Each control line has two or
three fields separated by colons. The first field says which server to control and is
called a *daemon_list*. The second field says what remote machines, domains, or
networks to control and is called a *client_list*. If commas appear in either field,
they separate multiple words. Some wildcards, such as ALL, are accepted in
either of these two fields.

The example in Fig. 9.2 shows several common uses of *tcpd*, illustrating what
would go in both the *hosts.allow* and the *hosts.deny* files. The first, *hosts.allow*,
permits incoming connections from any system inside the local domain,
ourco.com. The daemon_list in the first field, before the colon, is just ALL. This
means all services are permitted to any host that matches the client_list in the second field. The domain is listed twice in the client_list, with slightly different syn-
taxes. With the leading dot, as in *.ourco.com*, it matches any subdomain that ends
in that domain, such as *yourws.dev.ourco.com* or *gw.ourco.com*. But that word
does not match the domain *ourco.com* itself alone. The word without the leading
dot, *ourco.com*, matches exactly that domain, so those two words match the
domain and any subdomain within it. Some domain lookup methods do not
append the local domain to a remote hostname within the same domain, so the
most local hostname part may appear alone, for example, as *yourws*, and the wild
card *LOCAL* matches that case. All three words together permit any local system
to connect to any service.

Meanwhile, the line in the *hosts.deny* file prohibits access to the finger and
TELNET services from any system not already permitted in the *hosts.allow* file.
So nobody outside the local domain can use finger or TELNET, unless specifically
permitted to in the *hosts.allow* file. If you wanted to prohibit all access from outside to all services, you would want to change the *hosts.deny* line to

```
ALL: ALL
```

Figure 9.2 A Typical tcpd Example.

```
# hosts.allow
ALL: LOCAL, .ourco.com, ourco.com
in.telnetd: .governor.state.gov, 128.43.200.
ALL: .prest.edu EXCEPT open.dialups.prest.edu, 199.9.13.1

# hosts.deny
in.fingerd,in.telnetd: ALL
```

The second sample line for *hosts.allow* in Fig. 9.2 permits TELNET from the state governor's office, so they can use a service on your machine, but does not permit finger, so they won't be calling you as soon as you come in to work in the morning. The second word in the client_list permits access from any machine on a particular IP subnet at the governor's office. This often is necessary because of misconfigured Macintoshes that don't have DNS set up properly, so *tcpd* can't discover their domain names (if any). Note the trailing dot, which permits any string after it to match.

The third sample line for *hosts.allow* in Fig. 9.2 permits all services to be used from a prestigious university, except from a set of dialin modems that would be likely to harbor system crackers. We also know the specific IP address of that terminal server, and we do not want crackers coming in from it even when the university's DNS servers happen to have problems, so we explicitly disallow that address, as well.

The following lines would *not* work to disallow a particular host while permitting others within the same domain:

```
# hosts.allow
# Don't do this.
ALL: .prest.edu

# hosts.deny
# Don't do this.
ALL: open.dialups.prest.edu, 199.9.13.1
```

The first file would permit all access from all hosts at the prestigious university and the second file would never be searched for any such host.

Logging

Logging for *tcpd* is normally done through *syslog* using the same logging category as for mail (usually LOG_MAIL). So if your mailer daemon logs into */var/log/syslog*, so will *tcpd*. To find out where syslog is putting its output, look in the syslog configuration file, usually */etc/syslog.conf*. In addition to the usual syslog timestamp, *tcpd* logs the server name (for example, *in.fingerd*), and the remote domain name.

Traps

Denying access and logging aren't always enough. Sometimes you want to be notified more immediately when a likely cracking attempt occurs, to collect more information on the instigator, or even to set out bait. Examples of all three of these possibilities are shown in Fig. 9.3. These traps all use the optional third field, which is called the *shell_command,* and which can contain arbitrary shell commands to be executed when the first two fields match the incoming connection.

```
# in hosts.allow
# mail a notice
ALL: bad.guys.shady.edu: echo "%d from %c" | mail root
#
# reverse finger
ALL: bad.guys.shady.edu: finger @%h \
   | /usr/ucb/Mail -s "%d from %c" root
#
# No TFTPD from bad guys.
ALL EXCEPT in.tftpd: bad.guys.shady.edu: echo "%d from %c" \
   | mail root

# in hosts.deny
in.tftpd: ALL
```

Figure 9.3 Some tcpd Traps.

If you want to be notified when any connection attempt comes in from a particularly shady host, such as *bad.guys.shady.edu*, the first example in Fig. 9.3 would suffice; just put that line in *hosts.allow*. You (*root,* actually) will be mailed the name of the service (%d) and whatever is known (%c) about who tried to connect to it.

Suppose you want to know more about which user tried to connect. You can have *tcpd* finger the remote host to see who is logged on and mail the result to you, as shown in the second example in Fig. 9.3. This trap is not necessarily advisable because the remote system also can be monitoring incoming connections and might have a trap set to do something nasty to systems that finger it.... More passive monitoring as in the previous example is probably a better idea.

The third example in Fig. 9.3 involves both parameter files. Old versions of the UNIX TFTP daemon were notoriously insecure, and a knowledgeable system cracker might try that service just to see if you're running such an old daemon. Normally, you probably do not want to run TFTP at all, since its functions have mostly been taken over by various other protocols. To use the TFTP daemon as bait, you must first install it, but you can turn it off by default by using the *hosts.deny* line in Fig. 9.3. Then in *hosts.allow*, you can use the third example line to prohibit TFTP to the bad guys, too, while setting a trap to notify you if they try to use it.

Installation

Daemons that almost always should be run standalone include those for DNS (usually *in.named*), SMTP (often *sendmail*), and NNTP (in this book, *innd*). Almost any other IP server, whether for a TCP or a UDP service, can be put under *tcpd* control. There are even conditions under which the SMTP daemon can usefully be put under *tcpd* control.

There are two ways to put a program under *tcpd* control. Both use a parameter, REAL_DAEMON_DIR, which you must set in the Makefile to the pathname of the binary object files of the servers you want to control.

1. You can move the object file for the real server into the REAL_DAEMON_DIR directory, replacing it with a link to *tcpd*.

2. You can change the appropriate line in */etc/inetd.conf* to call *tcpd* from wherever you have put it.

The first method is simple, and there is not much more to be said about it. The second method is more flexible, and does not require moving the real server. Instead you make REAL_DAEMON_DIR point at its directory. The *tcpd* program then looks for the real server in the REAL_DAEMON_DIR directory. We always use the second method.

tcpd and inetd.conf

A service that is commonly put under *tcpd* control is *finger*. While *finger* is very useful in supplying information about individuals directly from primary sources (the individuals themselves and the system each is using), it often is perceived as a security problem for the same reason. The *finger* server is frequently called from *inetd* with a line in */etc/inetd.conf* like the following:

```
finger stream tcp nowait nobody /usr/etc/in.fingerd in.fingerd
```

To put *finger* under *tcpd* control, change that line by substituting the pathname of the *tcpd* server for that of the finger server, as in the following:

```
finger stream tcp nowait nobody /usr/local/etc/tcpd in.fingerd
```

Then *tcpd* will look for *in.fingerd* in REAL_DAEMON_DIR.

Servers controlled by *tcpd* using this method do not have to be in REAL_DAEMON_DIR. Instead, you can supply the pathname of the server as the first server argument in the *inetd.conf* string as follows:

```
finger stream tcp nowait nobody /usr/local/etc/tcpd \
    /usr/local/etc/in.fingerd
```

In this case, *tcpd* will use that pathname, stripping the prefix off it before passing it as the first argument of the server so found. This variation is useful in testing new versions of servers, while leaving undisturbed the old version that is known to work.

If you are getting repeated spurious error messages from a certain host or you think someone may be trying to break into your SMTP server from a certain host, you may want to put even your SMTP server under *tcpd* control. If your SMTP is served by *sendmail*, the following line will probably work in */etc/inetd.conf*:

```
smtp stream tcp nowait root /usr/etc/tcpd \
   /usr/lib/sendmail -bs
```

The *sendmail* program has many functions. You also will want to tell it to run the mail queue periodically, for example, by putting an entry like the following in root's crontab file:

```
13 * * * * /usr/lib/sendmail -q
```

Because *sendmail* is now under *tcpd* control, you can limit access to it from anywhere you consider inappropriate.

Options

Several options are worth your consideration.

PARANOID. The one thing that *tcpd* does not permit by default is any connection from a host whose domain name and IP address do not match. The IP address is immediately available from the operating system, and *tcpd* uses that address in a reverse DNS lookup to find the domain name for the host; this host name is used in logging. Next *tcpd* uses the host name in a forward DNS lookup to get an IP address. If that IP address does not match the one provided by the operating system, *tcpd* assumes either that the host is trying to spoof its name or address or that one of the DNS servers is lying. In this situation, *tcpd* logs the problem and drops the connection. If the reverse mapping fails, *tcpd* can't assume malice, since many hosts and domains just don't have their reverse mapping set up correctly.

But if the reverse mapping succeeds and the forward mapping fails, *tcpd* by default *does* act paranoid and drops the connection, logging it as for a mismatch of the type just described. To disable this paranoid assumption on the meaning of a failed forward DNS lookup, comment out -DPARANOID in the Makefile. We always leave this feature enabled.

RFC931. If someone breaks into your system, you are not as interested in knowing what organization's computers the person is using as in knowing who the individual is. The TCP protocol, the Domain Name System, and the host operating system permit *tcpd* to determine the remote host from the TCP connection itself. But *tcpd* does not actually read data on the connections it handles and so cannot directly determine the identity of the user who established the connection from the remote host. However, a typical host may be a workstation with only one user, so you often can make a good guess as to who the user is. But there are still enough large timesharing systems, particularly in universities in which a malicious system cracker can hide in a crowd.

An authentication service intended to help with this problem is specified in RFC 931 [StJohns 1985]. By setting the option -DRFC931 in the Makefile, you can make *tcpd* use RFC 931 to ask remote host who the remote user is. If the remote host is running an RFC 931 server (as many of the larger timesharing systems do), *tcpd* will log the result; if not, you've lost only a few seconds. The default is actually 30 seconds to wait for an RFC 931 response, so you may find this service more annoying to your legitimate users than it is worth. But *tcpd* is usually quite worth the small overhead it imposes on incoming connections.

9.8   Packet Filtering

Most networks of any size are interconnected with the Internet via a dedicated router. Because all packets must pass through a router to and from the Internet, it is an obvious place to put a first level of protection. Most modern routers provide packet filtering to some degree or another. All the firewalling techniques we describe in this section are based on router packet filtering. First, however, we need to explain what a router is and how it differs from a repeater and a bridge.

Routers, bridges, and repeaters transfer data between physical cable segments of a network. The more general term gateway is sometimes used for all three. Layering distinguishes these various kinds of gateways, as shown in Fig. 9.4.

Figure 9.4 Repeaters, Bridges, Routers, and Gateways.

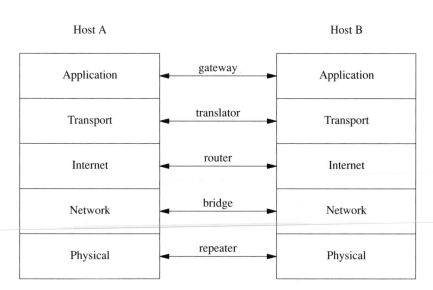

This concept is easier to understand with an example, so we offer one here using Ethernet. A **repeater** connects two Ethernet cable segments at the Physical Layer so that higher-layer protocols see the two segments as a single physical network. All traffic originating on either segment is transferred between the two segments. A **bridge** connects two cables at the Network Layer so that they appear as a single logical network. Bridges for Ethernet take data off one physical Ethernet and reintroduce them on another physical Ethernet as if they were new packets. This technique avoids physical segment length restrictions because the segments on either side of a bridge are separate Ethernets as far as the Ethernet specifications are concerned; however, they look like a single Ethernet to higher-protocol layers. A bridge also can connect two dissimilar LAN media. For example, bridges to interconnect Ethernets and Token Rings exist, since both datalink protocols share similar framing and addressing conventions. A **router** connects two networks at the Internet Layer; hence, they appear as separate logical networks. This setup avoids most of the restrictions of the lower-layer protocol specifications but requires the router to explicitly switch traffic for each higher-level protocol, such as IP.

Above the Internet Layer are translators and application gateways. A **translator** translates messages from one transport protocol to another transport protocol, although this is seldom seen. For example, it is possible to translate from TCP to ISO-OSI TP4, since both protocols support much the same functionality.

The term **gateway** is sometimes used to refer to routers, or even to bridges or repeaters, but it most commonly indicates an object that transfers data at the application layer. Today, most networks have mail gateways to other networks that sometimes use different lower-layer protocols. Many networks also support gateways for other application services such as USENET news.

To connect to the Internet, you very likely will use a dedicated router. While low-speed SLIP and PPP connectivity is becoming very popular and can be implemented on a general purpose UNIX system, modern multiprotocol routers provide a great deal of control over the packets that pass through them. Because they examine every packet in order to make the fundamental routing decision, most routers also allow you to selectively filter packets based on their contents. In this book, we concentrate on filtering TCP/IP packets because that is the dominant protocol used in the Internet. However, the same general principles apply to most other network protocols.

In the following examples, we refer to Fig. 9.5. Suppose your company IP networks are connected to the Internet by an intervening router, as shown in the figure. The Internet connection is via a serial line and the two internal networks are Ethernets, although any type of LAN technology will work equally well for filtering packets. Note that there is more than one internal network. This multiplicity allows us to describe how to selectively filter packets to give one internal network better Internet access (with less security) than the other internal network has. Observe the IP network numbers of each network and the IP addresses of the various hosts; they too are used in the examples. We use two Class C network numbers for clarity, although subnets of IP networks can work as well.

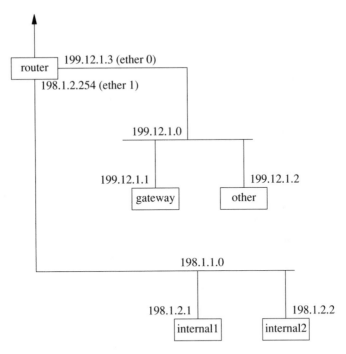

Figure 9.5 Example Network for ajax.com.

Filtering Basics

IP is used to move packets from their source to their final destination. Every IP packet contains a source and destination IP address. The source address is always that of the host from where the packet originated and the destination address is always that of the packet's final destination. Source and destination IP addresses are used by a router to forward a packet on the best path to its final destination.

Because every IP packet contains a source and destination IP address, packets bound for a particular host on a network can be selectively filtered based on their original source address or final destination address. Transport protocols such as TCP or UDP add a source and a destination port number to each packet as a part of the header they attach to each message. These numbers indicate which process on each host will receive the message encapsulated within the packet.

In general, routers normally don't look at port numbers when making routing decisions, but for filtering purposes, their knowing the source and destination port numbers allows selective filtering based on the service being used. For example, a TELNET server always uses port number 23 and an SMTP server always uses port number 25. Filtering selectively by port number also takes advantage of how port numbers are assigned. While a TELNET server always uses port number 23, a TELNET client's port number is not fixed but rather is assigned dynamically. In general, the client port number is assigned a number greater than 1023. For example, a user on host *procyon.acme.com* (128.84.1.2) who wants to access the

TELNET server on host *gateway.ajax.com* (199.12.1.1) TELNETs to the server with a command similar to the following:

```
telnet gateway.ajax.com
```

The *telnet* program first looks up the IP address of *gateway.ajax.com,* either with DNS or some other hostname-to-IP address mapping protocol. The client also gets a port number for its end of the connection. This address, assigned by the operating system, is an unused port number above 1023. Some systems assign this port number sequentially beginning with 1024; others assign a random number above 1023. The latter method makes it more difficult for a system cracker to guess the next likely port number a client will use. Let's say the client port number is 1026 and the client uses TCP as the transport protocol. The client sends an initial packet with source IP address 128.84.1.2, destination IP address 199.12.1.1, source port number 1026, and destination port number 23. *gateway.ajax.com* receives this packet and establishes a connection between the TELNET server (identified by port number 23) and the remote TELNET client. Once the connection is established, all traffic for this connection uses the same source and destination IP addresses and port numbers. The connection also is identified by the underlying transport protocol. So the connection can be uniquely identified by the 5-tuple

<128.84.1.2, 1026, 199.12.1.1, 23, TCP>.

If another TELNET connection is established between *procyon.acme.com* and *gateway.ajax.com*, then the client port number on *procyon.acme.com* will be different but still a port number greater than 1023. The server port number on *gateway.ajax.com* will always be 23.

You can verify this on a UNIX system by using the *netstat* utility, which gives the source and destination addresses and port numbers for established connections. Use the *-n* option to prevent the IP addresses and port numbers from being translated to their mnemonic names. Other operating systems have similar facilities. The following display shows a partial *netstat* output with two TELNET connections between the same hosts.

```
Active Internet connections
Proto Recv-Q Send-Q  Local Address     Foreign Address (state)
tcp        0      0   128.84.1.2.1026   199.12.1.1.23   ESTABLISHED
tcp        0      0   128.84.1.2.1028   199.12.1.1.23   ESTABLISHED
```

All other services (SMTP, etc.) use the same port assignment algorithm, so the filtering principles are identical.

If you want to disallow incoming TELNET connections on host *gateway.ajax.com* from any other host not on the same network, then a packet filter on the router interface *ether 0* simply needs to look at the destination address and destination port number of each packet. If the destination address is 199.12.1.1, the transport protocol is TCP, and the destination port number is 23, then the router should be instructed not to forward that packet on interface *ether 0*. This procedure effectively disallows incoming TELNET access to host *gateway.ajax.com*. If you wanted to disallow TELNET to all hosts on network 199.12.1.0, then the router only needs to match the network part of the IP destination address against network number 199.12.1.0.

Selective filtering of the source of IP packets allows TELNET service only from selected remote hosts. For example, if you want to allow TELNET only from host 135.84.12.2, the packet filter would check the source IP address and let packets from that host pass, while dropping all other TELNET packets.

Common Filter Types

Packet filters can be very flexible, but some common types have emerged, which we discuss here and in the next section.

- Secure subnet
  A Secure Subnet is an intermediate subnetwork between an internal network and the outside world. TCP connections are allowed on the secure network both from the internal network and the outside. Access to the secure network is controlled by limiting accounts on the machine or machines on the secure subnet and having tight password security. TCP connections are allowed only from the secure subnet to the internal network. A user on the outside who wants to access the internal network must first log in to the secure subnet and then from there are allowed to log in to the internal network. Users on the internal network can connect only to the secure subnet and from there can connect to the outside.

- Connection diode with secure subnet
  A connection diode disallows incoming connections but allows outbound connections from the internal network. This technique exploits the way client ports are assigned for TCP services.

- Permeable filter
  A permeable filter allows certain types of services or protocols to pass through the router while disallowing others. The filter may have less permeability in one direction than in another. The connection diode is a special type of permeable filter; for example, you might use one when you want to completely disallow TELNET but permit SMTP connections from your network to the outside world and vice versa. Or you might want to restrict *finger* access to only selected hosts. This is done by checking the port numbers in each packet.

Building Packet Filters

In this section, we assume you already have a router connected to the Internet and you now want to know how to turn it into a firewall. We present techniques for several kinds of firewalls, note which threats they can counter, and offer real-world examples of their usage.

Filter Syntax. For packet filtering, we borrow the filtering syntax used by cisco routers. Cisco routers use a fairly simple syntax to define a packet filter. Each network interface on a router is assigned an *access-group,* which is an integer number that identifies an *access-list.* This list comprises a sequence of filtering commands. For example, the following configuration commands would allow TELNET connections to be established only to host 199.12.1.1 from outside the local network:

```
interface ether 0
ip address 199.12.1.254 255.255.255.0
access-group 101
access-list 101 permit tcp 0.0.0.0 255.255.255.255 199.12.1.1 0.0.0.0   eq 23
access-list 101 deny   tcp 0.0.0.0 255.255.255.255 199.12.1.0 0.0.0.255 eq 23
```

The access-list is associated with a particular interface (the access-group command). It checks in order against each member of the access-list each packet routed to the interface. For example, the first member of access-list 101 says to permit TCP connections from anywhere to IP address 199.12.1.1, where the destination port number is 23. The IP addresses are given in dotted decimal notation followed by a mask. The mask tell which bits the list should ignore when checking the IP address. So the source IP address and mask of {0.0.0.0 255.255.255.255} says to match any address. The destination address and mask {199.12.1.1 0.0.0.0} will match only the IP address 199.12.1.1. Finally an optional port expression (eq 23 in lines 4 and 5) is compared against the destination port in the TCP header. If the values of these fields in the packet match, then the operator (permit) allows the packet to pass. If the operator is denied, the packet it dropped. Each access-list command is followed in order until a match occurs. If there is no match, then the packet is dropped.

Next, we lead you through a number of examples that show you how to filter connections.

Secure Subnet. The following commands let network 199.12.1.0 act as a secure subnet for our example network. We allow only TELNET to a single host on the secure network (199.12.1.1).

```
interface ether 0
ip address 199.12.1.254 255.255.255.0
access-group 102

interface ether 1
ip address 198.1.2.254 255.255.255.0
access-group 103

access-list 102 permit tcp 0.0.0.0 255.255.255.255 199.12.1.1 0.0.0.0 eq 23
access-list 102 permit tcp 0.0.0.0 255.255.255.255 199.12.1.1 0.0.0.0 gt 1023

access-list 103 permit tcp 199.12.1.1 0.0.0.0 198.1.2.0 0.0.0.255 eq 23
access-list 103 permit tcp 199.12.1.1 0.0.0.0 198.1.2.0 0.0.0.255 gt 1023
```

Access-list 102 is for the secure subnet. Line 1 permits incoming TELNET connections from anywhere (port 23); line 2 permits outbound services (ports>1023). This configuration permits TELNET as the only incoming service, hence effectively limiting connections to the TELNET protocol. Line 2 is needed for outbound TELNET connections, since an outbound TELNET client on *gateway.ajax.com* will have a local port number greater than 1023 and packets from the remote host's TELNET server will have a destination address of 199.12.1.1 and use the client's port number.

Access-list 103 is for the internal network. It is identical to access-list 102, except that inbound TELNET connections are permitted only from the single host on the internal network and outbound TELNET connections are allowed only to *gateway.ajax.com* (199.12.1.1). This restriction is enforced by the source IP address in the line 2 of the list. If an outbound TELNET connection is attempted to any other host, the packets from the remote server will be dropped.

TELNET Connection Diode. The TELNET connection diode filter is a variation on the secure subnet. It permits outbound TELNET connections but denies inbound TELNET connections from anywhere. The following packet filter demonstrates this for network 198.1.2.0:

```
interface ether 0
ip address 199.12.1.254 255.255.255.0
access-group 102

interface ether 1
ip address 198.1.2.254 255.255.255.0
access-group 104

access-list 102 permit tcp 0.0.0.0 255.255.255.255 199.12.1.1 0.0.0.0 eq 23
access-list 102 permit tcp 0.0.0.0 255.255.255.255 199.12.1.1 0.0.0.0 gt 1023

access-list 104 permit tcp 0.0.0.0 255.255.255.255 198.1.2.0 0.0.0.255 gt 1023
```

The single access-list command for the internal network (access-list 104) permits outbound TELNET connections. All inbound TELNET connections are denied to the internal network. If you want to permit inbound TELNETs from the secure subnet (ether 0), access-list 104 would be as follows:

```
access-list 104 permit tcp 199.12.1.1 0.0.0.0 198.1.2.0 0.0.0.255 eq 23
access-list 104 permit tcp 0.0.0.0 255.255.255.255 198.1.2.0 0.0.0.255 gt 1023
```

This is a more convenient way to restrict incoming TELNET to a specific host, while permitting anybody to use TELNET when going outside. However, this method provides less administrative control than the secure subnet case does, since any internal user can use TELNET to go anywhere, rather than being required to use an intermediate login on a host on the secure subnet. Also, any internal service on a port number above 1023 can be connected to by an external client. This means an internal user can more easily create potential security holes.

RLOGIN, the Berkeley remote terminal facility, uses client port numbers less than 1024. So an equivalent filter cannot be built for RLOGIN without modification. RLOGIN assigns unused port numbers starting at 1023. The following addition to access-list 104 allows outbound RLOGIN connections from network 198.1.2.0:

```
access-list 104 permit tcp 0.0.0.0 255.255.255.255 198.1.2.0 0.0.0.255 gt 1000
```

Note that no well-known services should be in the port number range above 1000. These port numbers are used by RLOGIN clients. The port numbers are under 1024 because of the authentication method used in RLOGIN. On systems, ports below 1024 can be assigned only if a process is run as *root*. RLOGIN authentication uses this trick to verify the true identity of the user. Setting the port number greater than 1000 allows 23 simultaneous RLOGIN connections from a single host. If you have more than this number of connections, you must set the port number in the filter lower. Be careful when you do this, however, or you will start to run into some well-known ports and inadvertently permit remote access to an internal service.

Permeable Filter. A permeable filter permits certain services inbound and denies other inbound services. Depending on the service restrictions, these filters can become very complex. Again, the selective filtering depends on all services using well-known ports.

A good example of using a permeable filter is a situation in which you permit both inbound and outbound SMTP connections from a single mail gateway host while denying other inbound services to other hosts including SMTP, as the following code illustrates:

```
interface ether 0
ip address 199.12.1.254 255.255.255.0
access-group 105

interface ether 1
ip address 198.1.2.254 255.255.255.0
access-group 106

access-list 105 permit tcp 0.0.0.0 255.255.255.255 199.12.1.1 0.0.0.0 eq 25
access-list 105 permit tcp 0.0.0.0 255.255.255.255 199.12.1.0 0.0.0.255 gt 1023

access-list 106 permit tcp 0.0.0.0 255.255.255.255 198.1.2.0 0.0.0.255 gt 1023
access-list 106 permit tcp 199.12.1.1 0.0.0.0 198.1.2.0 0.0.0.255 eq 25
```

Access-list 105 allows both inbound and outbound SMTP connections (port 25) to host *gateway.ajax.com*. Access-list 106 allows outbound connections but restricts inbound SMTP connections to those from *gateway.ajax.com*.

Putting It All Together. A more complex filter example involves more than a single service. For example, if you run DNS you need to allow DNS connectivity. DNS servers uses both TCP port 53 and UDP port 53. A DNS client (for bulk zone transfers) uses port numbers greater than 1023. NTP (the Network Time Protocol) uses UDP port 123. So an example filter for internal network 198.1.2.0, which allows only SMTP, DNS, and NTP access inbound, is as follows:

```
interface ether 1
ip address 198.1.2.254 255.255.255.0
access-group 107

access-list 107 permit tcp 0.0.0.0 255.255.255.255 198.1.2.0 0.0.0.255 gt 1023
access-list 107 permit tcp 0.0.0.0 255.255.255.255 198.1.2.0 0.0.0.255 eq 25
access-list 107 permit tcp 0.0.0.0 255.255.255.255 198.1.2.0 0.0.0.255 eq 53
access-list 107 permit udp 0.0.0.0 255.255.255.255 198.1.2.0 0.0.0.255 eq 53
access-list 107 permit udp 0.0.0.0 255.255.255.255 198.1.2.0 0.0.0.255 eq 123
```

The first access-list element takes care of the outbound connections. Line 2 takes care of inbound SMTP connections, while lines 3 and 4 handle both TCP and UDP for DNS. Line 5 deals with NTP. Generally speaking, punching an inbound hole requires adding a permit filter for the service's well-known port number.

Filter Caveats

Most servers use well-known port numbers under 1023. However, some servers use port numbers above 1023; in this case, if you allow outbound connections you must explicitly close that hole. For example, X Windows servers use a high port number (6000). If you don't want somebody on the outside to access an X Windows server, you need to filter out packets to that server's port number. The following example shows denying access to TCP port number 6000 while still allowing other inbound connections:

```
interface ether 0
ip address 199.12.1.254 255.255.255.0
access-group 107

interface ether 1
ip address 198.1.2.254 255.255.255.0
access-group 108

access-list 107 deny tcp 0.0.0.0 255.255.255.255 199.1.2.0 0.0.0.255 eq 6000
access-list 107 permit tcp 0.0.0.0 255.255.255.255 199.1.2.0 0.0.0.255 gt 1023

access-list 108 deny tcp 0.0.0.0 255.255.255.255 198.1.2.0 0.0.0.255 eq 6000
access-list 108 permit tcp 0.0.0.0 255.255.255.255 198.1.2.0 0.0.0.255 gt 1023
```

If you run X Windows among your local networks, you will need to permit packets for the X Window server port for those specific networks, as follows:

```
interface ether 0
ip address 199.12.1.254 255.255.255.0
access-group 107

interface ether 1
ip address 198.1.2.254 255.255.255.0
access-group 108

access-list 107 permit tcp 198.1.2.0 0.0.0.255 199.12.2.0 0.0.0.255 eq 6000
access-list 107 deny tcp 0.0.0.0 255.255.255.255 199.1.2.0 0.0.0.255 eq 6000
access-list 107 permit tcp 0.0.0.0 255.255.255.255 199.1.2.0 0.0.0.255 gt 1023

access-list 108 permit tcp 199.12.1.0 0.0.0.255 198.1.2.0 0.0.0.255 eq 6000
access-list 108 deny tcp 0.0.0.0 255.255.255.255 198.1.2.0 0.0.0.255 eq 6000
access-list 108 permit tcp 0.0.0.0 255.255.255.255 198.1.2.0 0.0.0.255 gt 1023
```

Packet filters can become quite complex, and it's easy to make mistakes or introduce typing errors. You should check your filters carefully before installing them. A good method to use is some type of source control methodology like the UNIX SCCS system so that you track the changes as a filter is updated. Once the filter is installed, again check the filter carefully for any potential holes or mistakes.

Firewalls can help prevent system crackers from penetrating your network, but remember, protection in depth is always better than relying on a thin, but strong, packet filter. Relying solely on a firewall to protect your systems is risky. Any firewall can be defeated with enough effort. However, if the effort required is very time consuming, the system cracker, like a house burglar, will find a more vulnerable target.

References

Carl-Mitchell & Quarterman 1992.   Carl-Mitchell, Smoot, & Quarterman, John S., "Internet Firewalls," *UNIX World* **IX**(2), pp. 93–102, McGraw-Hill, Inc. (February 1992).

Carl-Mitchell & Quarterman 1993a.   Carl-Mitchell, Smoot, & Quarterman, John S., "Datagrams: Protection per Host," *RS/Magazine* **2**(2), pp. 20-26, Computer Publishing Group, Inc. (February 1993).

Carl-Mitchell & Quarterman 1993b.   Carl-Mitchell, Smoot, & Quarterman, John S., "Local Protection for Networked Systems," *UNIX/World* **10**(7), Tech Valley Publishing (July 1993).

StJohns 1985.   StJohns, Mike, *Authentication Server (RFC931)*, January 1985.

CHAPTER 10

Setting Up Resource Discovery Services

So many indexing, categorizing, and organizational services have appeared in the past few years that we do not have space to discuss all of them in this book. Instead, in this chapter we provide the basics of setting up some of the most common services. We discuss setting up the client end of most of these services, and for a few services, we also describe how to set up the server end. The reason for this asymmetrical approach is that some clients, such as FTP, come configured with TCP/IP implementations, while some servers, such as archie, are appropriate only for organizations that wish to provide a public service for many clients. We describe the clients and servers we think you are most likely to need.

10.1 Finding People

The Internet has more ways of finding people than it needs. In this section we discuss three of the most common: *finger*, WHOIS, and *netfind*.

finger

The *finger* command, with no arguments, normally displays a list of the users that are logged in at the moment. This is its least interesting use. Given an argument, the command will list more detailed information about any user whose login name or real first or last name matches the argument (see Fig. 10.1.) The user's full name is normally kept in the */etc/passwd* file, and may be changed with the *chfn* command. Some versions of *finger* also attempt to encode various other information, such as office telephone number and address, into the name field in */etc/passwd*. Instead, we recommend creating a *.plan* or *.project* file in your home directory for more copious information about yourself. The contents of these files appear in finger output as shown in Fig. 10.1, beginning with the tags `Project:` and `Plan:`.

```
% finger jsq
Login name: jsq    In real life: John S. Quarterman
Directory: /usr/users/tic/jsq Shell: /bin/csh
On since Jul 30 12:20:21 on console
No unread mail
Project: network and open systems consulting
with particular emphasis on TCP/IP networks,
UNIX systems and standards.
Plan:
Texas Internet Consulting (TIC)
+1-512-451-6176
fax: +1-512-452-0127
1106 Clayton Lane, Suite 500W
Austin, TX 78723
U.S.A.
```

Figure 10.1 Finger.

If the argument to *finger* includes an "at" sign (@), the finger client takes the part to the right of the "at" sign to be a domain name, and attempts to connect across the Internet to the specified host, supplying the part to the left of the "at" sign as an argument to the remote finger server. So

```
finger jsq@tic.com
```

would normally produce output like that of Fig. 10.1 from any machine on the Internet that supports such a finger client. This capability is useful for people to tell what their colleagues and friends are doing. It also is the principal method the *netfind* protocol uses to find information about Internet users. But remote fingers are also a favorite of system crackers, since they provide information on who is logged in when. So don't be surprised if a remote system you attempt to finger turns out to have used *tcpd* to refuse remote fingers, as discussed in Chapter 9, *Security Issues*.

WHOIS

The general public WHOIS service run by *rs.internic.net* (see Chapter 4, *Registering Domain Names and IP Numbers*) is mostly limited to network, domain, or system administrators. If you are connecting your host or network to the Internet for full Internet access (see Chapter 3, *Types of Internet Access*), you are such an administrator and you should register. If you registered an IP network number or a domain and you provided information about yourself as an administrative or technical contact, you should already be registered. If not, use anonymous FTP to retrieve the file *templates/user-template.txt* from *rs.internic.net,* fill out a copy of

```
% telnet rs.internic.net 43
jsq
Quarterman, John S. (JSQ1)      jsq@TIC.COM
   1106 Clayton Lane, Suite 500W
   Austin, TX 78723
   (512) 451-6176

   Record last updated on 20-Nov-92.
%
```

Figure 10.2 WHOIS.

---

the file, and mail it electronically (not on paper) to *hostmaster@internic.net*.

If you do not have a local WHOIS client, you can TELNET to *rs.internic.net* instead. You can do this either on the default TELNET port number 23 or on port number 43 as in Fig. 10.2.

Many modern UNIX systems come with a WHOIS client. Unfortunately, it often is configured to connect to *nic.ddn.mil* instead of *rs.internic.net*, since the change of authority for WHOIS that happened 1 April 1993 will take some time to reach every vendor's products. Most such clients have an option for supplying a hostname. Often WHOIS will produce the same output as in the previous example as follows:

```
% whois -h rs.internic.net jsq
```

You can also make a WHOIS client out of a shell script that uses the simple client/server program described in [Carl-Mitchell & Quarterman 1993].

netfind

The quickest way to use netfind is to TELNET to one of the netfind server hosts, such as *bruno.cs.colorado.edu,* and log in as *netfind* (no password is needed). There is a netfind client, but it is dependent on SunOS lightweight processes, so you may not be able to install it if you are running another operating system. In addition, the netfind client is not very distinct from the netfind server: The server just calls the client to make it available via TELNET. (However, the netfind team is in the process of debugging a true client/server architecture for netfind.) You will also need about 10 megabytes of disk space to hold the seed database that netfind uses to deduce domain names from organization keywords. Frankly, unless you have a compelling reason for running your own netfind server, such as for internal use on your own large enterprise network, there is not much reason to install the netfind software. The easiest way to use netfind is with TELNET.

10.2 Finding Files

The possiblities for distributing, finding, and organizing files on the Internet are numerous, and include distributed file systems such as NFS (Network File System) and AFS (Andrew File System) and packages for TFA (Transparent File Access) like Alex and Prospero. We can't describe all of them here, and you would not want to run all of them at once, anyway. Instead, we describe how to set up an anonymous FTP server and archie clients. These are the two most commonly used file distribution and location methods.

Anonymous FTP Server

We describe in Chapter 4, *Registering Domain Names and IP Numbers* how to use FTP to retrieve files from another organization's anonymous FTP server; no local configuration on your machine is needed for such client use of the FTP protocol. However, you may want to run your own anonymous FTP server, and that does require local configuration, as we describe in this section.

Anonymous FTP is a very useful and popular convention. You can use it to distribute software, documents, or other information from your system to the Internet at large. You may want to do this as a service to your customers, thus permitting them to obtain distributions and updates conveniently and with minimum cost to them and you. You may also want to provide information as a way of participating in the Internet community, thus gathering good will and increasing the value of the network. Anonymous FTP is also one of the simplest Internet information distribution services to maintain, once you have set it up.

What to Watch Out For. Anonymous FTP can also produce problems. Any one of more than 10 million users of more than a million computers in more than 50 countries can access your anonymous FTP server. Never put anything in the least bit private up for anonymous FTP. You may consider distributing private information by anonymous FTP if you encrypt it, but even that use of this service is not as safe as you might think, since anyone can retrieve the information and have an arbitrary amount of time to decrypt it. For example, anonymous FTP is the *wrong* facility to use to distribute review copies of drafts of articles or book chapters, unless you want the whole world to be reading them. Your files would be more private as a sheaf of papers lying in the main concourse at Dallas-Fort Worth Airport. If you want to distribute information to someone by FTP, consider a restricted FTP facility; contact *tic@tic.com* for details.

Anonymous FTP is a favorite target of system crackers, in at least the ways that follow [CERT 1993]:

1. As a means of breaking into your system, by taking advantage of configuration errors

2. As a way of denying service to your system, by filling a file system

3. As a mechanism for distributing illicit files to other parties, by putting them on your server for someone else to pick up

You can prevent these problems, but to do so you must be aware of them, and you must carefully configure preventatives.

Levels of FTP Service

Consider these four levels of FTP server functionality [CIAC 1993]:

1. None at all

2. FTP without anonymous FTP

3. Anonymous FTP without writes

4. Anonymous FTP with writes

Let's examine each of these levels in more detail.

No FTP Service. Consider whether you need an FTP server at all. If you are using dialup IP, you may well want to disable FTP completely. You can do this on most UNIX systems by commenting out the line for FTP in *letc/inetd.conf* and then restarting *inetd*.

On many DOS systems, setting

```
ftp=no
```

in *config.tel* will disable FTP. You only need to worry about FTP on an DOS system if you have installed TCP/IP software on that system, using software such as NCSA TELNET or the Clarkson (Crynwr) package.

FTP without Anonymous FTP. You may want FTP without anonymous FTP. On most UNIX systems, this is accomplished by simply not having a user named *ftp*. In some related systems (e.g., MultiNet), you need to ensure there is no user named *anonymous*.

Many DOS TCP/IP packages accept anonymous FTP connections by default. To turn them off, you must create a file, often called *ftpusers*, with usernames and passwords for FTP users. This file is usually maintained with the *telpass* utility.

Anonymous FTP Without Writes. If you really do want anonymous FTP service to be available from your machine, be sure to set the login directory for the user *ftp* to a carefully selected directory subtree. On the Macintosh, similar protection can be accomplished with the *FTPd* facility.

Anonymous FTP With Writes. If you set up an anonymous FTP server, consider whether you have any need for anonymous users to *write* files onto your server, for example, to answer a questionnaire or to supply drafts of software or documents. Unless you really need anonymous write capability, be careful to prohibit it by making sure all anonymous FTP directories are not writable by the anonymous FTP user.

If you do need anonymous writes, permit them only in a carefully selected directory.

Anonymous FTP Server Configuration

This section is intended to help you configure a secure anonymous FTP service, but it can only provide guidelines. Your organization or site may have local policies that require modifications or extensions to what we provide here. Also these guidelines do not guarantee security. We have found them useful, and have cross-checked them against guidelines from CERT and CIAC, but neither we nor they can guarantee that any set of rules will prevent breakins. Use at your own risk.

Be sure to use the most recent version of FTP available for your system, to take advantage of any previous bug fixes. The details below are for FTP servers derived from the 4.2BSD FTP server, *ftpd*.

FTP Parameter Files. First, check some parameter files for the general FTP service. Only shells usable by your users on your system should be listed in */etc/shells*; otherwise that file should not exist at all. The file */etc/ftpusers* should contain a list of login names of users to *prohibit* from using FTP. This file should exist and should include at least the two lines:

```
root
uucp
```

Set up a user named *ftp* in */etc/passwd*, like this:

```
ftp:*:123:65533:FTP:/usr/spool/ftp:!
```

This user should have an unusable password and an unusable shell, such as those given in the example. The login directory for the *ftp* user, which is specified in the example as */usr/spool/ftp*, and which we will refer to as ~*ftp*, should be a directory hierarchy created specifically for use by anonymous FTP. No files in this directory should be used for any system functions.

Preventing Anonymous FTP Writes. The easiest way to ensure the anonymous FTP user can write no files is to have no files owned by that user, or in the login group of that user. Otherwise, you might accidentally, as *root,* change modes of a group of files and add write permission for the anonymous FTP user or group. You should make *root* own most of the basic directories under ~*ftp*, as well as make those directories unwritable so that ordinary users cannot change their protection modes or contents.

Anonymous FTP Directories. *ftpd* does a *chroot* system call to change the root directory to ~*ftp*for file system accesses, hence directory listings cannot use UNIX system commands or parameter files from the normal system directories. For directory listings to work properly, you will need directories ~*ftp/bin* and ~*ftp/etc*. The ~*ftp/bin* directory should normally contain nothing but a copy of the */bin/ls* command. If your system uses shared libraries, you may also need a ~*ftp/dev* and ~*ftp/usr/lib*; if so, see the manual page for *ftpd* on your system. Alternatively, and preferably, you can recompile an *ls* command that does not use shared libraries.

The ~*ftp/etc* directory should contain only truncated versions of the */etc/passwd* and */etc/group* files to look up login names or group names. Do *not* use copies or links to the actual */etc/passwd* or */etc/group* files, because those files contain much information of use to system crackers. A version of ~*ftp/etc/passwd* as brief as the following will work:

```
root:*:0:0:root:/:!
ftp:*:123:65534:FTP:/:!
```

Also make sure you replace the password field with * for any entries you put in ~*ftp/etc/passwd*. A version of ~*ftp/etc/group* as brief as the following will work:

```
wheel:*:0:
ftpgroup:*:65533:
```

Anonymous FTP service will work even with both of these files completely missing; directory listings will simply use numeric uids or gids instead of login names or group names. These files are not used for access control; *ftpd* sets up anonymous FTP access according to parameters it finds in the real */etc/passwd* file, not in ~*ftp/etc/passwd*.

All the files under ~*ftp* so mentioned far should be owned by root, in the system group, and not writable by anyone.

Public Anonymous FTP Files. The point of anonymous FTP is to make files publicly available, so you will want a directory ~*ftp/pub* for such files. Directories and files under ~*ftp/pub* can be owned by you or whoever else will be updating them and may be in any group, provided they are not owned by the *ftp* user or in the *ftp* user's group. You may also have local policies on who is permitted to distribute files by anonymous FTP, and you may want to further limit permissions on such files and directories accordingly.

Permitting Anonymous FTP Writes. Consider carefully before permitting anonymous FTP users to write files. That capability is potentially dangerous not only to you and your organization, but also to the Internet at large. This is due to the widespread use of writable anonymous FTP directories for distribution of contraband password files and stolen software, in addition to Trojan horses and software viruses and bombs.

To permit anonymous writes, create a directory, such as *ˉftp/incoming*, that is owned and writable by the *ftp* user. Usually, you will also want to make that directory unreadable by the anonymous FTP user and its group, so that one anonymous user cannot see what another anonymous user has left in the directory. However, you must leave execute permission on for the *ftp* user for that directory.

You can also use obscure subdirectory names to limit access to only certain people to whom you have told the names. But this method is equivalent to using unencrypted passwords. The restricted FTP facility mentioned above is preferable.

If your system has a disk quota facility, consider setting a disk quota for the anonymous FTP user. Also consider putting the anonymous FTP user on its own mounted disk partition so that excess anonymous FTP writes cannot fill up disk space needed for other purposes. Do not put the area writable by the anonymous FTP on a system disk. A malicious user could deny your system service by filling up your system disk.

Be very careful using any files written by the anonymous FTP user; inspect them only with a safe editor and do not compile or execute any uninspected source code. Do not permit any of your users to use anything from the writable anonymous FTP area before your system personnel have inspected it.

Log every anonymous FTP file written to your system. However, your FTP server may not be able to do this. For this and other reasons, you may want to install a more sophisticated FTP server, such as one of those listed in Appendix C, *Software and Other Information*. Finally, monitor your *ˉftp/incoming* directory carefully and frequently to be sure it is not producing problems.

archie

Even when you know a file is available by anonymous FTP, you still need to know which anonymous FTP server provides the file, and archie is very useful for this. You can use archie with nothing but TELNET on your end (for example, to *archie.sura.net*). However, you will find a local archie client to be more convenient, and those who run archie servers will thank you for reducing the load on their machines. Simply retrieve one of the several possible clients from the location indicated in Appendix C, *Software and Other Information* and follow the installation instructions.

10.3 Finding Documents

Perhaps the most flexible method of finding documents and other information by keyword search of the actual item on the Internet is **WAIS (Wide Area Information Servers).** WAIS is a client/server protocol for accessing textual documents. While there are other specialized retrieval systems, notably library card catalogues, they all tend to use customized interfaces. WAIS lets you use a single interface to access many databases simultaneously.

Configuring WAIS

Three versions of WAIS are generally available:

- **WAIS-8-b5,** a free version, and the oldest of the three

- **freeWAIS,** a free package from **CNIDR (Clearinghouse for Networked Information Discovery and Retrieval).**

- **WAIS,** a commercial product from WAIS, Inc.

In this section, we discuss freeWAIS, although WAIS is in some ways more capable and has a company to support it. These versions of WAIS are closely related, since freeWAIS is largely derived from WAIS-8-b5, which was written by people who later joined WAIS, Inc.

The version of freeWAIS we discuss here is freeWAIS 0.1. Although it is possible to configure and install only a WAIS client from this software, the distribution does not recognize much separation between the client and server. In addition, installing the server is not much for difficult than installing clients, so we assume here that you will do both.

For compilation configuration of this version of freeWAIS, you only need to edit the *Makefile.* You must set TOP to a pathname for the program source directory, as in:

```
TOP=/usr/src/local/freewais
```

This must be done because some sources for some reason want to refer to other sources by absolute pathname. You must comment out all lines or rules that contain

```
comment-me
```

This turns out to mean one rule immediately after the place you need to set the TOP variable.

The default *Makefile* comes with most of the useful options set. We added –DUSE_SYSLOG to make WAIS log with *syslog.*

Three clients come with this freeWAIS distribution: *waissearch,* which is a really simple command line interface, *swais,* which uses curses to handle character-cell terminals, and *Xwais,* which is an X Window System client. If you plan to use *swais,* and you want your common *wais-sources* directory to be somewhere other than the default location, you will also want to set

```
-DCOMMON_SOURCE_DIR=\\\"/usr/local/lib/wais-sources/\\\"
```

Note the three backslashes before each double quote character. Also note that this source directory is not the directory containing the sources for the WAIS programs (that one is called $TOP). This source directory is a repository for descriptions of

WAIS databases. Examples may be found in *$TOP/wais-sources*, that is, in a subdirectory of the program source directory.

To make WAIS applications to use with the X Window System, you will need to use the *makefile* provided with freeWAIS. Since X configurations vary widely, we do not say more about *Xwais* here.

Installing WAIS

Unfortunately, release 0.1 of freeWAIS does not implement the common convention for using `make install`, so you must install the programs manually. A simple way to do this is by creating a symbolic link like the following:

```
ln -s /usr/src/local/freewais/bin /usr/local/bin/wais
```

and then making sure */usr/local/bin/wais* is in everyone's PATH environment variable. If you plan to use any of the *display shell scripts, and your WAIS binaries are anywhere other than */big/wais/bin*, you will need to edit each of those scripts.

You also will need to copy or link *waisserver* to a directory for server daemons, such as */usr/local/etc.* Put a line in your */etc/services* file like the following:

```
z3950 210/tcp # wide area information server (WAIS)
```

If you are running NIS, remember to rebuild the NIS database files with something like the following:

```
cd /var/yp; make
```

You can either run *waisserver* as a standalone daemon or out of */etc/inetd.conf.* To run the WAIS server as a standalone daemon, call it with arguments similar to the following:

```
waisserver -p 210 -d /usr/spool/ftp/matrix/news \
    -e /var/log/wais
```

An invocation line like this needs to go in */etc/rc.local* if you want WAIS to be served after system reboot. To run the WAIS server from *inetd*, you will need a line in *inetd.conf* as follows:

```
z3950 stream tcp nowait root /etc/waisserver waisserver.d \
    -d /usr/local/lib/wais-sources -e /var/log/wais
```

Note that the zeroth argument to the server must be *waisserver.d*, not *waisserver*, since the program looks at the name it is called to decide whether it should act as if called by *inetd*. Remember to send a SIGHUP to *inetd* so it will know to look again at */etc/inetd.conf.*

The −*d* option tells the server which directory to search for **.src* files. The −*e* option tells the server where to log errors.

You will also need to copy *doc/original-TM-wais/man1/*.1* to be either */usr/local/man/man1/*.1* or some other directory for local manual pages.

Building a WAIS Database

An example of a WAIS database as seen from *swais* is shown in Fig. 10.3. To create a WAIS database, apply to *waisindex* a description of the database and the files to index. Put the result in the directory your WAIS server expects to find databases, such as */usr/local/lib/wais-sources*.

Figure 10.3 Using swais.

```
SWAIS                                    Source Selection              Sources: 435
 #            Server                                    Source              Cost
262:     [        zenon.inria.fr]   lp-bibtex-zenon-inria-fr             Free
263:     [        wais.fct.unl.pt]   lp-proceedings                       Free
264:     [             cs.uwp.edu]   lyrics                               Free
265:     [      next2.oit.unc.edu]   mac.FAQ                              Free
266:     [ cmns-moon.think.com]      macintosh-news                       Free
267:     [ cmns-moon.think.com]      macintosh-tidbits                    Free
268:     [     gopher.stolaf.edu]    MacPsych                             Free
269:     [          wais.cic.net]    mailing-lists                        Free
270:***[*********ftp.tic.com]**matrix_news*********************Free
271:     [          nic.merit.edu]   merit-archive-mac                    Free
272:     [          nic.merit.edu]   merit-nsfnet-linkletter              Free
273:     [        zenon.inria.fr]    meval-bibtex-zenon-inria-fr          Free
274:     [          nic.merit.edu]   michnet-news                         Free
275:     [        sol.acs.unt.edu]   midi                                 Free
276:     [          wais.cic.net]    midwest-weather                      Free
277:     [        munin.ub2.lu.se]   miljodatabas                         Free
278:     [   theory.lcs.mit.edu]     MIT-algorithms-bug                   Free
279:     [   theory.lcs.mit.edu]     MIT-algorithms-exercise              Free
280:     [   theory.lcs.mit.edu]     MIT-algorithms-suggest               Free
281:     [ cmns-moon.think.com]      Molecular-biology                    Free
282:     [daneel.rdt.monash.ed]      monashuni-phonedir                   Free
283:     [gourd.srv.cs.cmu.edu]      movie-lists                          Free
284:     [             cs.uwp.edu]   music-surveys                        Free
285:     [     gopher.stolaf.edu]    MuTeX                                Free
286:     [ndadsb.gsfc.nasa.gov]      NASA-directory-of-servers            Free
287:     [techreports.larc.nas]      nasa-larc-abs                        Free
288:     [         ncgia.ucsb.edu]   NCGIA-Technical-Reports              Free
289:     [stone.ucs.indiana.ed]      netbib                               Free
290:     [wais.unidata.ucar.ed]      netcdf-group                         Free

Keywords:

<space> selects, w for keywords, arrows move, <return> searches, q quits, o ?
```

```
(:source
   :version  3
   :ip-address "192.135.128.129"
   :ip-name "ftp.tic.com"
   :tcp-port 210
   :database-name "matrix_news"
   :cost 0.00
   :cost-unit :free
   :maintainer "jsq@ftp.tic.com"
   :keyword-list ( matrix matrixinformatio matrixnews mids tic vol)
   :description "Server created with freeWAIS Release 0.1 beta
 on Jul 30 17:14:25 1993 by jsq@ftp.tic.com
 "
 )
```

Figure 10.4 A WAIS Database Description (matrix_news.src).

The following are some typical examples of using *waisindex*:

```
db=matrix_news
waisindex -d $db -export -t one_line -a key
waisindex -d $db -export -t text -a 0* Matrix_News v[1-9]/*
```

The *-t* option specifies the type of document. The first example indexes the file named *key* line by line, that is, it takes each line in the file as a separate entity to index and retrieve. The second example indexes various files, including some in subdirectories, as text documents, meaning the whole document is indexed and retrieved as a single item. The *-d* option takes the name of the database, which is then used as a prefix in generating files like the following: **.src, *.dct, *.cat, *.inv, *.doc, *.fn,* and **.hl*. The *-a* option means to append new index entries to an existing index. The program will actually update duplicate entries, but will not remove old entries that are not among the new additions.

The *waisindex* program will create a *$db.src* file if there isn't one already. This file contains a description of the database, similar to the one illustrated in Fig. 10.4. The *waisindex* program will update many of the fields for you, including, annoyingly, the *ip-name* field (really a DNS name field), which the program made to be *akasha.tic.com* in Fig. 10.4.

We edited the example database description manually to change the domain name to *ftp.tic.com* everywhere. You also would want to add address and other contact information to the *description* field; be sure to put all new text inside the quotation marks.

To make your database known to the Internet at large, you must register it by mailing its **.src* file to *directory-of-servers@quake.think.com*.

10.4 Front Ends

In the past few years, widely deployed Internet applications have expanded from variations on the old Big Three of TELNET, FTP, and mail (plus mailing lists and news) to include all the applications mentioned so far in this book, in addition to some others. Keeping track of which service to use to find which piece of information is a problem. To help alleviate this situation, further applications have been developed to tie previous applications together. The two most common of these front end applications are Gopher and WWW (World Wide Web). We describe how to set up Gopher clients and servers, and how to set up the NCSA Mosaic WWW client.

Gopher Distributions

At least three implementations of Gopher exist, as follows:

- **Gopher** (also known as **base Gopher**) is the original Gopher protocol, in its latest version.

- **Gopher+** is a set of extensions to the base Gopher protocol, specified and implemented by the same people who wrote Gopher.

- The **gn** Gopher server is a reimplementation of Gopher by a different group.

In addition, there are more implementations of Gopher clients for various software and hardware platforms.

The most widespread server implementations are Gopher and Gopher+. The following is a partial list of things Gopher+ can do that Gopher can not:

- Attach attributes to Gopher objects, including size, date, author, and abstract

- Request and collect information from the user

- Provide alternate views of a Gopher object, for example plain text alternating with PostScript, or English alternating with French

- Provide better security

By design, base Gopher clients can interact with Gopher+ servers but only Gopher+ clients can use extended Gopher+ features [Riddle 1993]. Because Gopher is still much more widespread than Gopher+, we describe Gopher, not Gopher+, in the rest of this chapter. We describe Gopher v1.12S, but later subversions of Gopher v1 should provide similar features by similar methods.

```
          Internet Gopher Information Client v1.12S

             Root gopher server: gopher.tic.com

-->   1.  About the TIC gopher server.
      2.  About TIC and MIDS.
      3.  Texas Internet Consulting (TIC)/
      4.  Matrix Information and Directory Services (MIDS)/
      5.  Online Bookstore (OBS)/
      6.  General public files/
      7.  Bruce Sterling's agitprop/
      8.  EFF-Austin, a non-profit Texas educational corporation/
      9.  Electronic Frontiers Houston, nonprofit Texas corporation/
     10.  List of directories and files from this server (long).
     11.  All the gophers in Texas, and the rest of the world, too/

Press ? for Help, q to Quit, u to go up a menu          Page: 1/1
```

Figure 10.5 Using gopher (gopher gopher.tic.com).

Gopher Client

The Gopher distribution is partitioned into client and server directories, so you can install one without the other. Installing a Gopher server is appreciably more work than installing a Gopher client, so we assume here that you might want to install just a client. In either case, the *doc/INSTALL* documentation is easy to follow and mostly complete. An example of the default Gopher client is shown in Fig. 10.5.

Gopher configuration is done in two files: *Makefile.config* and *conf.h*. You must specify several directories, including:

- where the client executable program should be installed, for example, */usr/local/bin*

- where the Gopher help file should be installed, for example, */usr/local/lib*

- where to put the manual pages, for example */usr/local/man*.

In addition, you need to give a default hostname and port number for initial Gopher connections. If you are installing your own Gopher server, make these parameters point at your server. To make a client, type

```
make client
```

Gopher Server

To install a Gopher server, you must also set the following variables in addition to the configuration information needed for a Gopher client:

- SERVERDIR

  The directory for the executable Gopher server, for example, */usr/local/etc*

- SERVERDATA

  The default server directory, for example, */usr/spool/ftp*

- SERVERPORT

  The default server port, for example, 70

To make a server, type

```
make server
```

The Gopher server daemon can be run either standalone or by *inetd*. In either case, you will need the following line in */etc/services*:

```
gopher 70/tcp gopher
```

If you are using NIS, don't forget to tell it about this change.

A standalone invocation of the Gopher server might include a line like the following in */etc/rc.local*:

```
/usr/local/etc/gopherd -u gopherd -l /usr/log/gopherd.log
```

This example uses several important options; those, and one more option are described as follows:

- *−u*

  Tells the server to run as the specified user. By default, the server will do a *chroot* system call to the directory compiled in as SERVERDATA, or passed as the first nonoption argument. The server must start as *root* for the *chroot* system call to succeed. However, the server should not run as *root* while it is actually retrieving data.

- *−l*

  Tells the server to log into the specified file.

An *inetd* invocation might involve a line in */etc/inetd.conf* like this:

```
gopher stream tcp nowait root /usr/local/etc/gopherd gopherd \
    -I -u gopherd
```

The *−I* option tells the Gopher server it is running from *inetd*. Don't forget to send SIGHUP to inetd.

Setting Up a Gopher Tree

The interesting part of Gopher configuration is not in arranging to compile the source files; rather it is in setting up the various parameter files that determine types, names, and orders of objects served. The simplest types of objects are directories and text files. All you need to set up a rudimentary Gopher tree for your Gopher server is to make ordinary UNIX directories and filenames. Gopher will ignore any filename beginning with a dot, as well as the specific file or directory names *etc*, *usr*, *bin*, *dev*, and *core*. All other directories and filenames will be made visible to Gopher clients.

A major advantage of Gopher is that its clients normally list items one per line, with a long name for each item. By default, the name for an item is simply its filename. To make an item have a long name, you must put an entry for it in a subdirectory called *.cap* (note the leading dot). This capability file has the same name as the file it describes. For example, *0README* might have a capability file *.cap/0README*, with contents like the following:

```
Name=About these sample articles from Matrix News
Numb=4
```

Each capability is indicated by a keyword and an equals sign, followed by a value. In this example, the capability file gives *0README* a long name and a number. The number establishes a position in the menu listing. By default, the server presents items in a directory in alphabetical order, ignoring differences between uppercase and lowercase letters.

Various special cases are recognized automatically, such as files ending in *.Z* (these are assumed to be text files) and mailbox files (the server represents a mailbox as a directory and each message as a file).

Figure 10.6 Linking Gopher to TELNET-based Servers.

```
Name=WAIS demo by TELNET: log in as user wais
Type=8
Port=23
Path=wais
Host=quake.think.com
#
Name=netfind
Type=8
Port=23
Path=netfind
Host=bruno.cs.colorado.edu
```

More sophisticated types of objects are normally described in *.Links* files (actually, any plain text file with a name starting with dot will do). Figure 10.6 shows two examples of Type 8, for TELNET. The first example will connect to a WAIS demo, the other example to a *netfind* server. Other types include binary files, sound, GIF files, and WAIS databases.

For WAIS databases to work with Gopher, you must configure your Gopher server sources to use some WAIS source code. Depending on the version of the Gopher sources you have, you may need to use WAIS-8-b5* sources.

Gopher and Anonymous FTP

In the earlier discussion about configuring a Gopher server, we suggested setting SERVERDATA to */usr/spool/ftp*. Doing this makes the Gopher tree the same as the anonymous FTP tree. This double use of one filesystem subtree reduces disk space usage and avoids synchronization problems between divergent databases. Only a small amount of extra configuration is needed. We recommend running the Gopher server as a user other than the anonymous FTP user (we used the username *gopherd* in the Gopher configuration and installation examples).

To avoid naming and sorting each item every time the directory is accessed by a client, Gopher normally stores this information in a file called *.cache* in each directory. Since the Gopher server user should not be able to write into the anonymous FTP directory, you will want to set up all the *.cache* files beforehand. This can be done easily by having a script run daily by *cron* to set up ownership and modes on the cache files.

You also need to limit who can access your Gopher tree. Be careful about creating writable files or directories because the anonymous FTP user can write into those even though Gopher clients cannot. Other than these considerations, the main problem with a combined anonymous FTP and Gopher directory subtree is forgetting to add long Gopher names when putting up files for anonymous FTP.

NCSA Mosaic

You can use **WWW (World Wide Web)** as a front end to Gopher. The reverse is not true, since WWW handles bitmapped hypertext in a way that Gopher cannot. Installing a WWW server is probably not something you want to tackle immediately. On DOS and Macintosh systems, the usual WWW clients are called WWW.

One WWW UNIX client is relatively easy to install. This is **NCSA Mosaic.** from the **National Center for Supercomputing Applications (NCSA)**. This client program understands not only the WWW protocol, but also the Gopher, FTP, WAIS, NNTP, and some other protocols, and can speak directly to corresponding servers.

10.5 Checking It Out

For any server you have set up, the first step is always to try to connect to it your-self using your own client software from your own host. Then try getting a remote colleague to connect and report the results.

For any client you have set up, first try connecting to your own server (if you have one). Then try connecting to a remote server.

In this section, we provide some pointers to remote servers that can be used for checking out your software. Because available servers tend to change, most of the servers we suggest are ones we run ourselves.

Finding People

finger. The simplest test is to finger your own account. This demonstrates that your finger client and server both work, and gives you a chance to examine your own finger information. Next, ask a distant colleague to finger your account and try to finger that colleague's account. Finally, try:

```
finger @aw.com
```

WHOIS. Use WHOIS to check your own domain registration information. For example, if your domain is *bigco.com*, do the following:

```
whois -h rs.internic.net bigco.com
```

In the domain information you get back, you will find listed your domain's techni-cal and administrative contacts, along with their registration handles. Use WHOIS and their handles to check their personal registration information, as well.

netfind. TELNET to one of the *netfind* servers and look for yourself.

Finding Files

Anonymous FTP. FTP to *ftp.tic.com*, log in as *anonymous*, and try the anony-mous FTP convention there. Try changing into the *matrix/news* directory and see what you find there. Look at the **OBS (Online BookStore)** subdirectory for infor-mation on a use of restricted FTP.

archie. TELNET to one of the archie servers and search for the archie client software. Once you have retrieved and installed an archie client, use it to search again for the same software.

Finding Documents

WAIS. Look at the WAIS source *matrix_news* (it's on *ftp.tic.com*, port 210) and see how this access method compares to the same information you saw previously using anonymous FTP.

Front Ends

Gopher. Try Gopher to *gopher.tic.com* and look under MIDS, then under *Matrix News*. Compare this Gopher access method to the WAIS and anonymous FTP methods mentioned immediately above.

NCSA Mosaic. Use this front end to connect to each of the Gopher, WAIS, and anonymous FTP servers already mentioned immediately above, and compare the presentation techniques.

References

Carl-Mitchell & Quarterman 1993.   Carl-Mitchell, Smoot, & Quarterman, John S., *Practical Internetworking with TCP/IP and UNIX,* Addison-Wesley, Reading, MA (1993). ISBN 0-201-58629-0.

CERT 1993.   CERT, "Anonymous FTP Activity," *CERT Advisory* (CA-93:10), Computer Emergency Response Team (July 14, 1993).

CIAC 1993.   CIAC, "Wide-spread Attacks on Anonymous FTP Servers," *CIAC Information Bulletin*(D-19), The Computer Incident Advisory Capability (July 15, 1993).

Riddle 1993.   Riddle, Prentiss, "GopherCon '93:," *Matrix News* **3**(6), p. 1, MIDS (June 1993).

Internet Providers

In this appendix, we present lists of Internet connectivity providers worldwide, plus contact information for some related organizations. Most, but not all, of the providers listed here are commercial. All, so far as we know, provide Internet access, perhaps with restrictions, to the public.

A.1 Internet Connectivity Providers

In this section we list each provider of interactive TCP/IP connectivity three ways:

• By country and other geographical regions served.

• By telephone country code and area code.

• By name, in alphabetical order.

In each section, we note for each provider:

Name   The brief common name of the system.

Login Host   Whether the system lets users dial up, log in, and use the system to access Internet services.

Dialup IP   Whether the system lets the user dial up and establish an IP connection to the user's computer or network.

Direct IP   Whether the system lets the user establish a dedicated IP connection to the user's computer or network.

CIX   Whether the provider is a member of the **CIX (Commercial Internet Exchange).**

The first two sections contain only the information so far described, and are indexes into the third section, which contains more detailed information about each provider. We discussed the first three categories in detail in Chapter 3, *Types of Internet Access*, and CIX in Chapter 3 and in Chapter 2, *The Internet and Other Networks*. For an online list of providers, use anonymous FTP or Gopher to *ftp.tic.com*.

Several providers serve more than one geographical region, and we list such a provider in each region served (where known). If your specific city or area code is not listed, that does not necessarily mean there is no service available. You can almost certainly reach a **point of presence (PoP)** for some provider, even though you may need to make a long distance telephone call or put in a remote leased line to do it. Also, being in the same city or area code does not necessarily determine whether you will need to pay long distance rates, or what those rates might be. For example, interstate night dialup rates may be lower than intrastate daytime rates. In addition, some providers accept connections through WATS lines, X.25 PDNs, or other means that may have lesser or greater charges. Inquire directly of any potential provider as to telephone rates and other access details.

Providers by Geography

In this section we list providers by country, by state or province, and by city. Many providers serve more than one geographical region; we list each such provider under each region they serve (where known). Some providers are hard to represent accurately. In particular, EUnet provides services via 27 separate national networks throughout Europe and North Africa. The information included about EUnet is therefore representative for the typical EUnet service provider; some services may not be available in all countries. Several of its related national providers are also listed. A few major regional providers chose not to be listed, for example because of not providing service to the general public, and we may not know of some others. However, here is an extensive geographical listing of most of the IP connectivity providers in the world.

For login hosts, a list of specific basic services is shown, such as

FTP in, FTP out, mail in, mail out.

In such lists, "in" refers to towards the login host, and "out" means towards the Internet. So "mail in" means "mail from the Internet to the system" and "mail out" means "mail from the system to the Internet."

Place	System Name	Login Host	Dialup IP	Direct IP	CIX
Argentina	CCC			Dir. IP	
	Proyecto Wamani	Host			
	RECyT			Dir. IP	
	UNdIP			Dir. IP	

Place	System Name	Login Host	Dialup IP	Direct IP	CIX
Australia					
Australian Capital Territory					
Canberra	AARnet			Dir. IP	
New South Wales					
Sydney	AARnet			Dir. IP	
	Pactok	Host		Dir. IP	
Northern Territory					
Darwin	AARnet			Dir. IP	
Queensland					
Brisbane	AARnet			Dir. IP	
	Pegasus Networks	Host			
South Australia					
Adelaide	AARnet			Dir. IP	
Tasmania					
Hobart	AARnet			Dir. IP	
Victoria					
	connect.com.au	Host	Dial IP		
Melbourne	AARnet			Dir. IP	
Western Australia					
Perth	AARnet			Dir. IP	
Austria	EBONE			Dir. IP	
Bolivia	BOLNET			Dir. IP	
Brazil	Fapesp/CNPq			Dir. IP	
Canada					
Alberta					
Kananaskis	BCnet			Dir. IP	
British Columbia					
Victoria	Victoria FreeNet	Host			
Manitoba					
Winnipeg	MBnet	Host	Dial IP	Dir. IP	
New Brunswick					
Fredericton	NB*net			Dir. IP	
Nova Scotia					
Bedford	NSTN			Dir. IP	
	PEInet		Dial IP	Dir. IP	
Ontario					
Ottawa	National Capital FreeNet	Host			
	ONet			Dir. IP	
Toronto	ONet			Dir. IP	

Place	System Name	Login Host	Dialup IP	Direct IP	CIX
Quebec					
Brossard	cam.org	Host	Dial IP		
Montreal	RISQ		Dial IP	Dir. IP	
	SASK#net	Host		Dir. IP	
Chile	PUC			Dir. IP	
	REUNA		Dial IP	Dir. IP	
	UDC			Dir. IP	
	UTFSM			Dir. IP	
Costa Rica	CRnet			Dir. IP	
	Proyecto HURACAN	Host		Dir. IP	
Croatia	CARNet			Dir. IP	
Cuba	CENIAI	Host		Dir. IP	
Denmark	DENet			Dir. IP	
	DKnet	Host	Dial IP	Dir. IP	
Dominican Republi	REDID			Dir. IP	
Ecuador	ECUANET	Host	Dial IP	Dir. IP	
	Intercon			Dir. IP	
Finland	CSC	Host	Dial IP		
	DataNet			Dir. IP	
France	EBONE			Dir. IP	
	PIPEX		Dial IP	Dir. IP	CIX
Germany	EUnet Deutschland			Dir. IP	
	netmbx	Host	Dial IP	Dir. IP	
	uropax.contrib.de	Host	Dial IP		
Greece	FORTHnet		Dial IP	Dir. IP	
Hong Kong	Hong Kong Supernet	Host	Dial IP	Dir. IP	CIX
Ireland	IEunet		Dial IP	Dir. IP	
Israel	Actcom			Dir. IP	
	Dataserve	Host	Dial IP	Dir. IP	
	Goldnet	Host	Dial IP	Dir. IP	
	Kav Manche			Dir. IP	
Japan	IIJ			Dir. IP	
	InterAccess	Host		Dir. IP	CIX
	SPIN		Dial IP	Dir. IP	
	TWICS	Host	Dial IP		
Mexico	CONACYT			Dir. IP	
	MEXnet			Dir. IP	
Netherlands	EUnet	Host	Dial IP	Dir. IP	
	NLnet	Host	Dial IP	Dir. IP	

Place	System Name	Login Host	Dialup IP	Direct IP	CIX
	SURFnet			Dir. IP	
New Zealand	Actrix	Host			
	Wellington Citynet	Host		Dir. IP	
Peru	Red Cientifica Peruana	Host	Dial IP	Dir. IP	
Puerto Rico	CRACIN			Dir. IP	
Spain	Goya-EUnet Spain		Dial IP	Dir. IP	
Sweden	EBONE			Dir. IP	
	SWIPnet	Host	Dial IP	Dir. IP	
Switzerland	EUnet Switzerland	Host	Dial IP	Dir. IP	
	SWITCH	Host	Dial IP	Dir. IP	
United Kingdom	Demon Internet	Host	Dial IP	Dir. IP	CIX
	EUnet GB	Host	Dial IP	Dir. IP	
	PIPEX		Dial IP	Dir. IP	CIX
	UK PC User's Group	Host			
United States					
Arizona					
Phoenix	PSINet	Host	Dial IP	Dir. IP	CIX
Tempe	Westnet			Dir. IP	
Tucson	Westnet			Dir. IP	
California					
Alameda	Netcom	Host	Dial IP	Dir. IP	
Alpine	Netcom	Host	Dial IP	Dir. IP	
Anaheim	Netcom	Host	Dial IP	Dir. IP	
Bakersfield	CSUnet		Dial IP	Dir. IP	
Ben Lomond	Netcom	Host	Dial IP	Dir. IP	
Berkeley	AlterNet		Dial IP	Dir. IP	CIX
	BARRnet		Dial IP	Dir. IP	CIX
	HoloNet	Host	Dial IP		
Carson	Netcom	Host	Dial IP	Dir. IP	
Chico	CSUnet		Dial IP	Dir. IP	
Cupertino	BARRnet		Dial IP	Dir. IP	CIX
	The Portal System	Host	Dial IP		
Daly City	Netcom	Host	Dial IP	Dir. IP	
El Cajon	crash.cts.com	Host	Dial IP	Dir. IP	
Encinitas	The Cyberspace Station	Host	Dial IP		
Fresno	CSUnet		Dial IP	Dir. IP	
Fullerton	CSUnet		Dial IP	Dir. IP	
Hayward	CSUnet		Dial IP	Dir. IP	
Humboldt	CSUnet		Dial IP	Dir. IP	
Irvine	CERFnet	Host	Dial IP	Dir. IP	CIX

Place	System Name	Login Host	Dialup IP	Direct IP	CIX
Larkspur	CR Labs Dialup Internet A	Host	Dial IP	Dir. IP	
Los Angeles	AlterNet		Dial IP	Dir. IP	CIX
	ANS CO+RE Services		Dial IP	Dir. IP	
	CERFnet	Host	Dial IP	Dir. IP	CIX
	CSUnet		Dial IP	Dir. IP	
	PSINet	Host	Dial IP	Dir. IP	CIX
Marina del Rey	Los Nettos			Dir. IP	
Menlo Park	BARRnet		Dial IP	Dir. IP	CIX
Moffett Field	BARRnet		Dial IP	Dir. IP	CIX
Monterey	CSUnet		Dial IP	Dir. IP	
Monterrey	BARRnet		Dial IP	Dir. IP	CIX
Orange County	Express Access	Host	Dial IP	Dir. IP	
Palo Alto	AlterNet		Dial IP	Dir. IP	CIX
	ANS CO+RE Services		Dial IP	Dir. IP	
	BARRnet		Dial IP	Dir. IP	CIX
Pasadena	CERFnet	Host	Dial IP	Dir. IP	CIX
Pleasanton	Netcom	Host	Dial IP	Dir. IP	
Riverside	CERFnet	Host	Dial IP	Dir. IP	CIX
Sacramento	BARRnet		Dial IP	Dir. IP	CIX
	CSUnet		Dial IP	Dir. IP	
	Netcom	Host	Dial IP	Dir. IP	
San Diego	AlterNet		Dial IP	Dir. IP	CIX
	ANS CO+RE Services		Dial IP	Dir. IP	
	CERFnet	Host	Dial IP	Dir. IP	CIX
	CSUnet		Dial IP	Dir. IP	
	SDSCnet			Dir. IP	
San Francisco	ANS CO+RE Services		Dial IP	Dir. IP	
	BARRnet		Dial IP	Dir. IP	CIX
	CSUnet		Dial IP	Dir. IP	
	PSINet	Host	Dial IP	Dir. IP	CIX
San Jose	a2i communications	Host	Dial IP		
	AlterNet		Dial IP	Dir. IP	CIX
	CERFnet	Host	Dial IP	Dir. IP	CIX
	class	Host			
	CSUnet		Dial IP	Dir. IP	
San Luis Obispo	CSUnet		Dial IP	Dir. IP	
Santa Clara	Quack	Host			
Santa Cruz	BARRnet		Dial IP	Dir. IP	CIX
Sausalito	The WELL	Host			
Sonoma	CSUnet		Dial IP	Dir. IP	
Stanislaus	CSUnet		Dial IP	Dir. IP	
Stockton	BARRnet		Dial IP	Dir. IP	CIX

Place	System Name	Login Host	Dialup IP	Direct IP	CIX
Sunnyvale	PSINet	Host	Dial IP	Dir. IP	CIX
Colorado					
Boulder	ANS CO+RE Services		Dial IP	Dir. IP	
	Colorado SuperNet	Host	Dial IP	Dir. IP	
	Westnet			Dir. IP	
Colorado City	Colorado SuperNet	Host	Dial IP	Dir. IP	
Colorado Springs	Colorado SuperNet	Host	Dial IP	Dir. IP	
	Community News Service	Host	Dial IP		
	oldcolo	Host	Dial IP		
	Westnet			Dir. IP	
Denver	ANS CO+RE Services		Dial IP	Dir. IP	
	Colorado SuperNet	Host	Dial IP	Dir. IP	
	Denver Free-Net	Host			
	Nyx	Host			
	PSINet	Host	Dial IP	Dir. IP	CIX
	Westnet			Dir. IP	
Connecticut					
Bridgeport	JvNCNet	Host	Dial IP	Dir. IP	CIX
Hartford	ANS CO+RE Services		Dial IP	Dir. IP	
	PSINet	Host	Dial IP	Dir. IP	CIX
New Haven	JvNCNet	Host	Dial IP	Dir. IP	CIX
	PSINet	Host	Dial IP	Dir. IP	CIX
Stamford	PSINet	Host	Dial IP	Dir. IP	CIX
Storrs	JvNCNet	Host	Dial IP	Dir. IP	CIX
District of Columbia					
Washington	ANS CO+RE Services		Dial IP	Dir. IP	
	Express Access	Host	Dial IP	Dir. IP	
	SURAnet		Dial IP	Dir. IP	
Florida					
Jacksonville	PSINet	Host	Dial IP	Dir. IP	CIX
Miami	PSINet	Host	Dial IP	Dir. IP	CIX
Orlando	PSINet	Host	Dial IP	Dir. IP	CIX
Tallahassee	Tallahassee Free-Net	Host			
Tampa	PSINet	Host	Dial IP	Dir. IP	CIX
Georgia					
Acworth	Netcom	Host	Dial IP	Dir. IP	
Atlanta	AlterNet		Dial IP	Dir. IP	CIX
	ANS CO+RE Services		Dial IP	Dir. IP	
	PSINet	Host	Dial IP	Dir. IP	CIX
Hawaii					
Honolulu	PACCOM			Dir. IP	

Place	System Name	Login Host	Dialup IP	Direct IP	CIX
Idaho					
Boise	PSINet	Host	Dial IP	Dir. IP	CIX
	Westnet			Dir. IP	
Pocatello	Westnet			Dir. IP	
Illinois					
Chicago	AlterNet		Dial IP	Dir. IP	CIX
	ANS CO+RE Services		Dial IP	Dir. IP	
	CICnet			Dir. IP	
	MCSNet	Host	Dial IP		
	PSINet	Host	Dial IP	Dir. IP	CIX
Evanston	netILLINOIS			Dir. IP	
Peoria	Heartland Free-Net	Host			
Urbana-Champaign	ANS CO+RE Services		Dial IP	Dir. IP	
	CICnet			Dir. IP	
Indiana					
Indianapolis	CICnet			Dir. IP	
South Bend	CICnet			Dir. IP	
West Lafayette	ANS CO+RE Services		Dial IP	Dir. IP	
Iowa					
Iowa City	CICnet			Dir. IP	
Kentucky					
Louisville	OARnet	Host	Dial IP	Dir. IP	
Maine					
Portland	PSINet	Host	Dial IP	Dir. IP	CIX
Maryland					
Baltimore	Express Access	Host	Dial IP	Dir. IP	
	PSINet	Host	Dial IP	Dir. IP	CIX
College Park	ANS CO+RE Services		Dial IP	Dir. IP	
Massachusetts					
Boston	AlterNet		Dial IP	Dir. IP	CIX
	Netcom	Host	Dial IP	Dir. IP	
	The WORLD	Host			
Cambridge	ANS CO+RE Services		Dial IP	Dir. IP	
	DELPHI	Host			
	NEARnet		Dial IP	Dir. IP	CIX
Hanover	The WORLD	Host			
Hudson	DMConnection	Host	Dial IP		
Lowell	The WORLD	Host			
Westboro	The WORLD	Host			
Westford	PSINet	Host	Dial IP	Dir. IP	CIX
Michigan					

Place	**System Name**	**Login Host**	**Dialup IP**	**Direct IP**	**CIX**
Ann Arbor	ANS CO+RE Services		Dial IP	Dir. IP	
	CICnet			Dir. IP	
	MichNet	Host	Dial IP	Dir. IP	
	Msen	Host	Dial IP	Dir. IP	
	PSINet	Host	Dial IP	Dir. IP	CIX
Detroit	PSINet	Host	Dial IP	Dir. IP	CIX
Lansing	CICnet			Dir. IP	
Minnesota					
Duluth	MRnet		Dial IP	Dir. IP	
Mankato	MRnet		Dial IP	Dir. IP	
Minneapolis	CICnet			Dir. IP	
	MRnet		Dial IP	Dir. IP	
Moorhead	MRnet		Dial IP	Dir. IP	
Rochester	MRnet		Dial IP	Dir. IP	
St. Cloud	MRnet		Dial IP	Dir. IP	
Missouri					
Columbia	Columbia Online Informati	Host			
St. Louis	ANS CO+RE Services		Dial IP	Dir. IP	
Montana					
Dillon	Big Sky Telegraph	Host			
Nebraska					
Lincoln	ANS CO+RE Services		Dial IP	Dir. IP	
	MIDnet		Dial IP	Dir. IP	
Nevada					
Las Vegas	NevadaNet			Dir. IP	
Reno	NevadaNet			Dir. IP	
New Hampshire					
Manchester	mv.com	Host	Dial IP		
	PSINet	Host	Dial IP	Dir. IP	CIX
New Jersey					
New Brunswick	AlterNet		Dial IP	Dir. IP	CIX
	Express Access	Host	Dial IP	Dir. IP	
Newark	JvNCNet	Host	Dial IP	Dir. IP	CIX
Princeton	ANS CO+RE Services		Dial IP	Dir. IP	
	JvNCNet	Host	Dial IP	Dir. IP	CIX
	PSINet	Host	Dial IP	Dir. IP	CIX
New Mexico					
Albuquerque	Westnet			Dir. IP	
Las Cruces	Westnet			Dir. IP	
New York					
Albany	PSINet	Host	Dial IP	Dir. IP	CIX

Place	System Name	Login Host	Dialup IP	Direct IP	CIX
Binghamton	PSINet	Host	Dial IP	Dir. IP	CIX
Buffalo	Buffalo Free-Net	Host			
	PSINet	Host	Dial IP	Dir. IP	CIX
Corning	PSINet	Host	Dial IP	Dir. IP	CIX
Garden City	PSINet	Host	Dial IP	Dir. IP	CIX
Islip	PSINet	Host	Dial IP	Dir. IP	CIX
Ithaca	ANS CO+RE Services		Dial IP	Dir. IP	
	PSINet	Host	Dial IP	Dir. IP	CIX
Liverpool	NYSERnet		Dial IP	Dir. IP	
Long Island	JvNCNet	Host	Dial IP	Dir. IP	CIX
New York	AlterNet		Dial IP	Dir. IP	CIX
	ANS CO+RE Services		Dial IP	Dir. IP	
	JvNCNet	Host	Dial IP	Dir. IP	CIX
	MindVOX	Host			
	PANIX	Host			
	PSINet	Host	Dial IP	Dir. IP	CIX
Potsdam	PSINet	Host	Dial IP	Dir. IP	CIX
Poughkeepsie	PSINet	Host	Dial IP	Dir. IP	CIX
Rochester	PSINet	Host	Dial IP	Dir. IP	CIX
Syracuse	PSINet	Host	Dial IP	Dir. IP	CIX
Utica	PSINet	Host	Dial IP	Dir. IP	CIX
White Plains	PSINet	Host	Dial IP	Dir. IP	CIX
North Carolina					
Asheville	CONCERT-CONNECT	Host	Dial IP	Dir. IP	
Chapel Hill	CONCERT-CONNECT	Host	Dial IP	Dir. IP	
Charlotte	CONCERT-CONNECT	Host	Dial IP	Dir. IP	
Durham	CONCERT-CONNECT	Host	Dial IP	Dir. IP	
Greensboro	ANS CO+RE Services		Dial IP	Dir. IP	
	CONCERT-CONNECT	Host	Dial IP	Dir. IP	
Greenville	CONCERT-CONNECT	Host	Dial IP	Dir. IP	
Raleigh	CONCERT-CONNECT	Host	Dial IP	Dir. IP	
Wilmington	CONCERT-CONNECT	Host	Dial IP	Dir. IP	
Winston-Salem	CONCERT-CONNECT	Host	Dial IP	Dir. IP	
Ohio					
Akron	Netcom	Host	Dial IP	Dir. IP	
	OARnet	Host	Dial IP	Dir. IP	
Avon Lake	Lorain County Free-Net	Host			
Cincinnati	OARnet	Host	Dial IP	Dir. IP	
	Tristate Online	Host			
Cleveland	ANS CO+RE Services		Dial IP	Dir. IP	
	Cleveland Free-Net	Host			
	OARnet	Host	Dial IP	Dir. IP	

Place	System Name	Login Host	Dialup IP	Direct IP	CIX
	Wariat	Host			
Columbus	CICnet			Dir. IP	
	OARnet	Host	Dial IP	Dir. IP	
	PSINet	Host	Dial IP	Dir. IP	CIX
Dayton	OARnet	Host	Dial IP	Dir. IP	
Toledo	OARnet	Host	Dial IP	Dir. IP	
Youngstown	Youngstown Free-Net	Host			
Oregon					
Aloha	world.net			Dir. IP	CIX
Eugene	PSINet	Host	Dial IP	Dir. IP	CIX
Portland	AlterNet		Dial IP	Dir. IP	CIX
	Netcom	Host	Dial IP	Dir. IP	
	PSINet	Host	Dial IP	Dir. IP	CIX
Salem	PSINet	Host	Dial IP	Dir. IP	CIX
Tigard	agora.rain.com	Host			
Pennsylvania					
Harrisburg	PSINet	Host	Dial IP	Dir. IP	CIX
Philadelphia	JvNCNet	Host	Dial IP	Dir. IP	CIX
	PSINet	Host	Dial IP	Dir. IP	CIX
Pittsburgh	ANS CO+RE Services		Dial IP	Dir. IP	
	PREPnet	Host	Dial IP	Dir. IP	
	PSINet	Host	Dial IP	Dir. IP	CIX
	Telerama BBS	Host	Dial IP		
Rhode Island					
East Greenwich	The IDS World Network	Host	Dial IP		
Providence	JvNCNet	Host	Dial IP	Dir. IP	CIX
	PSINet	Host	Dial IP	Dir. IP	CIX
Texas					
Addison	Netcom	Host	Dial IP	Dir. IP	
Austin	AlterNet		Dial IP	Dir. IP	CIX
	Illuminati Online	Host			
	PSINet	Host	Dial IP	Dir. IP	CIX
	Real/Time	Host	Dial IP		
	SesquiNet		Dial IP	Dir. IP	
	Zilker Internet Park	Host	Dial IP		
Dallas	AlterNet		Dial IP	Dir. IP	CIX
	PSINet	Host	Dial IP	Dir. IP	CIX
	SesquiNet		Dial IP	Dir. IP	
Houston	AlterNet		Dial IP	Dir. IP	CIX
	ANS CO+RE Services		Dial IP	Dir. IP	
	BlackBox	Host	Dial IP		
	PSINet	Host	Dial IP	Dir. IP	CIX

Place	System Name	Login Host	Dialup IP	Direct IP	CIX
	SesquiNet		Dial IP	Dir. IP	
	SugarLand UNIX	Host			
Irving	Texas Metronet	Host	Dial IP		
Utah					
Provo	Westnet			Dir. IP	
Salt Lake City	ANS CO+RE Services		Dial IP	Dir. IP	
	Westnet			Dir. IP	
Virginia					
Blacksburg	ANS CO+RE Services		Dial IP	Dir. IP	
Charlottesville	VERnet			Dir. IP	
Falls Church	AlterNet		Dial IP	Dir. IP	CIX
Fredericksburg	PSINet	Host	Dial IP	Dir. IP	CIX
Herndon	PSINet	Host	Dial IP	Dir. IP	CIX
Norfolk	PSINet	Host	Dial IP	Dir. IP	CIX
	Wyvern	Host			
Reston	SURAnet		Dial IP	Dir. IP	
Richmond	PSINet	Host	Dial IP	Dir. IP	CIX
Vienna	grebyn	Host	Dial IP		
	Netcom	Host	Dial IP	Dir. IP	
Washington					
Aberdeen	Netcom	Host	Dial IP	Dir. IP	
Bellevue	Halcyon	Host	Dial IP	Dir. IP	
	NorthwestNet			Dir. IP	CIX
Bothell	Northwest Nexus	Host	Dial IP		
Olympia	PSINet	Host	Dial IP	Dir. IP	CIX
Seattle	ANS CO+RE Services		Dial IP	Dir. IP	
	Eskimo North	Host			
	PSINet	Host	Dial IP	Dir. IP	CIX
Spokane	PSINet	Host	Dial IP	Dir. IP	CIX
Tricities	PSINet	Host	Dial IP	Dir. IP	CIX
Yakima	PSINet	Host	Dial IP	Dir. IP	CIX
West Virginia					
Morgantown	WVNET			Dir. IP	
Wisconsin					
Madison	CICnet			Dir. IP	
Milwaukee	CICnet			Dir. IP	
Wyoming					
Laramie	Westnet			Dir. IP	
Uruguay	Chasque	Host	Dial IP		
	RAU			Dir. IP	

Providers by Area Code

This section lists providers sorted telephone area code. Here we only list providers in North America, since listing other providers by country code would merely duplicate the information presented in the previous section.

The plus (+) sign is the international standard way of indicating that the number immediately following is the country code. So +1 is not the U.S. direct dial prefix, it is country code 1, for North America, including Canada, the United States, much of the Caribbean (+1-809), and Guam (+1-671). We have listed the Caribbean +1-809 countries last, rather than between Hawaii and Indiana.

Remember that area codes do not completely determine telephone rates, as for example in Silicon Valley (+1-415 and +1-408). Ask any potential provider directly about rates and other access details.

Area Code	System Name	Login Host	Dialup IP	Direct IP	CIX
+1	**North America**				
+1-201 us.nj	JvNCNet	Host	Dial IP	Dir. IP	CIX
+1-203 us.ct	ANS CO+RE Services		Dial IP	Dir. IP	
	JvNCNet	Host	Dial IP	Dir. IP	CIX
	PSINet	Host	Dial IP	Dir. IP	CIX
+1-204 ca.mb	MBnet	Host	Dial IP	Dir. IP	
+1-206 us.or	world.net			Dir. IP	CIX
+1-206 us.wa	ANS CO+RE Services		Dial IP	Dir. IP	
	Eskimo North	Host			
	Halcyon	Host	Dial IP	Dir. IP	
	Netcom	Host	Dial IP	Dir. IP	
	Northwest Nexus	Host	Dial IP		
	NorthwestNet			Dir. IP	CIX
	PSINet	Host	Dial IP	Dir. IP	CIX
+1-207 us.me	PSINet	Host	Dial IP	Dir. IP	CIX
+1-208 us.id	PSINet	Host	Dial IP	Dir. IP	CIX
	Westnet			Dir. IP	
+1-209 us.ca	BARRnet		Dial IP	Dir. IP	CIX
	CSUnet		Dial IP	Dir. IP	
+1-212 us.ny	MindVOX	Host			
	PANIX	Host			
	PSINet	Host	Dial IP	Dir. IP	CIX
+1-213 us.ca	PSINet	Host	Dial IP	Dir. IP	CIX
+1-214 us.tx	AlterNet		Dial IP	Dir. IP	CIX
	Netcom	Host	Dial IP	Dir. IP	
	PSINet	Host	Dial IP	Dir. IP	CIX
	SesquiNet		Dial IP	Dir. IP	

Area Code	System Name	Login Host	Dialup IP	Direct IP	CIX
	Texas Metronet	Host	Dial IP		
+1-215 us.pa	JvNCNet	Host	Dial IP	Dir. IP	CIX
	PSINet	Host	Dial IP	Dir. IP	CIX
+1-216 us.oh	ANS CO+RE Services		Dial IP	Dir. IP	
	Cleveland Free-Net	Host			
	Lorain County Free-Net	Host			
	Netcom	Host	Dial IP	Dir. IP	
	OARnet	Host	Dial IP	Dir. IP	
	Wariat	Host			
	Youngstown Free-Net	Host			
+1-217 us.il	ANS CO+RE Services		Dial IP	Dir. IP	
	CICnet			Dir. IP	
+1-218 us.mn	MRnet		Dial IP	Dir. IP	
+1-219 us.in	CICnet			Dir. IP	
+1-282 us.mn	MRnet		Dial IP	Dir. IP	
+1-301 us.dc	Express Access	Host	Dial IP	Dir. IP	
+1-301 us.md	ANS CO+RE Services		Dial IP	Dir. IP	
+1-303 us.co	ANS CO+RE Services		Dial IP	Dir. IP	
	Colorado SuperNet	Host	Dial IP	Dir. IP	
	Denver Free-Net	Host			
	Nyx	Host			
	PSINet	Host	Dial IP	Dir. IP	CIX
	Westnet			Dir. IP	
+1-304 us.wv	WVNET			Dir. IP	
+1-305 us.fl	PSINet	Host	Dial IP	Dir. IP	CIX
+1-307 us.wy	Westnet			Dir. IP	
+1-309 us.il	Heartland Free-Net	Host			
+1-310 us.ca	Los Nettos			Dir. IP	
	Netcom	Host	Dial IP	Dir. IP	
+1-312 us.il	MCSNet	Host	Dial IP		
	PSINet	Host	Dial IP	Dir. IP	CIX
+1-313 us.mi	ANS CO+RE Services		Dial IP	Dir. IP	
	CICnet			Dir. IP	
	MichNet	Host	Dial IP	Dir. IP	
	Msen	Host	Dial IP	Dir. IP	
	PSINet	Host	Dial IP	Dir. IP	CIX
+1-314 us.mo	ANS CO+RE Services		Dial IP	Dir. IP	
	Columbia Online Informati	Host			
+1-315 us.ny	NYSERnet		Dial IP	Dir. IP	

Area Code	System Name	Login Host	Dialup IP	Direct IP	CIX
	PSINet	Host	Dial IP	Dir. IP	CIX
+1-317 us.in	ANS CO+RE Services		Dial IP	Dir. IP	
	CICnet			Dir. IP	
+1-319 us.ia	CICnet			Dir. IP	
+1-401 us.ri	JvNCNet	Host	Dial IP	Dir. IP	CIX
	PSINet	Host	Dial IP	Dir. IP	CIX
	The IDS World Network	Host	Dial IP		
+1-402 us.ne	ANS CO+RE Services		Dial IP	Dir. IP	
	MIDnet		Dial IP	Dir. IP	
+1-404 us.ga	AlterNet		Dial IP	Dir. IP	CIX
	ANS CO+RE Services		Dial IP	Dir. IP	
	Netcom	Host	Dial IP	Dir. IP	
	PSINet	Host	Dial IP	Dir. IP	CIX
+1-406 us.mt	Big Sky Telegraph	Host			
+1-407 us.fl	PSINet	Host	Dial IP	Dir. IP	CIX
+1-408 us.ca	a2i communications	Host	Dial IP		
	AlterNet		Dial IP	Dir. IP	CIX
	BARRnet		Dial IP	Dir. IP	CIX
	CERFnet	Host	Dial IP	Dir. IP	CIX
	class	Host			
	CSUnet		Dial IP	Dir. IP	
	Netcom	Host	Dial IP	Dir. IP	
	PSINet	Host	Dial IP	Dir. IP	CIX
	Quack	Host			
	The Portal System	Host	Dial IP		
+1-410 us.md	Express Access	Host	Dial IP	Dir. IP	
	PSINet	Host	Dial IP	Dir. IP	CIX
+1-412 us.pa	ANS CO+RE Services		Dial IP	Dir. IP	
	PREPnet	Host	Dial IP	Dir. IP	
	PSINet	Host	Dial IP	Dir. IP	CIX
	Telerama BBS	Host	Dial IP		
+1-414 us.wi	CICnet			Dir. IP	
+1-415 us.ca	AlterNet		Dial IP	Dir. IP	CIX
	ANS CO+RE Services		Dial IP	Dir. IP	
	BARRnet		Dial IP	Dir. IP	CIX
	CR Labs Dialup Internet A	Host	Dial IP	Dir. IP	
	CSUnet		Dial IP	Dir. IP	
	Netcom	Host	Dial IP	Dir. IP	
	PSINet	Host	Dial IP	Dir. IP	CIX
	The WELL	Host			

Area Code	System Name	Login Host	Dialup IP	Direct IP	CIX
+1-416 ca.on	ONet			Dir. IP	
+1-419 us.oh	OARnet	Host	Dial IP	Dir. IP	
+1-502 us.ky	OARnet	Host	Dial IP	Dir. IP	
+1-503 us.or	agora.rain.com	Host			
	AlterNet		Dial IP	Dir. IP	CIX
	Netcom	Host	Dial IP	Dir. IP	
	PSINet	Host	Dial IP	Dir. IP	CIX
+1-505 us.nm	Westnet			Dir. IP	
+1-506 ca.nb	NB*net			Dir. IP	
+1-507 us.mn	MRnet		Dial IP	Dir. IP	
+1-508 us.ma	DMConnection	Host	Dial IP		
	PSINet	Host	Dial IP	Dir. IP	CIX
	The WORLD	Host			
+1-509 us.wa	PSINet	Host	Dial IP	Dir. IP	CIX
+1-510 us.ca	AlterNet		Dial IP	Dir. IP	CIX
	BARRnet		Dial IP	Dir. IP	CIX
	CSUnet		Dial IP	Dir. IP	
	HoloNet	Host	Dial IP		
	Netcom	Host	Dial IP	Dir. IP	
+1-512 us.tx	AlterNet		Dial IP	Dir. IP	CIX
	Illuminati Online	Host			
	PSINet	Host	Dial IP	Dir. IP	CIX
	Real/Time	Host	Dial IP		
	SesquiNet		Dial IP	Dir. IP	
	Zilker Internet Park	Host	Dial IP		
+1-513 us.oh	OARnet	Host	Dial IP	Dir. IP	
	Tristate Online	Host			
+1-514 ca.qc	cam.org	Host	Dial IP		
	RISQ		Dial IP	Dir. IP	
	SASK#net	Host		Dir. IP	
+1-516 us.ny	JvNCNet	Host	Dial IP	Dir. IP	CIX
	PSINet	Host	Dial IP	Dir. IP	CIX
+1-517 us.mi	CICnet			Dir. IP	
+1-518 us.ny	PSINet	Host	Dial IP	Dir. IP	CIX
+1-602 us.az	PSINet	Host	Dial IP	Dir. IP	CIX
	Westnet			Dir. IP	
+1-603 us.nh	mv.com	Host	Dial IP		
	PSINet	Host	Dial IP	Dir. IP	CIX
+1-604 ca.ab	BCnet			Dir. IP	

Area Code	System Name	Login Host	Dialup IP	Direct IP	CIX
+1-604 ca.bc	Victoria FreeNet	Host			
+1-606 us.oh	OARnet	Host	Dial IP	Dir. IP	
+1-607 us.ny	ANS CO+RE Services		Dial IP	Dir. IP	
	PSINet	Host	Dial IP	Dir. IP	CIX
+1-608 us.wi	CICnet			Dir. IP	
+1-609 us.nj	ANS CO+RE Services		Dial IP	Dir. IP	
	JvNCNet	Host	Dial IP	Dir. IP	CIX
	PSINet	Host	Dial IP	Dir. IP	CIX
+1-612 us.mn	CICnet			Dir. IP	
	MRnet		Dial IP	Dir. IP	
+1-613 ca.on	National Capital FreeNet	Host			
	ONet			Dir. IP	
+1-614 us.oh	CICnet			Dir. IP	
	OARnet	Host	Dial IP	Dir. IP	
	PSINet	Host	Dial IP	Dir. IP	CIX
+1-617 us.ma	AlterNet		Dial IP	Dir. IP	CIX
	ANS CO+RE Services		Dial IP	Dir. IP	
	NEARnet		Dial IP	Dir. IP	CIX
	Netcom	Host	Dial IP	Dir. IP	
	The WORLD	Host			
+1-619 us.ca	AlterNet		Dial IP	Dir. IP	CIX
	ANS CO+RE Services		Dial IP	Dir. IP	
	CERFnet	Host	Dial IP	Dir. IP	CIX
	crash.cts.com	Host	Dial IP	Dir. IP	
	CSUnet		Dial IP	Dir. IP	
	Netcom	Host	Dial IP	Dir. IP	
	SDSCnet			Dir. IP	
	The Cyberspace Station	Host	Dial IP		
+1-702 us.nv	NevadaNet			Dir. IP	
+1-703 us.dc	ANS CO+RE Services		Dial IP	Dir. IP	
	SURAnet		Dial IP	Dir. IP	
+1-703 us.va	AlterNet		Dial IP	Dir. IP	CIX
	ANS CO+RE Services		Dial IP	Dir. IP	
	grebyn	Host	Dial IP		
	Netcom	Host	Dial IP	Dir. IP	
	PSINet	Host	Dial IP	Dir. IP	CIX
	SURAnet		Dial IP	Dir. IP	
+1-704 us.nc	CONCERT-CONNECT	Host	Dial IP	Dir. IP	
+1-707 us.ca	CSUnet		Dial IP	Dir. IP	
+1-708 us.il	AlterNet		Dial IP	Dir. IP	CIX

Area Code	System Name	Login Host	Dialup IP	Direct IP	CIX
	ANS CO+RE Services		Dial IP	Dir. IP	
	CICnet			Dir. IP	
	netILLINOIS			Dir. IP	
+1-713 us.tx	AlterNet		Dial IP	Dir. IP	CIX
	ANS CO+RE Services		Dial IP	Dir. IP	
	BlackBox	Host	Dial IP		
	PSINet	Host	Dial IP	Dir. IP	CIX
	SesquiNet		Dial IP	Dir. IP	
	SugarLand UNIX	Host			
+1-714 us.ca	CERFnet	Host	Dial IP	Dir. IP	CIX
	CSUnet		Dial IP	Dir. IP	
	Express Access	Host	Dial IP	Dir. IP	
	Netcom	Host	Dial IP	Dir. IP	
+1-716 us.ny	Buffalo Free-Net	Host			
	PSINet	Host	Dial IP	Dir. IP	CIX
+1-717 us.pa	PSINet	Host	Dial IP	Dir. IP	CIX
+1-718 us.ny	AlterNet		Dial IP	Dir. IP	CIX
	ANS CO+RE Services		Dial IP	Dir. IP	
	JvNCNet	Host	Dial IP	Dir. IP	CIX
+1-719 us.co	Colorado SuperNet	Host	Dial IP	Dir. IP	
	Community News Service	Host	Dial IP		
	oldcolo	Host	Dial IP		
	Westnet			Dir. IP	
+1-800 us.az	Westnet			Dir. IP	
+1-800 us.ma	DELPHI	Host			
+1-801 us.ut	ANS CO+RE Services		Dial IP	Dir. IP	
	Westnet			Dir. IP	
+1-804 us.va	PSINet	Host	Dial IP	Dir. IP	CIX
	VERnet			Dir. IP	
	Wyvern	Host			
+1-805 us.ca	CSUnet		Dial IP	Dir. IP	
+1-808 us.hi	PACCOM			Dir. IP	
+1-813 us.fl	PSINet	Host	Dial IP	Dir. IP	CIX
+1-813 us.nv	NevadaNet			Dir. IP	
+1-818 us.ca	AlterNet		Dial IP	Dir. IP	CIX
	ANS CO+RE Services		Dial IP	Dir. IP	
	CERFnet	Host	Dial IP	Dir. IP	CIX
	CSUnet		Dial IP	Dir. IP	
+1-902 ca.ns	NSTN			Dir. IP	
	PEInet		Dial IP	Dir. IP	

Area Code	System Name	Login Host	Dialup IP	Direct IP	CIX
+1-904 us.fl	PSINet	Host	Dial IP	Dir. IP	CIX
	Tallahassee Free-Net	Host			
+1-908 us.nj	AlterNet		Dial IP	Dir. IP	CIX
	Express Access	Host	Dial IP	Dir. IP	
+1-909 us.ca	CERFnet	Host	Dial IP	Dir. IP	CIX
+1-914 us.ny	PSINet	Host	Dial IP	Dir. IP	CIX
+1-916 us.ca	BARRnet		Dial IP	Dir. IP	CIX
	CSUnet		Dial IP	Dir. IP	
	Netcom	Host	Dial IP	Dir. IP	
+1-919 us.nc	ANS CO+RE Services		Dial IP	Dir. IP	
	CONCERT-CONNECT	Host	Dial IP	Dir. IP	
+1-809-689	**Dominican Republic**				
+1-809-689	REDID			Dir. IP	
+1-809-759	**Puerto Rico**				
+1-809-759	CRACIN			Dir. IP	

Providers by Name

In this section we provide details on each IP connectivity provider, sorted alpha-betically by service name. You will need to contact any potential provider and ask directly for current rates and other details not shown here. In addition, details that are shown here are subject to change, and you should also check those directly with any provider of interest, using the contact information provided here.

a2i communications. Login Host, Dialup IP.
Rahul Dhesi
1121 Park Avenue, Suite 202, San Jose, CA 95126-2924, USA
info@rahul.net, FTP: ftp.rahul.net:/pub/BLURB
Voice: +1-408-293-8078

Login Host: telephone, TELNET in, TELNET out, mail in, mail out, FTP in, FTP
   out, USENET news, IRC
  User interface: UNIX shell login, menu interface, command-line MS-DOS
  Dialup: PEP, 8N1, +1-408-293-9020
  To get a new account, log in as: guest

Dialup IP: SLIP, PPP, 2400bps, 9600bps, 14.4Kbps

AARnet. Direct IP.
Australian Academic and Research Network, Inc.
GPO Box 1142, Canberra, ACT 2601, Australia
aarnet@aarnet.edu.au, FTP: aarnet.edu.au:/pub/doc/*, Gopher: archie.au
Voice: +61-6-249-3385, Fax: +61-6-249-1369

Direct IP : Leased line, ISDN, Modem, 1200bps, 2400bps, 4800bps, 9600bps, 9600bps, 14.4Kbps, 64Kbps, 10Mbps, 2Mbps E-1

Actcom. Direct IP.
Active Communications, Ltd.
14 Pinsker Street Haifa 32715 Israel
amir@actcom.co.il, Voice: +972-4-676114, Fax: +972-4-676088
Direct IP : Leased line

Actrix. Login Host.
Actrix Information Exchange
root@actrix.gen.nz, FTP: actrix.gen.nz

Login Host: telephone, TELNET in, mail in, mail out, FTP in, USENET news
    User interface: menu interface
    Dialup: v.32, +64-4-389-5478
    To get a new account, log in as: bbs

agora.rain.com. Login Host.
RainDrop Laboratories
Pacific Systems Group, 10635 SW 127th Court, Tigard, OR 97223-1964, USA
info@agora.rain.com, FTP: agora.rain.com:/pub/gopher-data/agora/agora,
    Gopher: agora.rain.com
Voice: +1-503-524-7348

Login Host: telephone, TELNET in, TELNET out, mail in, mail out, FTP in, FTP
    out, USENET news, IRC
    User interface: UNIX shell login, menu interface
    Dialup: v.32bis, any, +1-503-293-2059
    To get a new account, log in as: apply
    Usage limitations: depends on service level

AlterNet. Dialup IP, Direct IP, CIX member.
UUNET Technologies, Inc.
3110 Fairview Park Drive, Suite 570, Falls Church, VA 22042, USA
alternet-info@uunet.uu.net, FTP: ftp.uu.net:/uunet-info/*
Voice: 1-800-4UU-NET3, +1-703-204-8000, Fax: +1-703-204-8001

Dialup IP : SLIP, PPP, 9600bps, 14.4Kbps

Direct IP : Leased line, Modem, 9600bps, 9600bps, 14.4Kbps, 56Kbps,
    1.544Mbps, 10Mbps

ANS CO+RE Services. Dialup IP, Direct IP.
ANS CO+RE Systems, Inc.
100 Clearbrook Road, Elmsford, NY, 10523, USA
info@ans.net, FTP: ftp.ans.net:/pub/info/*
Voice: +1-800-456-8267, Fax: +1-703-758-7717

Dialup IP : SLIP, PPP, 1200bps, 2400bps, 4800bps, 9600bps, 14.4Kbps

Direct IP : Leased line, SMDS, Modem, 56Kbps, 1.544Mbps, 10Mbps, 45Mbps

BARRnet. Dialup IP, Direct IP, CIX member.
WestREN Corporation
Pine Hall, Rm. 115, Stanford University, Stanford, CA 94305-4122, USA
info@nic.barrnet.net, FTP: ftp.barrnet.net:/barrnet/*, Gopher: gopher.barrnet.net
Voice: +1-415-725-1790, Fax: +1-415-723-0010
Dialup IP : SLIP, PPP, 14.4Kbps
Direct IP : Leased line, ISDN, SMDS, Modem, 14.4Kbps, 56Kbps, 1.544Mbps,
10Mbps, 45Mbps

BCnet. Direct IP.
407-6356 Agricultural Road, Vancouver, BC V6T 1Z2, Canada
mike@bc.net, FTP: ftp.bc.net:/BCnet/*
Voice: +1-604-822-3932, Fax: +1-604-822-5116
Direct IP : Leased line, ISDN, Modem, 2400bps, 9600bps, 9600bps, 14.4Kbps,
56Kbps, 1.544Mbps

Big Sky Telegraph. Login Host.
Western Montana College
710 S. Atlantic, Dillon, MT 59725, USA
franko@bigsky.dillon.mt.us, Voice: +1-406-683-7338, Fax: +1-406-683-7493
Login Host : telephone, TELNET in, TELNET out, mail in, mail out, FTP in, FTP
out, Gopher out, USENET news
User interface: menu interface
Dialup: v.32bis, 8N1, +1-406-683-7680
To get a new account, log in as: bbs
Membership restrictions: K-12 Educationally affiliated for full Internet access

BlackBox. Login Host, Dialup IP.
Mark K. Newman
PO Box 591822, Houston, Texas, 77259-1822, USA
mknewman@blkbox.com, Voice: +1-713-480-2684
Login Host : telephone, public data network, TELNET in, mail in, mail out, FTP
in, FTP out, Gopher out, USENET news, IRC
User interface: UNIX shell login, menu interface, GUI interface
Dialup: v.32bis, 8N1, +1-713-480-2686
To get a new account, log in as: guest, for information only
Dialup IP : SLIP, PPP, 1200bps, 2400bps, 4800bps, 9600bps, 14.4Kbps

BOLNET. Direct IP.
Avenida Meriscal
Santa Cruz #1175 (Plaza del obelisco), Facutad de Ingenieria, 3er Piso, la Paz,
Bolivia
clifford@unbol.bo, Voice: +591-2-359585, Fax: +591-2-391458

Direct IP : Leased line

Buffalo Free-Net. Login Host.

James Finamore

Town of Tonawanda, 1835 Sheridan Drive, Buffalo, NY 14223, USA

finamore@ubvms.cc.buffalo.edu, Voice: +1-716-877-8800x451

Login Host : telephone, mail in, mail out, FTP in
   User interface: UNIX shell login
   Dialup: +1-716-645-6128

cam.org. Login Host, Dialup IP.

Communications Accessibles Montreal

9025 Boulevard Rivard, Brossard, Quebec, J4X 1V5, Canada

info@cam.org, FTP: telnet to cam.org, login "info"

Voice: +1-514-923-2102

Login Host : telephone, TELNET in, TELNET out, mail in, mail out, FTP in, FTP
   out, USENET news, IRC
   User interface: UNIX shell login
   Dialup: v.32bis, HST 14.4, PEP, ZyXEL 19.2, 8N1, +1-514-671-6723
   To get a new account, log in as: interactive login not available.

Dialup IP : SLIP, PPP, 1200bps, 2400bps, 4800bps, 9600bps, 14.4Kbps, 16.8Kbps

CARNet. Direct IP.

Croatian Academic and Research Network

Ministry of Science, SRCE, J. Marohnica bb, 41000 Zagreb, Croatia

helpdesk@carnet.hr, Voice: +38-41-629-963

Direct IP : 9600bps

CCC. Direct IP.

Universidad de Buenos Aires

Centro de Comunicacion Cientifica, Buenos Aires, Argentina

julian@dcfcen.edu.ar, Voice: +54-1-783-0729, Fax: +54-1-311-0516

Direct IP : Leased line

CENIAI. Login Host, Direct IP.

Instituto de Intercambio de Automatizado de Informacion

Director Red CENIAI, Industria y San Jose Capitolio Nacional, Apartado 2213,
   Habana, Cuba

jemar@ceniai.cu, Voice: +53-7-62-6565, Fax: +53-7-33-8237

Login Host : telephone, public data network, mail in, mail out
   User interface: UNIX shell login, menu interface
   Dialup: v.32bis, 8N1, +53-7-62-0425
   To get a new account, log in as: nuevo
   Membership restrictions: Yes

Direct IP : Leased line

CERFnet. Login Host, Dialup IP, Direct IP, CIX member.
California Education & Research Foundation
PO Box 85608, San Diego, CA 92816-9784, USA
help@cerf.net, FTP: nic.cerf.net:/cerfnet/*, Gopher: nic.cerf.net
Voice: +1-800-876-CERF or +1-619-455-3900

Login Host : telephone, toll-free number, TELNET in, TELNET out, mail in, mail
   out, FTP in, FTP out, IRC
   User interface: UNIX shell login, menu interface

Dialup IP : SLIP, PPP, 9600bps, 14.4Kbps

Direct IP : Leased line, Modem, 14.4Kbps, 56Kbps, 1.544Mbps

Chasque. Login Host, Dialup IP.
Miguel Peirano, Gabriel Sere
J. Jackson 1136, Montevideo 11100, Uruguay
apoyo@chasque.apc.org, Voice: +598-2-496-192, Fax: +598-2-419-222

Login Host : telephone, public data network, mail in, mail out
   User interface: UNIX shell login, menu interface
   Dialup: v.32bis, 8N1, +598-2-420194
   To get a new account, log in as: send e-mail first

Dialup IP : SLIP, PPP, 1200bps, 2400bps, 4800bps, 9600bps, 14.4Kbps

CICnet. Direct IP.
Computing Center, 535 W. William St., Ann Arbor, MI 48103-4943, USA
maloff@merit.edu, FTP: ftp.cic.net, Gopher: gopher.cic.net
Voice: +1-313-998-6102, Fax: +1-313-998-6105

Direct IP : Leased line, 1.544Mbps

class. Login Host.
Cooperative Library Agency for Systems and Services
1415 Koll Circle, Suite 101, San Jose, CA 95112, USA
class@class.org, FTP: class.org
Voice: +1-800-488-4559, Fax: +1-408-453-5379

Login Host : toll-free number, TELNET in, TELNET out, mail in, mail out, FTP
   in, FTP out
   User interface: UNIX shell login
   Membership restrictions: Join CLASS, $135/yr.

Cleveland Free-Net. Login Host.
CWRU Community Telecomputing Laboratory
310 Wickenden Avenue, Cleveland, OH 44106, USA
jag@po.cwru.edu

Login Host : telephone, TELNET in, FTP in

User interface: menu interface
Dialup: +1-216-368-3888

Colorado SuperNet, Inc.. Login Host, Dialup IP, Direct IP.
Colorado SuperNet, Inc.
Colorado School of Mines, 1500 Illinois, Golden, CO 80401, USA
info@csn.org, FTP: csn.org:/CSN/reports/DialinInfo.txt
Voice: +1-303-273-3471, Fax: +1-303-273-3475

Login Host: telephone, toll-free number, TELNET in, TELNET out, mail in, mail
   out, FTP in, FTP out, USENET news, IRC
   User interface: UNIX shell login, menu interface, GUI interface
   Dialup: v.32bis, PEP, 8N1, revealed on registration
   Usage limitations: $250 max per month

Dialup IP: SLIP, PPP, 1200bps, 2400bps, 4800bps, 9600bps, 14.4Kbps

Direct IP: Leased line, ISDN, Frame Relay, SMDS, Modem, 9600bps, 19.2Kbps,
   56Kbps, 64Kbps, 1.544Mbps

Columbia Online Information Network. Login Host.
University of Missouri — Columbia
Campus Computing, 200 Hinkel Bldg., Columbia, MO 61211, USA
ccwam@mizzoui.missouri.edu, FTP: bigcat.missouri.edu, Gopher: big-
   cat.missouri.edu
Voice: +1-314-884-7000

Login Host: telephone, TELNET in, FTP in, Gopher out
   User interface: UNIX shell login
   Dialup: +1-314-884-7000

Community News Service. Login Host, Dialup IP.
Klaus Dimmler
1155 Kelly Johnson Blvd., Suite 400, Colorado Springs, CO 80920, USA
info@cscns.com, Gopher: cscns.com
Voice: +1-719-592-1240 (CO) or +1-800-748-1200, Fax: +1-719-592-1201,
   Dialup numbers+1-719-520-1700, +1-303-758-2656 (800 available)

Login Host: telephone, toll-free number, public data network, TELNET in,
   TELNET out, mail in, mail out, FTP in, FTP out, USENET news, IRC
   User interface: UNIX shell login, menu interface, GUI interface
   To get a new account, log in as: new, Password "newuser"

Dialup IP: SLIP, PPP, 1200bps, 2400bps, 4800bps, 9600bps, 14.4Kbps

CONACYT. Direct IP.
Consejo Nacional de Ciencia y Tecnologia CONACYT
Av. COnstituyentes 1046 Col. Lomas Altas, Mexico 11950, D.F., Mexico
conacyt@unamvm1.dgsca.unam.mx, Voice: +52-5-327-7400 ex. 7901, Fax:
   +52-5-327-7400 ex. 7132

Direct IP : Leased line

CONCERT-CONNECT. Login Host, Dialup IP, Direct IP.
MCNC Center for Communications
PO Box 12889, Research Triangle Park, NC 27709-2889, USA
info@concert.net, FTP: ftp.concert.net, Gopher: gopher.concert.net
Voice: +1-919-248-1999, Fax: +1-919-248-1405

Login Host :
   Dialup: v.32bis/PEP, 8N1, Availiable on request

Dialup IP : SLIP, PPP, 1200bps, 2400bps, 4800bps, 9600bps, 14.4Kbps

Direct IP : Leased line, Frame Relay, 9600bps, 19.2Kbps, 56Kbps, 64Kbps,
   1.544Mbps, 10Mbps

connect.com.au. Login Host, Dialup IP.
connect@connect.com.au, FTP: ftp.connect.com.au
Voice: +61-3-5282239, Fax: +61-3-5285887

Login Host : telephone, USENET news

Dialup IP : SLIP, PPP, 9600bps, 14.4Kbps, 64kbps ISDN

CR Labs Dialup Internet Access. Login Host, Dialup IP, Direct IP.
CR Laboratories
Box 326, Larkspur, CA 94977, USA
info@crl.com, Voice: +1-415-381-2800, Fax: +1-415-381-9578

Login Host : telephone, toll-free number, public data network, TELNET in,
   TELNET out, mail in, mail out, FTP in, FTP out, USENET news, IRC
   User interface: UNIX shell login, menu interface
   Dialup: v.32bis, 8N1, +1-415-389-8649
   To get a new account, log in as: guest

Dialup IP : SLIP, PPP, 1200bps, 2400bps, 4800bps, 9600bps, 14.4Kbps, 16.8Kbps

Direct IP : Leased line, ISDN, SMDS, Modem, 1200bps, 2400bps, 4800bps,
   9600bps, 9600bps, 14.4Kbps, 19.2Kbps, 56Kbps, 64Kbps, 1.544Mbps,
   10Mbps, 45Mbps, 100Mbps

CRACIN. Direct IP.
Corporacion para la Red Academica Cientifica y de Investigacion Nacional de
   Puerto Rico
Secretario de Relaciones Internacionales, PO Box 195355, San Juan, Puerto Rico
   00919-5355
erivera@mxruc.clu.net, Voice: +1-809-759-6891, Fax: +1-809-759-8117

Direct IP : Leased line

crash.cts.com. Login Host, Dialup IP, Direct IP.
CTS Network Services
1274 Vista del Monte, El Cajon, CA 92020-6830, USA
info@crash.cts.com, FTP: crash.cts.com:/ctsnet.info/*
Voice: +1-619-593-9597, Fax: +1-619-444-9247

Login Host : telephone, public data network, TELNET in, TELNET out, mail in, mail out, FTP in, FTP out, Gopher out, USENET news, IRC
  User interface: UNIX shell login
  Dialup: v.32bis, PEP, HST, 8N1, +1-619-593-6400
  To get a new account, log in as: help
  Usage limitations: 1hr/day

Dialup IP : SLIP, PPP, 1200bps, 2400bps, 9600bps, 14.4Kbps, 16.8Kbps

Direct IP : Leased line, Frame Relay, Modem, 1200bps, 2400bps, 9600bps, 9600bps, 14.4Kbps, 19.2Kbps, 56Kbps, 64Kbps, 10Mbps

CRnet. Direct IP.
Universidad de Costa Rica
Director Unidad de Redes, Apt. 2671, San Jose, Costa Rica
gdeter@inforisc.cr, Voice: +506-341013, Fax: +506-346001
Direct IP : Leased line

CSC. Login Host, Dialup IP.
Center for Scientific Computing
PO Box 405, Tietotie 6, Espoo SF-02101, Finland
kari.kankaala@csc.fi, FTP: nic.funet.fi:/FUNET/*, Gopher: gopher.csc.fi
Voice: +358-0-4572239, Fax: +358-0-4572302

Login Host : telephone, public data network, TELNET in, TELNET out, mail in, mail out, FTP in, FTP out, Gopher out, USENET news
  User interface: UNIX shell login
  Dialup: v.32bis, 8N1, +358-0-455 0399

Dialup IP : SLIP, PPP, 1200bps, 2400bps, 4800bps, 9600bps, 14.4Kbps

CSUnet. Dialup IP, Direct IP.
Chris Taylor
CSU Network User Services, California State University — Chancellor's office,
  PO Box 3842, Seal Beach, CA 90740-7842, USA
nethelp@csu.net, FTP: nic.csu.net:/csunet/*, Gopher: eis.calstate.edu
Voice: +1-310-985-9661, Fax: +1-310-985-9400

Dialup IP : SLIP, 1200bps, 2400bps, 4800bps, 9600bps, 14.4Kbps

Direct IP : Leased line, Frame Relay, 56Kbps, 1.544Mbps

The Cyberspace Station. Login Host, Dialup IP.
Robb Brock
204 N. El Camino Real, Suite E626, Encinitas, CA 92024, USA
help@cyber.net

Login Host : telephone, TELNET in, TELNET out, mail in, mail out, FTP in, FTP out, USENET news, IRC
  User interface: UNIX shell login
  Dialup: v.32bis, USR HST, 8N1, +1-619-634-1376

To get a new account, log in as: guest
Usage limitations: 1 hour/day if using dialin, unlimited for TELNET
Dialup IP : PPP, 1200bps, 2400bps, 9600bps, 14.4Kbps, 16.8Kbps

DataNet. Direct IP.
Telecom Finland
PO Box 228, Rautatienkata 10, 33101 TAMPERE, Finland
Seppo.Noppari@tele.fi, Voice: +358-31-243-2242, Fax: +358-31-243-2211
Direct IP : Leased line

Dataserve. Login Host, Dialup IP, Direct IP.
Dataserv Ltd Info. Services
Atidim Advanced Technology Center, POB 58064, Neve Sharet, Tel Aviv 61580,
     Israel
info@datasrv.co.il, Gopher: zeus.datasrv.co.il
Voice: +972-3-6474448, Fax: +972-3-6473833
Login Host : telephone, TELNET in, TELNET out, mail in, mail out, FTP in, FTP
     out, Gopher out, USENET news, IRC
   User interface: UNIX shell login, menu interface, GUI interface
   Dialup: v.32bis, 8N1, Availiable on registration
Dialup IP : SLIP, PPP, 2400bps, 9600bps, 14.4Kbps
Direct IP : Leased line, Modem, 14.4Kbps, 19.2kbps digital leased line

DELPHI. Login Host.
GVC Corp.
1030 Massachusetts Avenue, Cambridge MA 02138, USA
walthowe@delphi.com, Voice: +1-800-544-4005, Fax: +1-617-491-6642
Login Host : telephone, public data network, TELNET in, TELNET out, mail in,
     mail out, FTP out, USENET news, IRC
   User interface: menu interface, GUI interface
   Dialup: v.22, 8N1, +1-800-365-4636 (for registration & service only)
   To get a new account, log in as: JOINDELPHI, password INTERNETSIG

Demon Internet. Login Host, Dialup IP, Direct IP, CIX member.
Demon Systems
42 Hendon Lane, London N3 1TT, England
internet@demon.net, FTP: ftp.demon.co.uk:/pub/doc/Services.txt
Voice: +44-81-349-0063, Fax: +44-81-349-0309
Login Host : telephone, TELNET out, mail in, mail out, FTP in, FTP out,
     USENET news, IRC
   Dialup: v.32bis, 8N1, Availiable to members only Dialups in London, Warring-
   ton, and Edinburgh
   To get a new account, log in as: Mail or Phone for an account
Dialup IP : SLIP, PPP, 2400bps, 14.4Kbps

Direct IP : Leased line, SMDS, Modem, 2400bps, 9600bps, 9600bps, 14.4Kbps,
19.2Kbps, 64Kbps

DENet - Danish Academic Network. Direct IP.
UNI-C - Danish Computing Centre for Research and Education
DTH, Bygning 305, DK-2800 Lyngby, Denmark
Steen.Linden@uni-c.dk, Gopher: gopher.denet.dk
Voice: +45-45-93-83-55, Fax: +45-45-93-02-20
Direct IP : Leased line, 64Kbps, 128Kbps, 192Kbps, 2Mbps E-1

Denver Free-Net. Login Host.
University of Colorado
4200 East Ninth Avenue, Campus Box C-288, Denver, CO 80210, USA
drew@freenet.hsc.colorado.edu, Voice: +1-303-270-4865, Fax: +1-303-270-8660
    (Attn: Drew Mirque, Denver Free-Net)
Login Host : telephone, TELNET in, mail in, mail out, FTP in, USENET news
    User interface: UNIX shell login
    Dialup: v.32bis, 8N1, +1-303-270-4865
    To get a new account, log in as: guest
    Usage limitations: No IRC, limited newsgroups
    Membership restrictions: Must register as user to access all features

DKnet. Login Host, Dialup IP, Direct IP.
Fruebjergvej 3, 2100 Kobenhavn 0, Denmark
netpasser@dknet.dk, FTP: ftp.dknet.dk, Gopher: gopher.dknet.dk
Voice: +45-39-17-99-00, Fax: +45-39-17-98-97
Login Host : telephone, TELNET in, TELNET out, mail in, mail out, FTP in, FTP
    out, Gopher out, USENET news, IRC
    User interface: UNIX shell login
    Dialup: v.32bis, PEP, 8N1, unpublished
    To get a new account, log in as: new accounts availiable via fax/phone/mail.
Dialup IP : SLIP, PPP, 1200bps, 2400bps, 4800bps, 9600bps, 14.4Kbps
Direct IP : Leased line, ISDN, Frame Relay, SMDS, Modem, 1200bps, 2400bps,
    4800bps, 9600bps, 9600bps, 14.4Kbps, 19.2Kbps, 56Kbps, 64Kbps

DMConnection. Login Host, Dialup IP.
Doyle Munroe Consultants, Inc.
267 Cox St., Hudson, MA 01749, USA
info@dmc.com, FTP: dmc.com
Voice: +1-508-568-1618, Fax: +1-508-562-1133
Login Host : telephone, TELNET out, mail in, mail out, FTP in, FTP out,
    USENET news, IRC
    User interface: VMS
    Dialup: v.32bis, PEP, 8N1, On request

To get a new account, log in as: Mail for account

Dialup IP : SLIP, 2400bps, 9600bps, 14.4Kbps

EBONE. Direct IP.
c/o RARE, Singel 466-468, NL-1017 AW Amsterdam, Netherlands
raresec@rare.nl, FTP: ftp.rare.nl:/rare/liaisons/ebone/div/*, Gopher: gopher.rare.nl
Voice: +31-20-639-1131, Fax: +31-20-639-3289

Direct IP : Leased line, Frame Relay, 9600bps, 9600bps, 56Kbps, 64Kbps,
    1.544Mbps, 10Mbps, 100Mbps, 256Kbps, 512Kbps Yes

ECUANET. Login Host, Dialup IP, Direct IP.
Corporacion Ecuatoriana de Informacion
PO Box 988, Guayaquil, Ecuador
xbaquero@q.ecua.net.ec, Gopher: ecua.net.ec
Voice: +593-2-433-006 ext. 1410, Fax: +593-2-437-601

Login Host : telephone, TELNET in, TELNET out, mail in, mail out, FTP in, FTP
    out, Gopher out, USENET news
  User interface: UNIX shell login
  Dialup: v.32bis, 8N1, +593-2-464-046
  To get a new account, log in as: write for new account
  Usage limitations: Time restrictions
  Membership restrictions: Join organization

Dialup IP : SLIP, 1200bps, 2400bps, 4800bps, 9600bps, 14.4Kbps

Direct IP : Leased line, Modem, 1200bps, 2400bps, 4800bps, 9600bps, 9600bps,
    14.4Kbps

Eskimo North. Login Host.
Robert Dinse
PO Box 75284, Seattle, WA 98125-0284, USA
nanook@eskimo.com, FTP: eskimo.com:/read-me
Voice: +1-206-367-7457

Login Host : telephone, TELNET in, TELNET out, mail in, mail out, FTP in, FTP
    out, USENET news, IRC
  User interface: UNIX shell login, menu interface
  Dialup: +1-206-367-3837, +1-206-365-5458, +1-206-742-1150
  To get a new account, log in as: new

EUnet. Login Host, Dialup IP, Direct IP.
EUnet Ltd
Kruislaan 409, NL - 1098 SJ Amsterdam, The Netherlands
info@EU.net, FTP: ftp.EU.net:EUnet/info, Gopher: gopher.EU.net
Voice: +31-20-592-5109, Fax: +31-20-592-5163

Login Host : telephone, toll-free number, public data network, TELNET in,
    TELNET out, mail in, mail out, FTP in, FTP out, Gopher out, USENET
    news, IRC

User interface: UNIX shell login, POP3, for mail clients
Dialup: v.22, v.32, v.32bis, PEP, According to local practice, According to
  country
To get a new account, log in as: contact postmaster@<country>.EU.net

Dialup IP : SLIP, PPP, 9600bps, 14.4Kbps, X.25, ISDN

Direct IP : Leased line, ISDN, Modem, 9600bps, 9600bps, 14.4Kbps, 64Kbps,
  1.544Mbps

EUnet Deutschland. Direct IP.
EUnet Deutschland GmbH
Emil Figge Strasse 80, 44227 Dortmund, Germany
info@germany.eu.net, FTP: ftp.germany.eu.net:/pub/EUnet, Gopher:
  gopher.germany.eu.net
Voice: +49-231-972-2222, Fax: +49-231-972-1111

Direct IP : Leased line, ISDN, Frame Relay, Modem, 1200bps, 2400bps, 4800bps,
  9600bps, 9600bps, 14.4Kbps, 64Kbps, 19.2Kbps PEP, 2Mbps E-0, Others

EUnet GB. Login Host, Dialup IP, Direct IP.
GBnet Ltd.
KRDBC, Off Giles Lane, Canterbury, Kent CT2 7PB, UK
postmaster@britain.eu.net, Voice: +44-227-475497, Fax: +44-227-475478

Login Host : telephone, TELNET out, FTP in, FTP out
  User interface: UNIX shell login
  Dialup: v.32bis & PEP, 7N1, On request
  Membership restrictions: must already be uucp customer

Dialup IP : SLIP, PPP, 1200bps, 2400bps, 9600bps, 14.4Kbps, 16.8Kbps

Direct IP : Leased line, ISDN, Modem, 1200bps, 2400bps, 4800bps, 9600bps,
  9600bps, 14.4Kbps, 19.2Kbps, 64Kbps

EUnet Switzerland. Login Host, Dialup IP, Direct IP.
Zweierstrasse 35, CH-8004 Zuerich, Switzerland
info@eunet.ch, FTP: ftp.eunet.ch:/eunet/*, Gopher: gopher.eunet.ch
Voice: +41-1-291-45-80, Fax: +41-1-291-46-42

Login Host : telephone, public data network, TELNET in, TELNET out, mail in,
  mail out, FTP in, FTP out, Gopher out, USENET news, IRC
  User interface: UNIX shell login, menu interface
  Dialup: v.32bis, 8N1, Check with them for numbers
  To get a new account, log in as: pax, then new

Dialup IP : SLIP, PPP, 1200bps, 2400bps, 9600bps, 14.4Kbps

Direct IP : Leased line, ISDN, Frame Relay, Modem, 1200bps, 2400bps, 9600bps,
  14.4Kbps, 64Kbps

Express Access. Login Host, Dialup IP, Direct IP.
Digital Express Group, Inc.
6006 Greenbelt Road, Suite 228, Greenbelt MD 20770, USA

info@digex.net, Voice: +1-800-969-9090, +1-301-220-2020, Fax:
    +1-301-220-0477

Login Host: telephone, toll-free number, public data network, TELNET in,
    TELNET out, mail in, mail out, FTP in, FTP out, USENET news, IRC
  User interface: UNIX shell login
  To get a new account, log in as: new

Dialup IP: SLIP, PPP, 1200bps, 2400bps, 4800bps, 9600bps, 14.4Kbps

Direct IP: Leased line, Modem, 1200bps, 2400bps, 4800bps, 9600bps, 14.4Kbps,
    19.2Kbps, 56Kbps, 64Kbps, 1.544Mbps

Fapesp/CNPq. Direct IP.
R. Gerardo Amorin 222, Brasil
demi@fpsp.fapesp.br, Voice: +55-011-869-1041, Fax: +55-011-261-2167

Direct IP: Leased line

FORTHnet. Dialup IP, Direct IP.
Stelios Sartzetakis
36 Daidalou St., Heraklio, Crete GR71110, Greece
forthnet-pr@forthnet.gr, FTP: ftp.forthnet.gr, Gopher: gopher.forthnet.gr
Voice: +30-81-221171, Fax: +30-81-229342

Dialup IP: SLIP, PPP, 1200bps, 2400bps, 4800bps, 9600bps, 14.4Kbps, 16.8Kbps

Direct IP: Leased line, ISDN, Modem, 9600bps, 9600bps, 14.4Kbps, 64Kbps,
    10Mbps, 100Mbps

Goldnet. Login Host, Dialup IP, Direct IP.
Goldnet Communication Services
40 Namal Street, Tel Aviv 63506, Israel
zlevitan@attmail.com, Voice: +972-3-543-3777, Fax: +972-3-544-4199

Login Host: telephone, mail in, mail out
  User interface: UNIX shell login, menu interface, GUI interface
  Dialup: v.32bis, 8N1, +972-3-565-6622
  To get a new account, log in as: requires written contract
  Membership restrictions: must be R&D or educational user

Dialup IP: SLIP, 1200bps, 2400bps, 9600bps, 14.4Kbps

Direct IP: 1200bps, 2400bps, 9600bps, 9600bps, 14.4Kbps

Goya-EUnet Spain. Dialup IP, Direct IP.
Goya Servicios Telematicos SA
c/ Clara del Rey 8, 1-7. E-28002 Madrid. Spain
request@eunet.es (human), info@eunet.es, subject: help (auto), FTP:
    goya.eunet.es:/info/doc/EUnet/help
Voice: +34-1-413-48-56, Fax: +34-1-413-49-01

Dialup IP: SLIP, PPP, 1200bps, 2400bps, 4800bps, 9600bps, 14.4Kbps

Direct IP : Leased line, ISDN, Modem, 1200bps, 2400bps, 4800bps, 9600bps,
9600bps, 14.4Kbps, 19.2Kbps, 64Kbps

grebyn. Login Host, Dialup IP.
Grebyn Corporation
PO Box 497, Vienna, VA 22183-0497, USA
info@grebyn.com, Voice: +1-703-281-2194

Login Host : telephone, TELNET in, TELNET out, mail in, mail out, FTP in, FTP
out, USENET news, IRC
  User interface: UNIX shell login
  Dialup: v.32bis & PEP, 8N1, +1-703-281-7997
  To get a new account, log in as: apply

Dialup IP : SLIP, PPP, 1200bps, 2400bps, 4800bps, 9600bps, 14.4Kbps

Halcyon. Login Host, Dialup IP, Direct IP.
PO Box 40597, Bellevue, WA 98546-4597, USA
info@nwnexus.wa.com, FTP: halcyon.com:/pub/waffle/halcyon
Voice: +1-206-455-3505, Fax: +1-206-455-4672

Login Host : telephone, public data network, TELNET in, TELNET out, mail in,
mail out, FTP in, FTP out, USENET news, IRC
  User interface: UNIX shell login, menu interface, user-provided shells
  Dialup: v.32/v.32bis, 8N1, +1-206-382-6245
  To get a new account, log in as: new

Dialup IP : SLIP, PPP, 1200bps, 2400bps, 9600bps, 14.4Kbps

Direct IP : Leased line, Frame Relay, Modem, 1200bps, 2400bps, 9600bps,
9600bps, 14.4Kbps, 19.2Kbps, 56Kbps, 64Kbps, 1.544Mbps

Heartland Free-Net. Login Host.
Jobst North, Technology Center #415 C, D, Peoria, IL 61625, USA
xxadm@heartland.bradley.edu, Voice: +1-309-677-2544

Login Host : telephone, public data network, TELNET in, mail in, mail out
  User interface: menu interface
  Dialup: v.22bis, v.32bis, respectively, E71, +1-309-674-1100, +1-309-438-2300
  To get a new account, log in as: bbguest
  Usage limitations: Time limitations

HoloNet. Login Host, Dialup IP.
Information Access Technologies, Inc.
46 Shattuck Square, Suite 11, Berkeley, CA 94704-1152, USA
info@holonet.net, FTP: holonet.net:/info/*
Voice: +1-510-704-0160, Fax: +1-510-704-8019

Login Host : telephone, public data network, TELNET in, TELNET out, mail in,
mail out, FTP in, FTP out, USENET news, IRC
  User interface: menu interface

Dialup: 8N1, +1-510-704-1058

To get a new account, log in as: guest

Dialup IP : 1200bps, 2400bps, 4800bps, 9600bps, 14.4Kbps

Hong Kong Supernet. Login Host, Dialup IP, Direct IP, CIX member.

Hong Kong University of Science and Technology Research & Development Corporation, Ltd.

Clear Water Bay, Kowloon, Hong Kong

coggs@HK.Super.NET, FTP: ftp.hk.super.net, Gopher: gopher.hk.super.net

Voice: +852-358-7924, Fax: +852-358-7925

Login Host : Gopher out, USENET news, IRC

User interface: UNIX shell login

Dialup: 8N1, +852-719-4125 Modem type V.32bis/V.42bis, ZyXEL Proprietary, TurboPEP (Telebit Proprietary)

To get a new account, log in as: help

Dialup IP : SLIP, PPP, 1200bps, 2400bps, 9600bps, 14.4Kbps, ZyXEL:19.2Kbps and Telebit PEP 23Kbps

Direct IP : Leased line, ISDN, Modem, 1200bps, 2400bps, 9600bps, 9600bps, 14.4Kbps, 64Kbps, 1.544Mbps, 10Mbps, 45Mbps, Based on local availability in Hong Kong

The IDS World Network. Login Host, Dialup IP.

InteleCom Data Systems

3 Franklin Road, East Greenwich, RI 02818, USA

info@ids.net, FTP: ids.net:/ids.net, Gopher: gopher.ids.net

Voice: +1-408-884-7856

Login Host : telephone, public data network, TELNET in, TELNET out, mail in, mail out, FTP in, FTP out, USENET news, IRC

User interface: menu interface, VAX/VMS DCL shell

Dialup: v.22, v.32/PEP, respectively, 8N1, +1-401-884-9002, +1-401-884-7564

To get a new account, log in as: GUEST

Dialup IP : SLIP, 1200bps, 2400bps, 9600bps, 14.4Kbps

IEunet. Dialup IP, Direct IP.

Innovations Centre, Trinity College, Dublin 2, Ireland

info@ieunet.ie, FTP: ftp.ieunet.ie, Gopher: gopher.ieunet.ie

Voice: +353-1-6719361, Fax: +353-1-6798039

Dialup IP : SLIP, PPP, 1200bps, 2400bps, 4800bps, 9600bps, 14.4Kbps

Direct IP : Leased line, Modem, 1200bps, 2400bps, 4800bps, 9600bps, 9600bps, 14.4Kbps, 19.2Kbps, 64Kbps, 10Mbps, 45Mbps, 100Mbps, 1Gbps, 2Mbps E-1

IIJ. Direct IP.

Internet Initiative Japan, Inc.

2-11-2 Nagatacho, Hoshigaoka Bldg., Chiyoda-ku, Tokyo 100, Japan

info@iij.ad.jp, FTP: ftp.iij.ad.jp, Gopher: gopher.iij.ad.jp

Voice: +81-3-3580-3781, Fax: +81-3-3580-3782

Direct IP : Leased line, Modem, 9600bps, 64Kbps, 1.544Mbps, 10Mbps,
    128Kbps, 384Kbps, 512Kbps, 768Kbps, 1Mbps, V.32bis (no PEP), V.42bis

Illuminati Online. Login Host.
Steve Jackson Games, Inc.
PO Box 18957, Austin, TX 78760, USA
info@io.com, Voice: +1-512-447-7866, Fax: +1-512-447-1144

Login Host : telephone, TELNET in, TELNET out, mail in, mail out, FTP in, FTP
    out, Gopher out, USENET news, IRC
  User interface: UNIX shell login, menu interface, GUI interface, text-based VR
    interface through multiverse
  Dialup: +1-512-447-4449
  To get a new account, log in as: NEW

InterAccess. Login Host, Direct IP, CIX member.
InterCon International KK (IIKK)
205 Grand Chariot Yoyogi Kouen, 1-37-14 Tomigaya, Shibuya-ku, Tokyo 151,
    Japan
iikk@nic.inter.net, Voice: +81-3-5478-7601, Fax: +81-3-5478-7603
Login Host :
  User interface:

Direct IP : Leased line, ISDN, Frame Relay, 19.2Kbps, 56Kbps, 64Kbps,
    1.544Mbps, 500Kbps, 3.0Mbps

Intercon. Direct IP.
Ecuanex
Av. 12 de Octubre 622 y Patria, Quito, Ecuador
intercon@ecuanex.ec, Voice: +593-2-528-716, Fax: +593-2-505-073
Direct IP : Leased line

JvNCNet. Login Host, Dialup IP, Direct IP, CIX member.
Global Enterprise Services, Inc.
The John von Neumann Computer Network 3 Independence Way, Princeton, NJ
    08540, USA
info@jvnc.net, FTP: ftp.jvnc.net:/jvncnet-info/*
Voice: +1-800-35-TIGER, +1-609-897-7300, Fax: +1-609-897-7310

Login Host : telephone, toll-free number, TELNET out, mail in, mail out, FTP in,
    FTP out, USENET news
  User interface: SLIP software

Dialup IP : SLIP, PPP, 1200bps, 2400bps, 4800bps, 9600bps, 14.4Kbps

Direct IP : Leased line, SMDS, Modem, 1200bps, 2400bps, 4800bps, 9600bps,
    9600bps, 14.4Kbps, 19.2Kbps, 56Kbps, 64Kbps, 1.544Mbps

Kav Manche. Direct IP.
Trendline Ltd (Kav Manche)
22 Yavne Street, Tel Aviv, Israel
admin@vax.trendline.co.il, Voice: +972-3-290466, Fax: +972-3-200419
Direct IP : Leased line

Lorain County Free-Net. Login Host.
Thom Gould
32320 Stony Brook Dr., Avon Lake, OH 44012, USA
aa003@freenet.lorain.oberlin.edu, Voice: +1-800-227-7113x2451 or
    +1-216-277-2451
Login Host : telephone, TELNET in, FTP in
    Dialup: +1-216-366-9721
    To get a new account, log in as: guest

Los Nettos. Direct IP.
University of Southern California/ISI
4676 Admiralty Way, Marina del Rey, CA 90292-6995, USA
los-nettos-info@isi.edu, FTP: ftp.isi.edu:/in-notes/los-nettos-story
Voice: +1-310-822-1511, Fax: +1-310-823-6714
Direct IP : Leased line, 1.544Mbps

MBnet. Login Host, Dialup IP, Direct IP.
Manitoba Regional Network
c/o Computer Services, University of Manitoba, 15 Gillson St., Winnipeg, Mani-
    toba R3T 5V6, Canada
Gerry_Miller@MBnet.MB.CA, FTP: ftp.mbnet.mb.ca
Voice: +1-204-474-9590, Fax: +1-204-275-5420
Login Host : telephone, TELNET in, TELNET out, mail in, mail out, FTP in, FTP
    out, Gopher out, USENET news
    User interface: UNIX shell login, menu interface
    Dialup: v.32bis, 8N1, +1-204-275-6132
    To get a new account, log in as: mbnet, then guest
Dialup IP : SLIP, PPP, 1200bps, 2400bps, 9600bps, 14.4Kbps
Direct IP : Leased line, 1200bps, 2400bps, 9600bps, 9600bps, 14.4Kbps,
    19.2Kbps, 56Kbps, 10Mbps

MCSNet. Login Host, Dialup IP.
Macro Computer Solutions
3217 N. Sheffield, Chicago, IL 60657, USA
info@genesis.mcs.com, FTP: genesis.mcs.com:/mcsnet.info/*
Voice: +1-312-248-UNIX, Fax: +1-312-248-UNIXX
Login Host : telephone, public data network, TELNET in, TELNET out, mail in,
    mail out, FTP in, FTP out, USENET news, IRC

User interface: UNIX shell login, menu interface

Dialup: v.32, v.32bis & PEP, respectively, 8N1, +1-312-248-0900, +1-312-248-0970, +1-312-248-6295

To get a new account, log in as: follow prompts

Usage limitations: Detatched jobs & servers require approval

Dialup IP : 1200bps, 2400bps, 9600bps, 14.4Kbps

MEXnet. Direct IP.

ITESM Campus Monterrey

Depto do Telecomunicaciones y Redes, Garza Sada #2501, Monterrey NL, Mexico

hgarcia@mexnet.mty.itesm.mx, Voice: +52-83-582000, Fax: +52-83-692004

Direct IP : Leased line, Modem, 1200bps, 2400bps, 9600bps, 9600bps, 14.4Kbps, 56Kbps

MichNet. Login Host, Dialup IP, Direct IP.

Merit Network, Inc.

2200 Bonisteel Ave., Ann Arbor, MI 48109, USA

info@merit.edu, FTP: nic.merit.edu:/michnet/*, Gopher: nic.merit.edu

Voice: +1-313-764-9430, Fax: +1-313-747-3185

Login Host : telephone, toll-free number, public data network, TELNET in, TELNET out, mail in, mail out, FTP in, FTP out, USENET news, IRC

User interface: PPP, SLIP, TELNET service

Usage limitations: Must follow acceptable use policy

Dialup IP : SLIP, PPP, 1200bps, 2400bps, 9600bps

Direct IP : Leased line, ISDN, Frame Relay, SMDS, 9600bps, 14.4Kbps, 19.2Kbps, 56Kbps, 64Kbps, 1.544Mbps, 10Mbps, 45Mbps, 100Mbps

MIDnet. Dialup IP, Direct IP.

University of Nebraska

501 Building, Lincoln, NE 68588-0202, USA

dmf@westie.unl.edu, Voice: +1-402-472-8971, Fax: +1-402-472-8486

Dialup IP : SLIP

Direct IP : Leased line, Modem

MindVOX. Login Host.

Phantom Access Technologies, Inc.

1562 First Ave., Suite 351, New York, NY 10028, USA

info@phantom.com, Voice: +1-212-989-2418

Login Host : telephone, TELNET in, TELNET out, mail in, mail out, FTP out, IRC

Dialup: +1-212-989-4141

To get a new account, log in as: mindvox, pw: guest

MRnet. Dialup IP, Direct IP.
Dennis Fazio
511 11th Ave., Box 212, Minneapolis, MN 55415, USA
info@mr.net, FTP: ftp.mr.net, Gopher: gopher.mr.net
Voice: +1-612-342-2570, Fax: +1-612-344-1716
Dialup IP : SLIP, PPP, 1200bps, 9600bps, 14.4Kbps
Direct IP : Leased line, Frame Relay, 56Kbps, 64Kbps, 1.544Mbps, 10Mbps

Msen. Login Host, Dialup IP, Direct IP.
628 Brooks, Ann Arbor, MI, 48103, USA
info@msen.com, FTP: ftp.msen.com:/pub/vendor/msen, Gopher:
    gopher.msen.com
Voice: +1-313-998-4562, Fax: +1-313-998-4563
Login Host : telephone, toll-free number, TELNET in, TELNET out, mail in, mail
    out, FTP in, FTP out, Gopher out, USENET news, IRC
    User interface: UNIX shell login, menu interface
    Dialup: v.32bis, PEP, ISDN, 8N1, Availiable on request
Dialup IP : SLIP, PPP, 1200bps, 2400bps, 9600bps, 14.4Kbps
Direct IP : Leased line, ISDN, Frame Relay, Modem, 1200bps, 2400bps, 9600bps,
    14.4Kbps, 56Kbps, 64Kbps

mv.com. Login Host, Dialup IP.
MV Communications, Inc.
PO Box 4963, Manchester, NH 03108-4963, USA
info@mv.com (automated response), mv-admin@mv.com (human), FTP:
    ftp.mv.com:/pub/mv/*, Gopher: gopher.mv.com
Voice: +1-603-429-2233
Login Host : telephone, public data network, TELNET in, TELNET out, mail in,
    mail out, FTP in, FTP out, Gopher out, USENET news, IRC
    User interface: UNIX shell login, menu interface
    Dialup: Availiable on request
    To get a new account, log in as: info
Dialup IP : SLIP, PPP, 1200bps, 2400bps, 4800bps, 9600bps, 14.4Kbps

National Capital FreeNet. Login Host.
Carleton University, 1125 Colonel By Dr., Ottawa K1S 5B6, Canada
aa001@freenet.carleton.ca, Gopher: freenet.carleton.ca
Voice: +1-613-788-2600x3701
Login Host : telephone, TELNET in, mail in, mail out, Gopher out, USENET
    news
    User interface: freeport menu interface
    Dialup: v.22bis, 8N1, +1-613-780-3733
    To get a new account, log in as: guest

Usage limitations: No FTP, MUDS, 1 hour login limit

NB*net. Direct IP.
David MacNeil
dgm@unb.ca, Voice: +1-506-453-4573
Direct IP : Leased line

NEARnet. Dialup IP, Direct IP, CIX member.
BBN Technology Services, Inc.
10 Moulton Street, Cambridge, MA 02138, USA
nearnet-join@nic.near.net, FTP: ftp.near.net:/docs/*, Gopher: gopher.near.net
Voice: +1-617-873-8730, Fax: +1-617-873-5620
Dialup IP : SLIP, PPP, 9600bps, 14.4Kbps
Direct IP : Leased line, ISDN, Frame Relay, SMDS, Modem, 9600bps, 14.4Kbps,
    19.2Kbps, 56Kbps, 1.544Mbps, 10Mbps, 45Mbps

Netcom. Login Host, Dialup IP, Direct IP.
Netcom Online Communication Services
PO Box 20774, San Jose, CA 95160, USA
info@netcom.com, Voice: +1-408-554-UNIX, Fax: +1-408-241-9145
Login Host : telephone, TELNET in, TELNET out, mail in, mail out, FTP in, FTP
    out, USENET news, IRC
  User interface: UNIX shell login, menu interface
  Dialup: depends on dialup, 8N1, send mail to above address
  To get a new account, log in as: guest
  Usage limitations: No background processes
Dialup IP : SLIP, PPP, 1200bps, 2400bps, 4800bps, 9600bps, 14.4Kbps
Direct IP : Leased line, Frame Relay, Modem, 1200bps, 2400bps, 4800bps,
    9600bps, 9600bps, 14.4Kbps, 56Kbps, 1.544Mbps

netILLINOIS. Direct IP.
627 Dartmouth Place, Evanston, IL 60208, USA
p_roll@nwu.edu, FTP: illinois.net
Voice: +1-708-467-7655, Fax: +1-708-467-1786
Direct IP : Leased line, SMDS, 56Kbps, 1.544Mbps

netmbx. Login Host, Dialup IP, Direct IP.
Ralf Moritz
Feurbachstr. 47-49, D-12163 Berlin, Germany
trepex@netmbx.netmbx.de, Voice: +49-30-8555350, Fax: +49-30-8555395
Login Host : telephone, TELNET in, TELNET out, mail in, mail out, FTP in, FTP
    out, Gopher out, USENET news, IRC
  User interface: UNIX shell login
  Dialup: v.32bis/HST, 8N1, five lines - numbers on request

To get a new account, log in as: call or write us for account
Usage limitations: Only those imposed by account type

Dialup IP : SLIP, 14.4Kbps

Direct IP : Leased line, ISDN, Modem, 9600bps, 14.4Kbps, 56Kbps, 64Kbps

NevadaNet. Direct IP.
University and Community College System of Nevada
System Computing Services, 4505 Maryland Pkwy., Las Vegas, NV 89154, USA
mitch@nevada.edu, FTP: ftp.nevada.edu, Gopher: gopher.nevada.edu
Voice: +1-702-895-4580, Fax: +1-702-895-4580

Direct IP : Leased line, 56Kbps, 64Kbps, 1.544Mbps, 10Mbps

NLnet. Login Host, Dialup IP, Direct IP.
Kruislaan 413, 1098 SJ Amsterdam, The Netherlands
nlnet@nl.net, FTP: ftp.nl.net, Gopher: gopher.nl.net
Voice: +31-20-5924245, Fax: +31-20-5924199

Login Host : telephone, public data network, TELNET in, TELNET out, mail in,
mail out, FTP in, FTP out, Gopher out, USENET news, IRC
User interface: UNIX shell login
Dialup: v.32bis, ZyXEL 19.2, PEP, 8N1, on request
To get a new account, log in as: Telephone for new account

Dialup IP : SLIP, PPP, 1200bps, 2400bps, 4800bps, 9600bps, 14.4Kbps, ZyXEL
19.2Kbps

Direct IP : Leased line, Modem, 1200bps, 2400bps, 4800bps, 9600bps, 14.4Kbps,
10Mbps, 19.2Kbps ZyXEL, 64Kbps ISDN, 2Mbps E-1, 34Mbps E-3

Northwest Nexus. Login Host, Dialup IP.
info@nwnexus.wa.com, FTP: nwnexus.wa.com:/NWNEXUS.info.txt
Voice: +1-206-455-3505

Login Host : telephone, mail in, mail out, FTP in, FTP out, USENET news
Dialup: Availiable on request

Dialup IP : SLIP, PPP

NorthwestNet. Direct IP, CIX member.
Northwest Academic Computing Consortium, Inc.
15400 SE 30th Pl., Ste. 202, Bellevue, WA 98007, USA
info@nwnet.net, FTP: ftp.nwnet.net:/nic/nwnet/*
Voice: +1-206-562-3000, Fax: +1-206-562-4822

Direct IP : Leased line, Modem, 1200bps, 2400bps, 4800bps, 9600bps, 9600bps,
56Kbps, 1.544Mbps, 10Mbps, 45Mbps

NSTN. Direct IP.
Michael Martineau
martinea@hawk.nstn.ns.ca, Voice: +1-902-468-NSTN

Direct IP : Leased line

NYSERnet. Dialup IP, Direct IP.
200 Elwood Davis Rd., Ste. 103, Liverpool, NY 13088, USA
info@nysernet.org, FTP: nysernet.org:/pub/nysernet/*, Gopher: nysernet.org
Voice: +1-315-453-2912, Fax: +1-315-453-3052

Dialup IP : SLIP, 9600bps, 14.4Kbps

Direct IP : Leased line, Frame Relay, 19.2Kbps, 56Kbps, 1.544Mbps, 128 Kbps,
   256Kbps, 384Kbps, 512Kbps

Nyx. Login Host.
University of Denver
c/o Prof. Andrew Burt, Dept. of Math and Computer Science, Denver, CO 80208,
   USA
aburt@nyx.cs.du.edu, Fax: +1-303-871-3310 (Attn: Dr. Burt)

Login Host : telephone, TELNET in, mail in, mail out, FTP in, FTP out, USENET
   news, IRC
   User interface: UNIX shell login, menu interface
   Dialup: v.32bis, PEP, HST, 8N1, +1-303-871-3324
   To get a new account, log in as: new

OARnet. Login Host, Dialup IP, Direct IP.
1224 Kinnear Road, Columbus, OH, 43212-1154, USA
nic@oar.net, FTP: ftp.oar.net:/pub/OARnet/*, Gopher: gopher.oar.net
Voice: +1-614-292-8100, Fax: +1-614-292-7168

Login Host : telephone, toll-free number, TELNET in, TELNET out, mail in, mail
   out, FTP in, FTP out, Gopher out, USENET news
   User interface: UNIX shell login
   Dialup: availiable on request

Dialup IP : SLIP, PPP, 1200bps, 2400bps, 4800bps, 9600bps, 14.4Kbps

Direct IP : Leased line, ISDN, 9600bps, 19.2Kbps, 56Kbps, 1.544Mbps

oldcolo. Login Host, Dialup IP.
Old Colorado City Communications
2502 W. Colorado Ave. #203, Colorado Springs, CO 80904, USA
dave@oldcolo.com, FTP: oldcolo.com:/pub/info
Voice: +1-719-632-4848, Fax: +1-719-593-7521

Login Host : telephone, TELNET in, TELNET out, mail in, mail out, FTP in, FTP
   out, USENET news
   User interface: UNIX shell login, menu interface, GUI interface
   Dialup: v.32bis, +1-719-632-4111
   To get a new account, log in as: newuser

Dialup IP : SLIP, 2400bps, 9600bps, 14.4Kbps

ONet. Direct IP.
255 Huron Street, Toronto, Ontario M5S 1A1, Canada
herb@onet.on.ca, FTP: onet.on.ca:/ONET/*
Voice: +1-416-978-4589, Fax: +1-416-978-6620
Direct IP : Leased line

PACCOM. Direct IP.
Torben Nielsen
torben@hawaii.edu, Voice: +1-808-956-3499
Direct IP : Leased line

Pactok. Login Host, Direct IP.
Pacific Community Computer Networking Project
PO Box 49, Annandale NSW 2038, Australia
pactok@peg.apc.org, Voice: +61-2-692-0231, Fax: +61-2-660-1404
Login Host : telephone, mail in, mail out, FTP in
   Dialup: Varies
Direct IP : Modem

PANIX. Login Host.
Public Access UNIX of New York
c/o Alexis Rosen, 110 Riverside Dr., New York, NY 10024, USA
alexis@panix.com, Gopher: gopher.panix.com
Voice: +1-212-877-4854
Login Host : telephone, TELNET in, TELNET out, mail in, mail out, FTP in, FTP
   out, Gopher out, USENET news, IRC
   User interface: UNIX shell login
   Dialup: +1-212-787-3100
   To get a new account, log in as: newuser

Pegasus Networks. Login Host.
Pegasus Networks Communications
PO Box 284, Broadway, Brisbane 4006, Australia
pwilson@peg.apc.org, Voice: +61-7-257-1111, Fax: +61-7-257-1087,   ,
   Dialup Hosts
Login Host : telephone, public data network, TELNET in, TELNET out, mail in,
   mail out, FTP in, Gopher out, USENET news, IRC
   User interface: menu interface
   Dialup: v.32bis, 8N1, +61-7-257-1111

PEInet. Dialup IP, Direct IP.
PEInet, Inc.
Box 3126, Charlottetown, PEI C1A 7N9, Canada
gardiner@peinet.ca, Voice: +1-902-368-3305, Fax: +1-902-368-2446

Dialup IP : SLIP, 1200bps, 2400bps, 4800bps, 9600bps

Direct IP : Leased line, Modem, 1200bps, 2400bps, 4800bps, 9600bps, 9600bps, 14.4Kbps, 19.2Kbps, 56Kbps

PIPEX. Dialup IP, Direct IP, CIX member.
Richard Nutall
216 Cambridge Science Park, Cambridge, CB4 4WA, England
pipex@pipex.net, FTP: ftp.pipex.net:/pub/*
Voice: +44-223-250120, Fax: +44-223-250121

Dialup IP : SLIP, PPP, 1200bps, 2400bps, 4800bps, 9600bps, 14.4Kbps

Direct IP : Leased line, ISDN, Modem, 4800bps, 9600bps, 64Kbps, 1.544Mbps, 2Mbps E-1

The Portal System. Login Host, Dialup IP.
Portal Communications Company
20863 Stevens Creek Blvd., Ste. 200, Cupertino, CA 95014, USA
cs@cup.portal.com, FTP: ftp.portal.com:/portal-info/*
Voice: +1-408-973-9111

Login Host : telephone, public data network, TELNET in, TELNET out, mail in, mail out, FTP in, FTP out, USENET news, IRC
   User interface: UNIX shell login, menu interface
   Dialup: v.32bis, 8N1, +1-408-973-8091, +1-408-725-0561, +1-415-965-8059
   To get a new account, log in as: info

Dialup IP : SLIP, PPP, 1200bps, 2400bps, 4800bps, 9600bps, 14.4Kbps

PREPnet. Login Host, Dialup IP, Direct IP.
305 S. Craig St., Pittsburgh, PA, 15213, USA
FTP: ftp.prepnet.com:/prepnet/general/*
Voice: +1-412-268-7870, Fax: +1-412-268-7875

Login Host : telephone, TELNET in, TELNET out, mail in, mail out, FTP in, FTP out
   Dialup: Availiable on request

Dialup IP : SLIP

Direct IP : Leased line

Proyecto HURACAN. Login Host, Direct IP.
Theodore Hope
Apdo. 288-2050, Costa Rica
hope@huracan.cr, Voice: +506-241431, Fax: +506-534344

Login Host : telephone, public data network, mail in, mail out
   User interface: menu interface, spanish-language "elm" and "nn".
   Dialup: v.32, 8N1, +506-532000
   To get a new account, log in as: write to hope@huracan.cr

Direct IP : Leased line

Proyecto Wamani. Login Host.

Centro de Communicacion de Informacion — CCI

Talcahuano 325-3F, 1013 Buenos Aires, Argentina

info@wamani.apc.org, Voice: +54-1-382-6842 (+54-1-793-1502 for messages)

Login Host : telephone, public data network, mail in, mail out, USENET news

   User interface: UNIX shell login, menu interface

   Dialup: v.32bis, TurboPEP, ZyXEL, 8N1, Availiable on request

   To get a new account, log in as: register by mail

   Usage limitations: Yes, time

PSINet. Login Host, Dialup IP, Direct IP, CIX member.

Performance Systems International

P.O. Box 3850, Reston, VA 22091, USA

info@psi.com, FTP: ftp.psi.com

Voice: +1-800-82-PSI-82, +1-703-620-6651, Fax: +1-703-620-4586

Login Host : telephone, TELNET out, mail in, mail out, FTP in, FTP out

   User interface: menu interface

   Dialup: v.32, 8N1, Too many to mention

Dialup IP : SLIP, PPP, 9600bps, 14.4Kbps

Direct IP : Leased line, Frame Relay, Modem, 9600bps, 14.4Kbps, 19.2Kbps,

   56Kbps, 1.544Mbps, 10Mbps, 45Mbps, 100Mbps

PUC. Direct IP.

Pontificia Universidad Catolica de Chile

Vicuna Nackenna 4860, Santiago, Chile

ediaz@tolten.puc.cl, Voice: +56-2-5524703, Fax: +56-2-5542730

Direct IP : Leased line

Quack. Login Host.

Kentucky Fried Unix

2351 Sutter Ave. #6, Santa Clara, CA 95050, USA

postmaster@quack.kfu.com, FTP: quack.kfu.com:/pub/kfu/*

Login Host : telephone, TELNET in, TELNET out, mail in, mail out, FTP in, FTP

   out, Gopher out, USENET news, IRC

   User interface: UNIX shell login

   Dialup: v.32bis/PEP, 8N1, +1-408-249-9630

   To get a new account, log in as: guest

   Usage limitations: No per-use charges, but be reasonable

   Membership restrictions: Accounts may not be shared.

RAU. Direct IP.

Red Academica Uruguaya

Colonia 2066, Montevideo 11200, Uruguay

holz@seciu.uy, Voice: +598-2-41-3901, Fax: +598-2-41-5843

Direct IP : Leased line, 4800bps

Real/Time. Login Host, Dialup IP.
Bob Gostwick & Assoc.
8760-A Research Blvd., Suite 152, Austin, Texas, USA
hosts@wixer.bga.com, Voice: +1-512-451-0046

Login Host : telephone, TELNET in, TELNET out, mail in, mail out, FTP in, FTP
    out, Gopher out, USENET news, IRC
  User interface: UNIX shell login, menu interface, GUI interface
  Dialup: v.32bis, v.22bis, 8N1, +1-512-459-4391, 459-4396
  To get a new account, log in as: new

Dialup IP : SLIP, PPP, 1200bps, 2400bps, 9600bps, 14.4Kbps, 16.8Kbps, PEP &
    SuperPEP for UUCP only

RECyT. Direct IP.
Red Cientifica y Tecnologica Nacional
Av. Cordoba 831 3er. Piso, Buenos Aires, Argentina
ebarone@secyt.gov.ar, Voice: +54-1-312-8917, Fax: +54-1-312-414201-054
Direct IP : Leased line

Red Cientifica Peruana. Login Host, Dialup IP, Direct IP.
RCP
Alonso de Molina, 1698, Monterrico, Lima, Peru
js@rcp.net.pe, FTP: rcp.net.pe, Gopher: rcp.net.pe
Voice: +51-14-35-1760 ex. 527, Fax: +51-14-36-4067

Login Host : telephone, public data network, TELNET in, TELNET out, mail in,
    mail out, FTP in, FTP out, Gopher out
  User interface: UNIX shell login, menu interface
  Dialup: v.32bis, 8N1, +51-14-364445
  To get a new account, log in as: visita_rcp, your name as password
  Membership restrictions: Membership in non-profit RCP

Dialup IP : SLIP, PPP, 1200bps, 2400bps, 4800bps, 9600bps, 14.4Kbps

Direct IP : Leased line, ISDN, Frame Relay, Modem, 1200bps, 2400bps, 4800bps,
    9600bps, 9600bps, 14.4Kbps, 19.2Kbps, 56Kbps, 64Kbps, 10Mbps

REDID. Direct IP.
Red Dominicana de Intercambio para el Dessarrollo
Apantade 2972, Santo Domingo, Republica Dominicana
dpimient!pimienta!daniel@redid.org.de, Voice: +1-809-689-4973, Fax:
    +1-809-535-6646
Direct IP : Leased line

REUNA. Dialup IP, Direct IP.
Red Universitaria Nacional
Canada 308, 2o. piso Santiago, Chile
info-reuna@uchdciux.seci.uchile.cl, Voice: +56-2-274-4537, Fax:

+56-2-209-6729

Dialup IP : SLIP, PPP

Direct IP : Leased line, 4800bps, 9600bps

RISQ. Dialup IP, Direct IP.
Bernard Turcotte
1801, avenue McGill College, Bureau 800, Montreal, Quebec H3A 2N4, Canada
turcotte@crim.ca, FTP: ftp.risq.net:/risq, Gopher: gopher.crim.ca
Voice: +1-514-340-5700, Fax: +1-514-398-1244

Dialup IP : SLIP, PPP, 9600bps, 14.4Kbps

Direct IP : Leased line, 19.2Kbps, 56Kbps, 1.544Mbps, 10Mbps

SASK#net. Login Host, Direct IP.
University of Saskatchewan
Dean Jones, Computing Services, 56 Physics Bldg., Saskatoon, SK S7N 0W0,
    Canada
dean.jones@usask.ca, Voice: +1-514-340-5700

Login Host : telephone, TELNET in, TELNET out, mail in, mail out, FTP in, FTP
    out, Gopher out, USENET news
    User interface: UNIX shell login
    Dialup: v.32bis, 8N1, Availiable on registration
    Usage limitations: 1hr/day

Direct IP : Leased line, Modem, 9600bps, 9600bps, 19.2Kbps, 56Kbps

SDSCnet. Direct IP.
San Diego Supercomputer Center
PO Box 85608, San Diego, CA 92138, USA
loveep@sds.sdsc.edu

Direct IP : Leased line

SesquiNet. Dialup IP, Direct IP.
Rice University
ONS, Houston, TX 77251-1892, USA
info@sesqui.net, FTP: ftp.sesqui.net:/pub/*
Voice: +1-713-527-4988, Fax: +1-713-527-6099

Dialup IP : SLIP, PPP, 1200bps, 2400bps, 4800bps, 9600bps, 14.4Kbps

Direct IP : Leased line, Frame Relay, Modem, 1200bps, 2400bps, 4800bps,
    9600bps, 9600bps, 14.4Kbps, 56Kbps, 64Kbps, 1.544Mbps, 10Mbps,
    45Mbps, 100Mbps, 1Gbps

SPIN. Dialup IP, Direct IP.
AT&T Jens Corporation
Spin Project, AT&T Jens Corporation, No. 25 Mori Building, 1-4-30 Roppongi,
    Minato-ku, Tokyo 106, Japan
attjens@nic.inter.net, info@spin.ad.jp, Voice: +81 3 5561-3333, Fax: +81 3
    3584-0810,

Dialup IP : SLIP, PPP, 14.4Kbps, 64Kbps

Direct IP : Leased line, ISDN, Frame Relay, Modem

SugarLand UNIX. Login Host.
NeoSoft
3408 Mangum, Houston, TX 77092, USA
info@neosoft.com, Voice: +1-713-438-4964

Login Host : telephone, TELNET in, TELNET out, mail in, mail out, FTP in, FTP
    out, USENET news, IRC
  User interface: UNIX shell login, menu interface
  Dialup: +1-713-684-5900

SURAnet. Dialup IP, Direct IP.
Southern Universities Research Association
8400 Baltimore Blvd., College Park, MD 20740, USA
marketing@sura.net, FTP: ftp.sura.net:/pub/nic/*
Voice: +1-301-982-4600, Fax: +1-301-982-4605

Dialup IP : SLIP, 1200bps, 2400bps, 9600bps, 14.4Kbps

Direct IP : Leased line, ISDN, Frame Relay, SMDS, 9600bps, 56Kbps, 64Kbps,
    1.544Mbps, 10Mbps, 45Mbps, 100Mbps

SURFnet. Direct IP.
SURFnet bv
PO Box 19035, 3501 DA Utrecht, The Netherlands
info@surfnet.nl, FTP: ftp.nic.surfnet.nl, Gopher: gopher.nic.surfnet.nl
Voice: +31-30-310290, Fax: +31-30-340903

Direct IP : Leased line, 9600bps, 1.544Mbps

SWIPnet. Login Host, Dialup IP, Direct IP.
SwipNet AB
PO Box 62, S-164 94 Stockholm, Sweden
info@swip.net, Voice: +46-8-6324040, Fax: +46-8-632-4200

Login Host : telephone, public data network, TELNET in, mail in, mail out
  User interface: UNIX shell login
  Dialup: v.32bis, 8N1, on request
  To get a new account, log in as: call or write for account

Dialup IP : SLIP, 1200bps, 2400bps, 9600bps, 14.4Kbps, V.FAST 24Kbps

Direct IP : Leased line, Modem, 14.4Kbps, 64Kbps, 1.544Mbps, 10Mbps

SWITCH. Login Host, Dialup IP, Direct IP.
Swiss Research Network
Limmatquai 138, CH-8001 Zuerich, Switzerland
postmaster@switch.ch, FTP: nic.switch.ch, Gopher: gopher.switch.ch
Voice: +41-1-268-15-15, Fax: +41-1-261-15-68

Login Host: telephone, TELNET in, TELNET out, mail in, mail out, FTP in, FTP
   out, Gopher out, USENET news, IRC   ·
   User interface: VMS shell
   Dialup: v.32bis, 8N1, Availiable to customers only
Dialup IP: 2400bps, 9600bps, 14.4Kbps
Direct IP: Leased line, ISDN, Modem, 64Kbps, 1.544Mbps, 10Mbps, 100Mbps

Tallahassee Free-Net. Login Host.
Leon County Library, 200 W. Park Ave., Tallahassee, FL 32301, USA
wood@cs.fsu.edu, Voice: +1-904-644-1796
Login Host: telephone, TELNET in, mail in, mail out, Gopher out
   User interface: menu interface
   Dialup: v.32bis, 8N1, +1-904-488-5056
   To get a new account, log in as: visitor
   Usage limitations: 2 hrs/day

Telerama BBS. Login Host, Dialup IP.
Luce McQuillin Corp.
PO Box 60024, Pittsburgh, PA 15211, USA
info@telerama.lm.com, FTP: telerama.lm.com:/info/general.info, Gopher: tel-
   erama.lm.com
Voice: +1-412-481-3505, Fax: +1-412-481-8568
Login Host: telephone, public data network, TELNET in, TELNET out, mail in,
   mail out, FTP in, FTP out, Gopher out, USENET news, IRC
   User interface: UNIX shell login, menu interface
   Dialup: v.32bis, 8N1, +1-412-481-5302
   To get a new account, log in as: new
Dialup IP: 1200bps, 2400bps, 4800bps, 9600bps, 14.4Kbps

Texas Metronet. Login Host, Dialup IP.
860 Kinwest Parkway, Suite 179, Irving, TX 75063-3440, USA
info@metronet.com, FTP: metronet.com:/pub/info/*, Gopher:
   feenix.metronet.com
Voice: +1-214-401-2900, Fax: +1-214-401-2802
Login Host: telephone, TELNET in, TELNET out, mail in, mail out, FTP in, FTP
   out, USENET news, IRC
   User interface: UNIX shell login, menu interface
   Dialup: v.32bis, PEP, 8N1, +1-214-705-2901
   To get a new account, log in as: user: info, pw: info / user: signup, pw
   signup
   Usage limitations: Only those imposed by account type
Dialup IP: SLIP, 1200bps, 2400bps, 9600bps, 14.4Kbps

Tristate Online. Login Host.
Cincinnati Bell Directory, Inc.
Room 102-2000, 201 E. 4th St., Cincinnati, OH 45201-2301, USA
sysadmin@cbos.uc.edu, Voice: +1-513-397-1396, Fax: +1-513-721-5147
Login Host: telephone, TELNET in, mail in, mail out, FTP in, FTP out
  User interface: menu interface
  Dialup: v.32bis, 8N1, +1-513-579-1990
  To get a new account, log in as: "VISITOR", PIN 9999

TWICS. Login Host, Dialup IP.
Tim Burress
Twics Co., Ltd., International Education Center Bldg., 1-21 Yotsuya, Shinjuku-ku,
  Tokyo 160, Japan
info@twics.co.jp, FTP: ftp.twics.co.jp
Voice: +81-3-3351-5977, Fax: +81-3-3353-6096
Login Host: telephone, public data network, TELNET in, TELNET out, mail in,
  mail out, FTP in, FTP out, Gopher out, USENET news, IRC
  User interface: custom script
  Dialup: v.32bis, PEP, 8N1, +81-3-3351-8244 (v.32) +81-3-3351-7905 (v.32bis)
  To get a new account, log in as: GUEST
Dialup IP: SLIP, PPP, 1200bps, 2400bps, 4800bps, 9600bps, 14.4Kbps, ISDN

UDC. Direct IP.
Universidad de Concepcion
Jefe de Unidad de Servicios Informaticos Academicos, PO Box 1313, Concepcion, Chile
crobles@halcon.depi.udec.cl, Voice: +56-41-234985 ex. 2393, Fax:
  +56-41-246076
Direct IP: Leased line

UK PC User's Group. Login Host.
info@ibmpcug.co.uk, Voice: +44-81-863-6646
Login Host: telephone, TELNET in, TELNET out, mail in, mail out, FTP in, FTP
  out, USENET news, IRC
  Dialup: +44-81-863-6646

UNdIP. Direct IP.
Universidad Nacional de la Plata
Centro Superior Procesamiento de la Informacion, Director General Cientifico y
  Tecnico, CESPI, 50 y 115, 3er Piso, 1900 La Plata, Argentina
jdiaz@unlp.edu.ar, Voice: +54-21-35102, Fax: +54-21-257240
Direct IP: Leased line

uropax.contrib.de. Login Host, Dialup IP.
Thomas Kaulmann
info@contrib.de, FTP: contrib.de:/src/pub/README, Gopher: contrib.de

Voice: +49-30-694-6907, Fax: +49-30-694-6809

Login Host : telephone, TELNET in, TELNET out, mail in, mail out, FTP in, FTP
    out, Gopher out, USENET news, IRC
  User interface: UNIX shell login, menu interface
  Dialup: v.32bis, HST, 8N1, +49-30-694-6182
  To get a new account, log in as: guest
  Usage limitations: Monthly time limit

Dialup IP : SLIP, PPP, 2400bps, 9600bps, 14.4Kbps, 16.8Kbps

UTFSM. Direct IP.
Universidad tecnica Federico Santa Maria
Director de los Servicios Computacionales Academicos, Casilla 110-V, Val-
    paraiso, Chile
mjapke@disca.utfsm.cl, Voice: +56-32-665053

Direct IP : Leased line

VERnet. Direct IP.
University of Virginia
Acaqdemic Computing Center, Gilmer Hall, Charlottesville, VA 22903, USA
jaj@virginia.edu, FTP: ftp.ver.net:/ver_net/*
Voice: +1-804-924-0616

Direct IP : Leased line

Victoria FreeNet. Login Host.
Victoria FreeNet Association
c/o VIATC, Suite 203-1110 Government Street, Victoria, BC V8W 1Y2, Canada
vifa@freenet.victoria.bc.ca, Gopher: freenet.victoria.bc.ca
Voice: +1-604-389-6026

Login Host : telephone, TELNET in, mail in, mail out, Gopher out, USENET
    news, IRC
  User interface: menu interface
  Dialup: v.32bis, 8N1, +1-604-595-2300
  To get a new account, log in as: guest
  Usage limitations: 1hr./session

Wariat. Login Host.
Zbigniew J. Tyrlik
zbig@wariat.org, FTP: wariat.org:pub/user.new
Voice: +1-216-481-9428, Fax: +1-216-338-3315

Login Host : telephone, TELNET in, TELNET out, mail in, mail out, FTP in, FTP
    out, Gopher out, USENET news, IRC
  User interface: UNIX shell login, menu interface
  Dialup: v.22, v.32bis/SPEP, respectively, 8N1, +1-216-481-9436
    +1-216-481-9425

To get a new account, log in as: bbs
Usage limitations: No jobs can remain running after logout

The WELL. Login Host.
Whole Earth 'Lectronic Link, Inc.
27 Gate Five Rd., Sausalito, CA 94965, USA
info@well.sf.ca.us, Gopher: gopher.well.sf.ca.us
Voice: +1-415-332-4335, Fax: +1-415-332-4927

Login Host : telephone, public data network, TELNET in, TELNET out, mail in,
   mail out, FTP in, FTP out, Gopher out, USENET news
   User interface: UNIX shell login, picospan conferencing software (CLI)
   Dialup: v.22bis, v.32bis, respectively, depends on your software,
   +1-415-332-6106, +1-415-332-8410
   To get a new account, log in as: newuser

Wellington Citynet. Login Host, Direct IP.
Wellington City Council
PO Box 2199, Wellington, New Zealand
naylor@wcc.govt.nz, Gopher: gopher.wcc.govt.nz
Voice: +64-4-801-3303, Fax: +64-4-8010-3007

Login Host : telephone, public data network, TELNET in, mail in, mail out,
   Gopher out, USENET news, IRC
   User interface: menu interface
   Dialup: v.22bis, 8N1, +64-4-801-3060
   Usage limitations: 3 hrs/day
Direct IP : ISDN

Westnet. Direct IP.
Colorado State University
ACNS, Colorado St. University, Fort Collins, CO 80523, USA
info@westnet.net, FTP: westnet.net
Voice: +1-303-492-8560

Direct IP : Leased line, 14.4Kbps, 56Kbps, 1.544Mbps

The WORLD. Login Host.
Software Tool & Die
1330 Beacon St., Brookline, MA 02146, USA
office@world.std.com, FTP: world.std.com:/world-info/basic.info
Voice: +1-617-739-0202, Fax: +1-617-739-0914

Login Host : telephone, public data network, TELNET in, TELNET out, mail in,
   mail out, FTP in, FTP out, Gopher out, USENET news, IRC
   User interface: UNIX shell login
   Dialup: v.32bis, 8N1, +1-617-739-9753
   To get a new account, log in as: new

world.net. Direct IP, CIX member.
Internetworks, Inc.
PO Box 5127, Aloha, OR 97006, USA
info@world.net, FTP: ftp.world.net:/pub/world.net/*
Voice: +1-206-576-7147
Direct IP : Leased line

WVNET. Direct IP.
West Virginia Network for Educational Telecomputing
837 Chestnut Ridge Rd., Morgantown, WV 26505, USA
INFOREP@WVNVM.WVNET.EDU, Voice: +1-304-293-5192
Direct IP : Leased line

Wyvern. Login Host.
Wyvern Technologies, Inc.
211 East City Hall Ave., Suite 236, Norfolk, VA 23510, USA
system@wyvern.wyvern.com, Voice: +1-804-622-4289, Fax: +1-804-622-7158
Login Host : telephone, TELNET in, TELNET out, mail in, mail out, FTP in, FTP
    out, Gopher out, USENET news, IRC
  User interface: UNIX shell login, menu interface
  Dialup: v.32bis, +1-804-627-1828
  To get a new account, log in as: guest

Youngstown Free-Net. Login Host.
St. Elizabeth Hospital Medical Center and Lou Anschuetz
410 Wick Ave., Youngstown, OH 44555, USA
lou@yfn.ysu.edu, Voice: +1-216-742-3075
Login Host : telephone, TELNET in, mail in, mail out, Gopher out, USENET
    news, IRC
  User interface: freePort menu interface
  Dialup: v.22bis, 8N1, +1-216-742-3072
  To get a new account, log in as: visitor

Zilker Internet Park. Login Host, Dialup IP.
Texas Internet Consulting (TIC)
1106 Clayton Lane, Suite 500W, Austin, TX 78723, USA
zip@tic.com, FTP: ftp.tic.com:zip, Gopher: gopher.tic.com
Voice: +1-512-451-6176, Fax: +1-512-452-0127
Login Host : telephone, TELNET in, TELNET out, mail in, mail out, FTP in, FTP
    out, Gopher out, USENET news, IRC
  User interface: UNIX shell login
  Dialup: v.32bis, Available on request
  To get a new account, log in as: new
Dialup IP : SLIP, PPP, 1200bps, 2400bps, 4800bps, 9600bps, 14.4Kbps

A.2   Other

In Chapter 9, *Security Issues* and in Chapter 10, *Setting Up Resource Discovery Services* we mentioned CERT and CIAC. Here is contact information for them.

CERT: Computer Emergency Reponse Team

The number given here is for a 24-hour hotline. CERT personnel answer 8:30 AM – 5:00 PM EST(GMT–5) / EDT(GMT–4), 8:30 AM – 5:00 PM EST(GMT–5) / EDT(GMT–4), and are on call for emergencies during other hours.

cert@cert.org   CERT Coordination Center
ftp:cert.org   Software Engineering Institute
+1-412-268-7090   Carnegie Mellon University
                                     Pittsburgh, PA 15213-3890
                                     USA

FIRST: Forum of Incident Response and Security Teams

FIRST (Forum of Incident Response and Security Teams) maintains a list of contacts for its participating members for retrieval by anonymous FTP from *csrc.ncsl.nist.gov* as the file *pub/first/first-contacts*. They also have a mail server, which works like this:

```
To: docserver@first.org

send first-contacts
```

FIRST will also refer you to an appropriate response team. The general response team for the Internet is CERT.

first-sec@first.org   FIRST Secretariat
+1-301-975-5200   Attn: Dennis Steinauer
+1-301-975-3359   National Institute of Standards and Technology
                                     A-216 Technology Building
                                     Gaithersburg, MD 20899-0001
                                     USA

Registration Templates

We discussed registering DNS domain names and IP network numbers in Chapter 4, *Registering Domain Names and IP Numbers*. Here are examples of the templates you will need to register. The exact template required by your registrar may be somewhat different, but all are similar to these.

B.1   Domain Registration

The example here is from the InterNIC *domain-template.txt* template.

From domain-template.txt

(1) The name of the top-level domain to join (EDU, COM, MIL, GOV, NET, ORG).

    1. Top-level domain:

(2) The name of the domain (up to 12 characters). This is the name that will be used in tables and lists associating the domain with the domain server addresses. [While, from a technical standpoint, domain names can be quite long we recommend the use of shorter, more user-friendly names.]

    2. Complete Domain Name:

(3) The name and address of the organization establishing the domain.

    3a. Organization name:
    3b. Organization address:

(4) The date you expect the domain to be fully operational.

    4. Date operational:

(5) The handle of the administrative head of the organization — or this person's name, mailing address, phone number, organization, and network mailbox. This is the contact point for administrative and policy questions about the domain. In the case of a research project, this should be the principal investigator.

NOTE: Both the Administrative and the Technical/Zone contact of a domain MUST have a network mailbox, even if the mailbox is to be within the proposed domain.

    5a. Handle (if known) :
    5b. Name (Last, First) :
    5c. Organization:
    5d. Mail Address:

    5e. Phone Number:
    5f. Net Mailbox :

(6) The handle of the technical contact for the domain or the person's name, mailing address, phone number, organization, and network mailbox. This is the contact point for problems concerning the domain or zone, as well as for updating information about the domain or zone.

    Technical and Zone Contact
    6a. Handle (if known):
    6b. Name (Last, First):
    6c. Organization:
    6d. Mail Address:

    6e. Phone Number:
    6f. Net Mailbox:

(7) Domains must provide at least two independent servers on Government-sponsored networks that provide the domain service for translating names to addresses for hosts in this domain.

* If you are applying for a domain and a network number assignment simultaneously and a host on your proposed network will be used as a server for the domain, you must wait until you receive your network number assignment and have given the server(s) a netaddress before sending in the domain application. Sending in the domain application without complete information in Sections 7 and 8 of this template will result in the delay of the domain registration.

Also, establishing the servers in physically separate locations and on different PSNs and/or networks is strongly recommended.

    7a. Primary Server Hostname:
    7b. Primary Server Netaddress:
    7c. Primary Server Hardware:
    7d. Primary Server Software:

(8) The Secondary server information.

    8a. Secondary Server Hostname:
    8b. Secondary Server Netaddress:
    8c. Secondary Server Hardware:
    8d. Secondary Server Software:

(9) If any currently registered hosts will be renamed into the new domain, please specify old hostname, netaddress, and new hostname.

For example:

BAR-FOO2.XYZ.COM (26.8.0.193) -> FOO2.BAR.COM
BAR-FOO3.XYZ.COM (192.7.3.193) -> FOO3.BAR.COM
BAR-FOO4.ARPA (34.6.0.193) -> FOO4.BAR.COM

(10) Please describe your organization briefly.

For example: Our Corporation is a consulting organization of people working with UNIX and the C language in an electronic networking environment. It sponsors two technical conferences annually and distributes a bimonthly newsletter.

B.2   IP Network Number Registration

The example here is from the InterNIC *internet-number-template.txt* template.

From internet-number-template.txt

1) If the network will be connected to the Internet, you must provide the name of the governmental sponsoring organization, and the name, title, mailing address, phone number, net mailbox, and NIC Handle (if any) of the contact person (POC) at that organization who has authorized the network connection. This person will serve as the POC for administrative and policy questions about authorization to be a part of the Internet. Examples of such sponsoring organizations are: DISA DNSO, the National Science Foundation (NSF), or similar military or government sponsors.

NOTE: If the network will NOT be connected to the Internet, then you do not need to provide this information.

    1a. Sponsoring Organization:
    1b. Contact name (Lastname, Firstname):
    1c. Contact title:
    1d. Mail Address :

    1e.Phone :
    1f. Net mailbox :
    1g. NIC handle (if known):

2) Provide the name, title, mailing address, phone number, and organization of the technical POC. The online mailbox and NIC Handle (if any) of the technical POC should also be included. This is the POC for resolving technical problems associated with the network and for updating information about the network. The technical POC may also be responsible for hosts attached to this network.

    2a. NIC handle (if known):
    2b. Technical POC name (Lastname, Firstname):
    2c. Technical POC title:
    2d. Mail address :

    2e. Phone :
    2f. Net Mailbox :

3) Supply the short mnemonic name for the network (up to 12 characters). This is the name that will be used as an identifier in internet name and address tables.

    3. Network name:

4) Identify the network geographic location and the responsible organization establishing the network.

    4a. Postal address for main/headquarters network site:

    4b. Name of Organization:

5) Question #5 is for MILITARY or DOD requests, ONLY.

If you require that this connected network be announced to the NSFNET please answer questions 5a, 5b, and 5c.

    5a. Do you want MILNET to announce your network to the NSFNET? (Y/N):

5b. Do you have an alternate connection, other than MILNET, to the NSFNET? (please state alternate connection if answer is yes):

5c. If you've answered yes to 5b, please state if you would like the MIL-NET connection to act as a backup path to the NSFNET? (Y/N):

6) Estimate the number of hosts that will be on the network:

6a. Initially:
6b. Within one year:
6c. Within two years:
6d. Within five years:

7) Unless a strong and convincing reason is presented, the network (if it qualifies at all) will be assigned a class C network number. If a class C network number is not acceptable for your purposes state why. (Note: If there are plans for more than a few local networks, and more than 100 hosts, you are strongly urged to consider subnetting. [See RFC 950])

7. Reason:

8) Networks are characterized as being either Research, Defense, Government - Non Defense, or Commercial, and the network address space is shared between these four areas. Which type is this network?

8. Type of network:

9) What is the purpose of the network?

9. Purpose:

B.3   IP Number to Domain Registration

The example here is from the InterNIC *in-addr-template.txt* template.

From in-addr.arpa.txt

The Internet uses a special domain to support gateway location and Internet address to host mapping. The intent of this domain is to provide a guaranteed method to perform host address to host name mapping, and to facilitate queries to locate all gateways on a particular network in the Internet.

The following information is needed for delegation of registered networks in your domain for inclusion in the IN-ADDR.ARPA zone files:

• the IN-ADDR.ARPA domain

• the Network name

• the Hostnames of the two hosts on networks that will be acting as servers

IN-ADDR domains are represented using the network number in reverse. Network 123.45.67.0's IN-ADDR domain is represented as 67.45.123.IN-ADDR.ARPA. For example:

IN-ADDR domain	Network Name	IN-ADDR Servers (Hostname) (NetAddress) (CPUType/OpSys)
41.192.IN-ADDR.ARPA	NET-TEST-ONE	BAR.FOO.EDU 123.45.67.89 VAX-II/VMS ONE.ABC.COM 98.76.54.32 SUN/UNIX

Please have the Network Coordinator complete and return the following information for those networks needing IN-ADDR registration.

IN-ADDR domain	Network Name	IN-ADDR Servers

APPENDIX C

Software and Other Information

In this appendix we list specific anonymous FTP servers or other sources for every piece of software described in the book, plus other relevant information. We have already described Anonymous FTP in Chapter 4, *Registering Domain Names and IP Numbers*. We mentioned archie in Chapter 10, *Setting Up Resource Discovery Services*. For those not already familiar with it, we provide information on archie next. The bulk of this appendix consists of specific details on finding software.

C.1 Archie

Archie is an application that collects indexes of anonymous FTP servers (by polling them approximately monthly) and provides search access to those indexes to clients [Deutsch *et al.* 1992]. Archie is a good example of a widely used Internet service that was developed by essentially volunteer labor, and that has no organized means of support [Deutsch 1991; Barron 1992].

To try archie, TELNET to one of the archie server machines, such as *archie.sura.net*, and log in as archie. Try to pick a server close to you; there are currently servers on at least three continents and many countries. The archie command *servers* lists all archie servers. Archie has a help command that tells you how to actually use it. For real use, it's best to get an archie client. The source for the archie client may be retrieved by anonymous FTP to one of the archie servers. Look in the directory */archie/clients* or */pub/archie/clients*. Comments and bug reports may be sent to *archie-admin@bunyip.com* .

C.2   Software Access List

This is a list of most of the software packages mentioned or described in the book. The software is grouped by general topic area and each of the servers where the package may be obtained is listed. The list of sites is by no means complete, but is rather an attempt to point out the most common locations where the software may be obtained. For a more complete list install *archie* on your system and use it to search for specific software.

Software	Site	Pathname
DNS		
BIND	duke.cs.duke.edu	/dist/sources/bind/
	guardian.cse.psu.edu	/pub/src/bind/
	luga.latrobe.edu.au	/pub/network/bind/
	files1zrz.zrz.tu-berlin.de	/pub/net/bind/
	iraun1.ira.uka.de	/network/domain/bind/
	ftp.cfi.waseda.ac.jp	/pub/network/bind/
BIND tools		
nslookup	harpo.seas.ucla.edu	/mnt/fs01/nslookup/
	wasp.eng.ufl.edu	/pub/nslookup/
	files1zrz.zrz.tu-berlin.de	/pub/net/nslookup/
	inf.informatik.uni-stuttgart.de	/local/nslookup/
dig	uxc.cso.uiuc.edu	/net/dig/
	valhalla.ee.rochester.edu	/pub/src/dig/
	files1zrz.zrz.tu-berlin.de	/pub/net/dig/
	cs.tut.fi	/pub/src/utbind/tools/dig/

Software	Site	Pathname
Electronic Mail		
sendmail.cf templates	ftp.tic.com	/pub/cf.pn.tar.Z
POPmailer	mailer.fsu.edu	/pub/pc/popmail/
	pacific.mps.ohio-state.edu	/mac/comm/Mail/popmail
	luga.latrobe.edu.au	/pub/network/popmail/
	uniwa.uwa.oz.au	/pub/mac/popmail/
	sun.rz.tu-clausthal.de	/pub/msdos/networking/popmail/
	sun0.urz.uni-heidelberg.de	/pub/net/mac/popmail/
Eudora	mailer.fsu.edu	/pub/mac/eudora/
	dorm.rutgers.edu	/pub/Mac/eudora/
	luga.latrobe.edu.au	/pub/network/eudora/
	uniwa.uwa.oz.au	/pub/mac/freeware/eudora/
	nic.switch.ch	/mirror/eudora/
	gmdzi.gmd.de	/mac/eudora/
	miki.cs.titech.ac.jp	/pub/Mac/eudora/

Software	Site	Pathname
USENET News		
News Transport		
B News	ftp.uu.net	/networking/news/transport/bnews-2.11/
	ftp.denet.dk	/mirror1/unix/news/transport/bnews-2.11/
	sparc01.cc.ncsu.edu	/mirrors/wustl/mirrors/news/transport/bnews-2.11/
	toklab.ics.es.osaka-u.ac.jp	/net/news/Bnews/
	ftp.germany.eu.net	/pub/news/bnews/
	mcsun.eu.net	/news/transport/bnews-2.11/
	unix.hensa.ac.uk	/pub/uunet/networking/news/transport/bnews-2.11
C News	ftp.uu.net	/networking/news/transport/cnews/
	munnari.oz.au	/pub/news/cnews/
	ftp.germany.eu.net	/pub/news/cnews/
	sparc01.cc.ncsu.edu	/mirrors/wustl/mirrors/news/transport/cnews/
	mcsun.eu.net	/news/transport/cnews/
INN	ftp.uu.net	/networking/news/transport/inn/
	grasp1.univ-lyon1.fr	/pub/unix/news/inn/
	munnari.oz.au	/pub/news/inn
	src.doc.ic.ac.uk	/computing/usenet/software/transport/inn/
nntpd	emx.cc.utexas.edu	/pub/mnt/source/news/nntp-1.5.11t/
	cs.tut.fi	/pub/src/mail_and_news/news-stuff/nntp.1.5.11/
	lth.se	/pub/network/nntp/nn-nntpd/
nntplink	src.doc.ic.ac.uk	/computing/usenet/software/transport/nntplink
News Readers		
gnus	ftp.uu.net	/networking/news/readers/gnus/
	agate.berkeley.edu	/pub/usenet/gnus-3.14.1.tar.Z
	plaza.aarnet.edu.au	/gnu/Local/gnus-3.14.1.tar.Z
	files1zrz.zrz.tu-berlin.de	/pub/unix/gnu/gnus-3.14.1.tar.Z
	akiu.gw.tohoku.ac.jp	/pub/net/news/gnus/
nn	ftp.uu.net	/networking/news/readers/nn/
nov	ftp.uu.net	/networking/news/transport/cnews/nov/
readnews	gatekeeper.dec.com	/.0/usenet/comp.sources.unix/volume1/readnews.1.Z
	uxc.cso.uiuc.edu	/usenet/c-news/rna/
	toklab.ics.es.osaka-u.ac.jp	/net/news/Bnews/src/readnews.c
rn	ftp.uu.net	/networking/news/readers/rn/
tin	ftp.uu.net	/networking/news/readers/tin/
	gumby.dsd.trw.com	/pub/news/newsreaders/tin/
	files1zrz.zrz.tu-berlin.de	/pub/news/tin
	walhalla.germany.eu.net	/pub/news/tin/
	brolga.cc.uq.oz.au	/comp.sources.misc/volume31/tin/
	isfs.kuis.kyoto-u.ac.jp	/net/tin/
trn	ftp.uu.net	/networking/news/readers/trn/
	archive.cis.ohio-state.edu	/pub/rn/trn/
	walhalla.germany.eu.net	/pub/news/trn/

Software	Site	Pathname
	mcsun.eu.net	/news/readers/trn/
	huon.itd.adelaide.edu.au	/pub/news/readers/trn/
	brolga.cc.uq.oz.au	/comp.sources.unix/volume25/trn/
	ftp.cfi.waseda.ac.jp	/pub/archive/comp.sources.unix/volume25/trn/
vn	kirk.bu.oz.au	/pub/net/news/vn/
	gatekeeper.dec.com	/.0/usenet/comp.sources.unix/volume13/vn.jan.8:
	walhalla.germany.eu.net	/pub/news/vn/
vnews	uhunix2.uhcc.hawaii.edu	/pub/vms/vnews/
	cs.utk.edu	/pub/vnews/

Software	Site	Pathname
Security		
Password Checkers		
crack	swdsrv.edvz.univie.ac.at	/unix/security/cert/tools/crack/
	huon.itd.adelaide.edu.au	/pub/security/cert/tools/crack/
	bode.ee.ualberta.ca	/pub/unix/SECURITY/
	files1zrz.zrz.tu-berlin.de	/pub/unix/crack/
	cert.sei.cmu.edu	/pub/tools/crack/
	arthur.cs.purdue.edu	/pub/pcert/tools/unix/crack/
npasswd	ftp.cc.utexas.edu	/pub/npasswd/
	guardian.cse.psu.edu	/pub/src/npasswd/
	huon.itd.adelaide.edu.au	/pub/security/misc/npasswd/
	csc2.anu.edu.au	/pub/security/npasswd/
	files1zrz.zrz.tu-berlin.de	/pub/unix/npasswd/
	inf.informatik.uni-stuttgart.de	/pub/archive/comp.sources/unix/npass
	ftp.cfi.waseda.ac.jp	/pub2/security/npasswd/
passwd+	dartvax.dartmouth.edu	/pub/security/
	arthur.cs.purdue.edu	/pub/pcert/tools/unix/
	urec.urec.fr	/pub/Securite/Unix/Logiciels/
	krynn.efd.lth.se	/pub/security/
	ftp.cfi.waseda.ac.jp	/pub2/security/passwd+/
	huon.itd.adelaide.edu.au	/pub/security/dartmouth/
	brolga.cc.uq.oz.au	/cert/tools/
cops	ftp.cert.org	/pub/tools/cops
	nic.sura.net	/pub/security/programs/unix/cops/
	swdsrv.edvz.univie.ac.at	/unix/security/cert/tools/cops/
	walhalla.germany.eu.net	/pub/sysadmin/cops/
	huon.itd.adelaide.edu.au	/pub/security/cert/tools/cops/
	csc2.anu.edu.au	/pub/security/cops/
	ftp.cfi.waseda.ac.jp	/pub2/security/cops/
tcpd	ftp.cert.org	/pub/tools/tcp_wrappers
	coombs.anu.edu.au	/pub/net/log/tcpd6.0.tar.Z

Software	Site	Pathname
Resource Discovery		
Alex	alex.sp.cs.cmu.edu	/src/alex.tar.Z
	nctuccca.edu.tw	/packages/alex/
	src.doc.ic.ac.uk	/computing/archiving/alex/
Prospero	gum.isi.edu	/nfs/pub/prospero/
	msun.eu.net	/misc/prospero/
	ftp.uni-kl.de	/pub1/packages/prospero/
	huon.itd.adelaide.edu.au	/pub/misc/prospero.tar.Z
WAIS		
WHOIS	charon.mit.edu	/pub/whois/
archie	ashley.cs.widener.edu	/pub/archie/
	cs.huji.ac.il	/pub/archie
	isfs.kuis.kyoto-u.ac.jp	/net/archie
	ftp.germany.eu.net	/pub/packages/archie
finger	archive.cis.ohio-state.edu	/n/archive/0/extra-ftp/gnu/finger/
	unr.edu	/pub/unix/finger/
	brolga.cc.uq.oz.au	/comp.sources.unix/volume25/finger/
	toklab.ics.es.osaka-u.ac.jp	/net/unix/v25/finger/
freeWAIS	ftp.cnidr.org	/pub/NIDR.tools/freeWAIS-0.2.tar.Z
netfind	bruno.cs.colorado.edu	/pub/cs/distribs/netfind/
	rye.cs.ucla.edu	/pub/netfind/
	nuri.inria.fr	/network/netfind/
	ftp.denet.dk	/pub/infosys/netfind/
Gopher	boombox.micro.umn.edu	/pub/gopher/
	nisc.jvnc.net	/pub/packages/gopher/
	files1zrz.zrz.tu-berlin.de	/pub/unix/infosystems/gopher/
	mcsun.eu.net	/misc/gopher/
	plaza.aarnet.edu.au	/gopher/
	isfs.kuis.kyoto-u.ac.jp	/net/gopher/
Gopher+	boombox.micro.umn.edu	/pub/unix/gopher2.09.tar.Z
gn Gopher	ftp.acns.nwu.edu	/pub/gn/gn-1.0beta.tar.Z
		/pub/gopher/Unix/gn/gn-1.0beta.tar.Z
NCSA Mosaic	zaphod.ncsa.uiuc.edu	/Web/xmosaic-binaries/
WWW	archive.cis.ohio-state.edu	/pub/www/
	dorm.rutgers.edu	/pub/www/
	swdsrv.edvz.univie.ac.at	/network/misc/www/
	nxoc1.cern.ch	/pub/www/
	brain.vifp.monash.edu.au	/pub/src/infosystems/www/
	isfs.kuis.kyoto-u.ac.jp	/net/WWW/

Software	Site	Pathname
Miscellaneous		
patch	boulder.colorado.edu	/pub/patch/
	wayback.cs.cornell.edu	/pub/patch/
	groper.jcu.edu.au	/pub/patch/
	files1zrz.zrz.tu-berlin.de	/pub/unix/tools/patch/
	ftp.uni-kl.de	/pub1/packages/gnu/patch/
	akiu.gw.tohoku.ac.jp	/pub/unix/patch/

References

Barron 1992.   Barron, Billy, "The Left Hand Doesn't Know What the Right Hand Is Doing," *Matrix News* **2**(4), pp. 5–6, MIDS (April 1992).

Deutsch 1991.   Deutsch, Peter, "On the Need to Develop Internet User Services," *Matrix News* **1**(4), p. 3, MIDS (July 1991).

Deutsch et al. 1992.   Deutsch, P., Emtage, A., & Heelan, B., "Archie: An Internet Electronic Directory Service," *ConneXions—The Interoperability Report* **6**(2), pp. 2–9, Interop, Inc. (February 1992).

APPENDIX D

Further Reading

Here is a selection of books for new members of the Internet community.

Introductory Internet user guides range from the short and inexpensive [LaQuey & Ryer 1992; Kehoe 1992] to the long and relatively comprehensive [Krol 1992; Kochmer & NorthWestNet 1993; Dern 1993], then on to a travelog [Malamud 1992] and sociology [Benedikt 1991; Harasim 1993].

A few books (other than this one) are about connecting to the Internet [Marine 1992; Estrada 1993], or the way the Internet community functions [Quarterman & Wilhelm 1993; Lynch & Rose 1993]. Some books cover more networks than just the Internet, from the quick desk reference [Frey & Adams 1992] to the comprehensive [Quarterman 1990].

Real-life social and legal issues are found as history [Levy 1984] in a dictionary [Raymond & Steele 1991] in a true spy novel [Stoll 1989] and in documentary reporting [Denning 1990; Hafner & Markoff 1991; Sterling 1992]. Certain fictional works have influenced the networks, and the reverse [Delany 1969; Vinge 1987; Brunner 1975; Gibson 1984; Stephenson 1993].

References

Benedikt 1991.   Benedikt, Michael ed., *Cyberspace: First Steps,* MIT Press, Cambridge, MA (1991).

Brunner 1975.   Brunner, John, *Shockwave Rider,* Ballantine Books, New York (1975).

Delany 1969.   Delany, Samuel R., *Nova,* Bantam (November 1969).

Denning 1990.   Denning, Peter J. ed., *Computers Under Attack: Intruders, Worms, and Viruses,* ACM Press/Addison-Wesley, Reading, MA (1990).

Dern 1993.   Dern, Daniel P., *The New User's Guide to the Internet,* McGraw-Hill, New York (1993).

Estrada 1993.   Estrada, Susan, *Connecting to the Internet: An O'Reilly Buyer's Guide,* O'Reilly & Associates, Sebastopol, CA (1993).

Frey & Adams 1992.   Frey, Donnalyn, & Adams, Rick, *!%@: A Directory of Electronic Mail Addressing and Networks,* O'Reilly & Associates, Sebastopol, CA (1992).

Gibson 1984.   Gibson, William, *Neuromancer,* Ace, New York (1984).

Hafner & Markoff 1991.   Hafner, Katie, & Markoff, John, *Cyberpunk,* Simon & Schuster, New York (1991).

Harasim 1993.   Harasim, Linda M. ed., *Global Networks: Computers and International Communication,* MIT Press, Cambridge, MA (1993).

Kehoe 1992.   Kehoe, Brendan P., *Zen and the Art of the Internet: A Beginner's Guide to the Internet.,* Prentice-Hall, Englewood Cliffs, NJ (July 1992).

Kochmer & NorthWestNet 1993.   Kochmer, Jonathan, & NorthWestNet, *The Internet Passport: NorthWestNet's Guide to Our World Online, 4th ed.,* NorthWestNet, Bellevue, WA (1993).

Krol 1992.   Krol, Ed, *The Whole Internet: Catalog & User's Guide,* O'Reilly & Associates, Inc., Sebastopol, CA (13 September 1992).

LaQuey & Ryer 1992.   LaQuey, Tracy, & Ryer, Jeanne C., *The Internet Companion: A Beginner's Guide to Global Networking,* Addison-Wesley, Reading, MA (October 1992).

Levy 1984.   Levy, Steven, *Hackers: Heroes of the Computer Revolution,* Anchor Press/Doubleday, Garden City, NY (1984).

Lynch & Rose 1993.   Lynch, Daniel C. ed., & Rose, Marshall T. ed., *The Internet System Handbook,* Addison-Wesley, Reading, MA (1993).

Malamud 1992.   Malamud, Carl, *Exploring the Internet: A Technical Travelogue,* Prentice-Hall, Englewood Cliffs, NJ (August 1992).

Marine 1992.   Marine, April, *Internet: Getting Started,* SRI International, Menlo Park, CA (September 1992).

Quarterman 1990.   Quarterman, John S., *The Matrix: Computer Networks and Conferencing Systems Worldwide,* Digital Press, Bedford, MA (1990).

Quarterman & Wilhelm 1993.   Quarterman, John S., & Wilhelm, Susanne, *UNIX, POSIX, and Open Systems: The Open Standards Puzzle,* Addison-Wesley, Reading, MA (1993).

Raymond & Steele 1991.   Raymond, Eric S. ed., & Steele, Guy, *The New Hacker's Dictionary,* MIT Press, Cambridge, MA (1991).

Stephenson 1993.   Stephenson, Neal, *Snow Crash,* Bantam Books; Spectra, New York (May 1993).

Sterling 1992.   Sterling, Bruce, *The Hacker Crackdown: Law and Disorder on the electronic frontier,* Bantam, New York (1992).

Stoll 1989.   Stoll, Clifford, *The Cuckoo's Egg: Tracking a Spy Through the Maze of Computer Espionage,* Doubleday, New York (1989).

Vinge 1987.   Vinge, Vernor, "True Names," in *True Names and Other Dangers*, Baen Books (Simon & Schuster), New York (1987).

Glossary

A (Address) DNS resource type that maps from a domain name to an IP address.

AARNET (Australian Academic and Research Network) The main national backbone network of Australia.

Acceptable Use Policy *See* AUP.

address A symbol (usually numeric) that uniquely identifies the interface of a host attached to a network.

Address *See* A.

Address Resolution Protocol *See* ARP.

Advanced Network and Services *See* ANS.

Advanced Research Projects Agency *See* ARPA.

AFS (Andrew File System) A transparent file access system from CMU and Transarc.

Alex A resource discovery protocol that caches anonymous FTP files locally and makes them available via NFS.

alias A name with special meaning to an MTA; often used for mailing lists.

Alias *See* Cname.

alt USENET top level newsgroup about almost anything.

American Telephone and Telegraph *See* AT&T.

Andrew File System *See* AFS.

anonymous The anonymous FTP username on MultiNet for VMS.

Anonymous FTP A form of FTP that allows any user to access a restricted set of files without authentication.

ANS (Advanced Network and Services) A national Internet provider.

archie   An Internet resource discovery protocol that finds files in anonymous FTP archives.

ARP (Address Resolution Protocol)   A protocol used to discover the datalink (often Ethernet) address corresponding to an IP address.

ARPA (Advanced Research Projects Agency)   The agency of the U.S. Department of Defense that funded the ARPANET and 4.2BSD.

article   A USENET news message.

AT&T (American Telephone and Telegraph)   The provider of InterNIC directory and database services.

AT&T Jens   AT&T's Japanese subsidiary.

AUP (Acceptable Use Policy)   A policy for the types of traffic allowed on a specific network.

Australian Academic and Research Network   *See* AARNET.

BARRNet (San Francisco Bay Area Regional Research Network)   A regional Internet provider in the San Francisco area.

base Gopher   The original implementation of the Gopher protocol.

Because It's Time Network   *See* BITNET.

Berkeley Internet Name Daemon   *See* BIND.

Berkeley mail   An early line-oriented mail user agent.

BIND (Berkeley Internet Name Daemon)   The most popular implementation of DNS for systems.

bionet   USENET top level newsgroup about biology.

bit   USENET top level newsgroup for gatewayed BITNET LISTSERV lists.

BITNET (Because It's Time Network)   A network formed in May 1981 to interconnect educational and research institutions; merged with CSNET in CREN in 1989.

biz   USENET top level newsgroup about business.

bridge   A device that forwards datalink layer frames.

California Education and Research Foundation   *See* CERF.

California Education and Research Foundation Network   *See* CERFnet.

Carnegie-Mellon University   *See* CMU.

CCITT (International Consultative Committee on Telegraphy and Telephony)   A committee for telecommunications standards.

CERF (California Education and Research Foundation)   A federation of California research and educational institutions.

CERFnet (California Education and Research Foundation Network)   A commercial Internet access provider based in San Diego.

CERT (Computer Emergency Response Team) A group charged with disseminating information about Internet security.

circuit switching A method of data communication whereby a communications path involving communications media, buffers, and other resources, is constructed between two entities that wish to communicate.

CIX (Commercial Internet Exchange) A cooperative organization of a variety of networks that range from regional to global in extent.

clari USENET top level newsgroup for ClariNet for-pay newsgroups.

ClariNet A for-pay news service using USENET newsgroups for distribution.

CMC (Computer Mediated Communication) Communication among people that is aided by computer systems.

CMU (Carnegie-Mellon University) A university with one of the leading Computer Science departments.

Cname (Alias) A DNS resource record that maps an alias domain name to its real domain name.

Commercial Internet Exchange *See* CIX.

COmmercial plus Research and Educational *See* CO+RE.

comp USENET top level newsgroup about computer science, software source, hardware and software systems.

Computer Emergency Response Team *See* CERT.

Computer Mediated Communication *See* CMC.

Computer Science Network *See* CSNET.

Computer Systems Research Group *See* CSRG.

Configure A configuration script for large software packages; used with trn.

connectionless protocol A protocol where the switching nodes of the network attempt to deliver the packet without any guarantees.

connection-oriented protocol A protocol that requires the setup of a complete path between two nodes before data can be exchanged.

CO+RE (COmmercial plus Research and Educational) A commercial Internet provider that is a subsidiary of ANS.

CoREN (Corporation for Regional and Enterprise Networking) A group of U.S. regional networks that have banded together to facilitate wide area interconnectivity to the Internet.

CREN (Corporation for Research and Education Networking) The organization that was the merger of BITNET and CSNET.

cron A UNIX program scheduler.

CSNET (Computer Science Network) A network established in 1981 to facilitate research in computer science and engineering; merged with BITNET in CREN in 1989; retired 1990.

CSRG (Computer Systems Research Group) The research group at the University of California at Berkeley that developed the 4.2BSD version of the UNIX operating system and later developed 4.3BSD and 4.4BSD.

ctlinnd The INN program that advises innd of parameter file status changes.

curses A software package for screen oriented use of ASCII character-cell terminals.

DARPA (Defense Advanced Research Projects Agency) A research agency of the U.S. Department of Defense.

datagram A discrete chunk of data with sufficient addressing information that it can be routed independently in an internetwork.

dbm A simple database format found on UNIX.

DCA (Defense Communications Agency) The early name of DISA.

Defense Advanced Research Projects Agency *See* DARPA.

Defense Communications Agency *See* DCA.

Defense Information Systems Agency *See* DISA.

Demon Internet Systems *See* DIS.

Department of Defense *See* DoD.

Department of Energy *See* DOE.

dig A debugging tool for DNS.

DIS (Demon Internet Systems) A CIX member in the United Kingdom.

DISA (Defense Information Systems Agency) The DoD agency that oversees the operation of the military portion of the Internet.

DNS (Domain Name System) The resource naming system of the Internet.

DNS Mail System All hosts that exchange mail using domain names.

DoD (Department of Defense) The U.S. Department of Defense.

DOE (Department of Energy) The U.S. Department of Energy.

domain name A unique identifier for a single node in the DNS naming tree.

Domain Name System *See* DNS.

duplicate A news article that a news systems recognizes as having seen before and rejects.

EARN (European Academic and Research Network) The European academic community NJE network; equivalent to BITNET in the United States.

EC (European Commission) The council of the European Community.

EInet (Enterprise Integration Network) A project of MCC.

electronic mail *See* email.

elm A screen-oriented mail user agent.

Emacs A text editor.

e-mail A short name for electronic mail.

email (electronic mail)   A computer network service that provides one-to-one communications by the exchange of asynchronous messages.

Enterprise Integration Network   *See* EInet.

enterprise IP network   A TCP/IP network inside a corporation that is used for the business of the corporation.

/etc/rc.local   A common name for the main UNIX system startup local configuration script.

EUnet (European UNIX network)   A European UUCP and IP network connectivity provider.

European Academic and Research Network   *See* EARN.

European Commission   *See* EC.

European UNIX network   *See* EUnet.

expire   A USENET news maintenance program that deletes old news articles.

expireover   The program that expires articles from the news overview database. *See* nov.

Federal Networking Council   *See* FNC.

Fido   The protocol suite used by FidoNet.

FidoNet   A mostly dialup network of mostly DOS machines that use the FidoNet protocols.

File Transfer Protocol   *See* FTP.

finger   A simple protocol for obtaining information about users on the Internet.

FIRST (Forum of Incident Response and Security Teams)   A coordinating body for incident response and security teams. *See* CERT.

FNC (Federal Networking Council)   A council that coordinates networking activity among U.S. Federal agencies.

Forum of Incident Response and Security Teams   *See* FIRST.

forward domain   The DNS domain that maps from a domain name to principally IP addresses.

forward zone database   The database that contains information pricipally about domain name to IP address mappings.

4.2BSD (Fourth.2 Berkeley Software Distribution)   A popular implementation of the UNIX operating system with full TCP/IP networking support.

FQDN (fully qualified domain name)   A domain name that completely traverses the path from a node in the DNS tree to the root of the tree.

Free Software Foundation   *See* FSF.

freeWAIS   A freeware implementation of the WAIS system.

FSF (Free Software Foundation)   A nonprofit foundation that coordinates writing and distribution of free software.

ftp   The anonymous FTP username on most UNIX systems.

FTP (File Transfer Protocol)   The remote file transfer protocol in the TCP/IP suite.

ftpd   The name of the FTP server process on most UNIX systems.

fully qualified domain name   *See* FQDN.

gateway   A generic term for a machine or software that transfers data between two entities at different layers in a protocol stack.

GIX (Global Internet Exchange)   A proposal (not yet implemented) for routing exchange in the Internet for international traffic.

gn   A reimplementation of a Gopher server.

gnu   USENET top level newsgroup about GNU.

GNU (GNU's Not UNIX)   A free software collection.

gnus   A USENET interface that works within Emacs.

GNU's Not UNIX   *See* GNU.

Gopher+   A set of extensions to the base Gopher protocol.

Gopher   A menu-oriented Internet resource discovery protocol.

handle   A unique identifier used in NIC databases.

High Performance Computing Act   *See* HPCA.

HKS (Hong Kong Supernet)   An Internet provider in Hong Kong.

host   A computer system used for application processing on a network.

HPCA (High Performance Computing Act)   The U.S government act that authorized the NREN.

IAB (Internet Activities Board)   The old name of the IAB.

IAB (Internet Architecture Board)   The technical policy board of the Internet.

IAB Standards Process   The process that produces Internet Standards.

IESG (Internet Engineering Steering Group)   The coordinating body for the IETF.

IETF (Internet Engineering Task Force)   The IAB committee that oversees the development and deployment of TCP/IP protocols.

IIJ (Internet Initiative Japan)   An Internet provider in Japan.

IIKK (InterCon International, KK)   An Internet provider in Japan.

inet   A news distribution used to explicitly carry articles over the Internet.

inetd   A super server that efficiently multiplexes many network services.

inews   The USENET B news master database manager program.

info   A top level newsgroup for gatewayed mailing lists.

INN (InterNet News)   A recent implementation of USENET news, intended for use over TCP/IP in the Internet.

innd   The INN news server daemon.

innxmit   An NNTP transmission program that comes with INN.

InterCon International, KK   *See* IIKK.

Inter-Exchange Carriers   *See* IXCs.

International Consultative Committee on Telegraphy and Telephony   *See* CCITT.

International Organization for Standardization   *See* ISO.

internet   A collection of networks perhaps using different underlying network technology, but all tied into a virtual network by use of an internet protocol that provides a common address space and routing.

on the Internet   A host that has direct IP connectivity to any well-known Internet host.

the Internet   The worldwide interconnected collection of networks that predominantly use the TCP/IP protocol suite.

Internet Activities Board   *See* IAB.

Internet Architecture Board   *See* IAB.

Internet Engineering Steering Group   *See* IESG.

Internet Engineering Task Force   *See* IETF.

Internet Initiative Japan   *See* IIJ.

Internet Mail System   Another name for the DNS mail system.

InterNet News   *See* INN.

Internet Protocol   *See* IP.

Internet Registry   *See* IR.

Internet Relay Chat   *See* IRC.

Internet Research Steering Group   *See* IRSG.

Internet Research Task Force   *See* IRTF.

Internet Society   *See* ISOC.

Internet Standards   Protocol specifications produced by the IAB Standards Process.

InterNIC   A NIC service sponsored by the U.S. National Science Foundation (NSF) to provide and coordinate services for the NSFNET community (and by default to the Internet at large).

IP (Internet Protocol)   The single protocol at the Internet Layer of the TCP/IP protocol model.

IR (Internet Registry)   A registry for IP numbers. InterNIC is the global IR; the RIPE NCC is the European regional IR; there are local IRs for many countries; and many Internet connectivity providers are also local IRs.

IRC (Internet Relay Chat)   A protocol that allows multiple users to interactively participate in a discussion simultaneously.

IRSG (Internet Research Steering Group)   The coordinating body for the IRTF.

IRTF (Internet Research Task Force)   The IAB committee that coordinates Internet research activities.

ISO (International Organization for Standardization)   The international standards body.

ISOC (Internet Society)   A nonprofit professional society that houses the IAB.

IXCs (Inter-Exchange Carriers)   Long-distance telephone companies.

JAIN (Japan Academic Inter-university Network)   A research and academic network in Japan.

Japan UNIX Network   *See* JUNET.

John von Neuman Computer Center Network   *See* JvNCNet.

JUNET (Japan UNIX Network)   A research and academic network in Japan.

JvNCNet (John von Neuman Computer Center Network)   An Internet provider in the Northeastern U.S.

link   A communication path between two network nodes.

list   The NNTP command that lists active newsgroups.

mail   The common name for electronic mail.

Mail Exchanger   *See* MX.

mail forwarder   A host responsible for forwarding mail for a domain from the Internet to some other network.

Mail User's Shell   *See* MUSH.

mailbox   A repository for incoming electronic mail.

mailer   Another name for an MTA.

mailing list   A list of electronic mail addresses, accessed by mail to a single alias.

mailx   A variant of Berkeley mail found on System V UNIX systems.

makegroup   The INN script for creating a newsgroup.

makehistory   The INN command that makes a blank history file.

Martian packets   An IP packet from an unregistered network number.

in the Matrix   A host that can exchange electronic mail with a host in the Matrix.

the Matrix   All computer networks that exchange electronic mail.

MCC (Microelectronics and Computer Corporation)   The consortium that is promoting EInet.

message transfer agent   *See* MTA.

MFS (Metropolitan Fiber Systems)   A provider of 100Mbps wide area IP service.

MH   An older line-oriented mail user agent that uses the UNIX shell as its user interface.

Microelectronics and Computer Corporation   *See* MCC.

MIME (Multipurpose Internet Mail Extensions)   Extensions to Internet electronic mail that permit sending non-ASCII documents over a 7-bit ASCII channel by using specific encoding standards.

misc   USENET top level newsgroup about topics that don't fit elsewhere.

moderated   A USENET newsgroup or an electronic mailing list is moderated if a specific person is responsible for deciding what gets posted on it.

moderator   The person who controls postings to a USENET newsgroup or an electronic mailing list.

MTA (message transfer agent)   A program that transfers mail to and from another computer on a network.

mthreads   The program trn originally used to keep track of threads of conversation in news articles. *See also* nov.

Multipurpose Internet Mail Extensions   *See* MIME.

MUSH (Mail User's Shell)   A screen-oriented enhanced version of Berkeley mail.

MX (Mail Exchanger)   A DNS resource record that maps a domain name to a mail gateway host.

nameless host   A host with an IP address, but no corresponding domain name.

Nameserver   *See* NS.

NASA (National Aeronautics and Space Agency)   Agency that funded one of the early Internet backbone networks.

National Center for Supercomputing Applications   *See* NCSA.

National Information Infrastructure   *See* NII.

National Institutes of Health   *See* NIH.

National Research and Education Network   *See* NREN.

National Science Foundation   *See* NSF.

NCC (Network Coordination Center)   The regional Internet Registry for Europe.

NCSA (National Center for Supercomputing Applications)   The creator of the WWW client interface called Mosaic.

NCSA Mosaic   A WWW client implementation.

NEARnet (New England Academic and Research network)   An Internet provider in the New England part of the U.S.

netfind   A protocol for obtaining information about Internet users.

Network Coordination Center   *See* NCC.

Network File System   *See* NFS.

Network Information Center   *See* NIC.

Network Information Service   *See* NIS.

Network Job Entry   *See* NJE.

Network News Reading Protocol   *See* NNRP.

Network News Transfer Protocol   *See* NNTP.

Network Solutions, Inc   *See* NSI.

New England Academic and Research network   *See* NEARnet.

newgroup   The USENET protocol command for creating a newsgroup on multiple systems.

A news   The first implementation of USENET news; now long obsolete.

B news   A series of intermediate implementations of USENET news.

C news   A complete rewrite of USENET news.

news   A UNIX system group for administrative convenience in installing and maintaining USENET news software.

news   A UNIX user to own news article database and administrative files.

news   USENET top level newsgroup about the news network and its software.

news overview   *See* nov.

news.daily   The INN script that performs daily automatic news administration and provides a daily summary of news activity.

newsgroup   A USENET news discussion topic.

news.newsgroups   A USENET newsgroup used to coordinate voting on new newsgroups.

NFS (Network File System)   A transparent file access system from Sun Microsystems.

NIC (Network Information Center)   An organization or service that provides information about networks.

NIH (National Institutes of Health)   A participant in the FNC.

NII (National Information Infrastructure)   A proposed commercially-supported U.S. national networking infrastructure.

NIS (Network Information Service)   A resource mapping protocol developed by Sun Microsystems.

NJE (Network Job Entry)   The remote job entry protocol used on the IBM VM/370 operating system. It was the original underlying transport protocol used by BITNET. *See also* RSCS.

nn   A visual USENET news interface.

NNRP (Network News Reading Protocol)   A portion of NNTP that allows an individual user to read news articles from a remote server.

nnrpd   The INN NNRP (news reading part of NNTP) server daemon.

NNTP (Network News Transfer Protocol)   The standard protocol for transporting USENET News articles over TCP/IP.

nntplink   A program for fast transmission of USENET news articles using NNTP over the Internet.

node   Any computer attached to a network.

non-service provider   An organization that handles IP number registration requests from other organizations that have no Internet connections.

NorthWestNet   An Internet provider in the Northwestern U.S.

nov (news overview)   A software package that keeps track of threads of conversation in news articles for use by various news readers.

NREN (National Research and Education Network)   The follow on network to NSFNET.

NS (Nameserver)   A DNS resource record that maps a domain name to the nameserver that serves that domain.

NSF (National Science Foundation)   The U.S. agency that took over funding of the major U.S. Internet backbone, NSFNET. Also seed-funded a number of regional networks that all tied into the backbone network.

NSFNET   The backbone network funded by the National Science Foundation.

NSI (Network Solutions, Inc.)   The provider of InterNIC registration services.

nslookup   A DNS debugging tool.

OBS (Online BookStore)   An electronic bookstore run by Editorial, Inc. and Texas Internet Consulting.

OSI (Open Systems Interconnection)   The basic reference model for the ISO networking protocols.

overchan   A program that enters articles in the news overview database. *See* nov.

packet   A discrete chunk of data, usually no more than a few thousand bytes long. Each packet is self-contained and holds all the information required to send it to its final destination. *See also* packet switching.

packet switching   A method of data communication where one entity divides data sent to another entity into discrete chunks or packets, and each packet travels to its destination independently of all other packets.

patch   A program that applies difference listings to source files in order to patch bugs.

path   The route taken by a data packet through a network.

PDNs (Public Data Networks)   Networks intended to provide host-to-host connectivity for remote login, often using X.25.

Pine   A screen-oriented mail user agent.

Pipex   A CIX member in the United Kingdom.

Pnews   The trn news posting program.

point of presence   *See* PoP.

Pointer *See* PTR.

Point-to-Point Protocol *See* PPP.

PoP (point of presence) An Internet providers local attachment point.

POP (Post Office Protocol) A protocol that allows mail to be retrieved from a mailbox on a remote server.

Post, Telephone, and Telegraph *See* PTT.

PPP (Point-to-Point Protocol) A standard datalink protocol that allows the encapsulation of multiple higher layer protocols over the same point-to-point interface.

Prospero A resource discovery protocol that allows transparent access to anonymous FTP archives.

protocol stack A selection of protocols from a protocol suite that supports a specific application.

protocol suite The entire set of protocols that are a part of a protocol model.

PTR (Pointer) A DNS resource record that maps a domain back to another domain.

PTT (Post, Telephone, and Telegraph) A national monopoly telephone company, or a similar company of national scale.

Public Data Networks *See* PDNs.

RARE (Reseaux Associés pour la Recerche Européenne) Associated European Research Networks, a coordinating body for European networking.

RCP (Remote Copy Protocol) A remote file copying protocol for a network of UNIX systems.

readnews An old line-oriented USENET news interface.

rec USENET top level newsgroup about recreational activities.

reference model A common model for talking about how the components of a complex system fit together.

relaynews The USENET C news master database manager program.

Remote Copy Protocol *See* RCP.

Remote Login Protocol *See* RLOGIN.

Remote Spooling Communications Subsystem *See* RSCS.

repeater A device that forwards physical layer signals.

Request for Comment *See* RFC.

Reseaux Associés pour la Recerche Européenne *See* RARE.

Reseaux IP Européens *See* RIPE.

resolver A set of routines that lets an application program send queries to a DNS server.

resource record A record in a DNS database that defines the type and value of a domain name resource.

Resource sharing Remote access to resources like supercomputers and file servers through a network.

reverse domain The DNS domain that maps from an IP addres to a domain name.

reverse zone database DNS database that contains resource records that point an IP address back to its associated domain.

RFC (Request for Comment) A document published by the IAB.

RIPE (Reseaux IP Européens) The coordinating body for Internet activity in Europe.

RLOGIN (Remote Login Protocol) A virtual terminal protocol specific to UNIX systems.

rn A visual USENET news interface.

root node The top-most node of the DNS hierarchy.

route Same as a path. Also used as a verb to describe what a router does.

router A computer dedicated to routing packets.

Royal Signals and Radar Establishment *See* RSRE.

RSCS (Remote Spooling Communications Subsystem) The most common implementation of NJE.

RSRE (Royal Signals and Radar Establishment) The research organization in the U.K. that developed an early implementation of the TCP retransmission algorithm.

San Francisco Bay Area Regional Research Network *See* BARRNet.

sci USENET top level newsgroup for technical discussions about sciences.

secondary nameserver A DNS nameserver that copies authoritative information for a DNS zone and becomes an authoritative copy of that zone.

sendmail The most common UNIX electronic mail message transfer agent.

Serial Line IP *See* SLIP.

server A process that offers a service to a client process, or an entire machine that offers a specific service, such as filesharing.

service provider An organization that provides Internet connectivity and handles IP number registration requests.

SGML (Simplified Generic Markup Language) A standard method of specifying keywords and other features of a document.

Simple Mail Transfer Protocol *See* SMTP.

Simplified Generic Markup Language *See* SGML.

SLIP (Serial Line IP) A standard protocol for encapsulating IP packets over low-speed serial interfaces.

SMI (Sun Microsystems, Inc.) A vendor of popular UNIX workstations.

SMTP (Simple Mail Transfer Protocol)   The Internet standard protocol for moving mail messages from one host to another.

SOA (Start of Authority)   The DNS resource record that defines where a new zone starts.

soc   USENET top level newsgroup about social issues and socializing.

SPIN   Name under which AT&T Jens is providing Internet service in Japan.

SprintLink   A commercial Internet provider.

Start of Authority   *See* SOA.

subdomains   The descendants of any node in the DNS hierarchy.

Sun Microsystems, Inc   *See* SMI.

swais   A screen-oriented cient interface to the WAIS system.

syslog   The UNIX system logger.

talk   USENET top level newsgroup for debates and lengthy discussions.

TCP (Transmission Control Protocol)   The reliable two-way byte stream protocol in the TCP/IP protocol suite.

TCP/IP (Transmission Control Protocol / Internet Protocol)   The name of the protocol suite that is the dominant protocol in the worldwide Internet.

TELNET (Virtual Terminal Protocol)   The remote virtual terminal protocol in the TCP/IP suite.

templates   Registration forms.

Texas Higher Education network   *See* THEnet.

TFA (Transparent File Access)   Filesystem protocols that access files from remote servers and make them appear local to the end-user application.

TFTP (Trivial File Transfer Protocol)   A very simple file transfer protocol with minimal authentication.

THEnet (Texas Higher Education network)   A research and educational Internet provider in Texas.

ticket   In the Kerberos authentication system, an encrypted message that authenticates the identity of the client.

tin   A visual USENET news interface.

TISN (Todai International Science Network)   A research and academic backbone network in Japan.

to   A top level newsgroup for testing news links.

Todai International Science Network   *See* TISN.

top-level domains   The domains that are the immediate descendants of the root node in the DNS tree.

translator   A device that translates from one transport protocol to another.

Transmission Control Protocol   *See* TCP.

Transmission Control Protocol / Internet Protocol   *See* TCP/IP.

Transparent File Access   *See* TFA.

transport protocols   A protocol that guarantees certain features about the transport of data.

Trivial File Transfer Protocol   *See* TFTP.

trn   A visual USENET news interface with explicit threads of conversation.

UA (user agent)   A program used to compose, send, read, file, and retrieve mail messages.

UCB (University of California at Berkeley)   The university that developed the 4.2BSD version of the UNIX operating system that incorporated full TCP/IP support.

UDP (User Datagram Protocol)   An unrelaible packet oriented protocol where ordering or delivery is not guaranteed.

UNIX Seventh Edition   An early version of the UNIX operating system first distributed in the late 1970s.

UNIX to UNIX CoPy   *See* UUCP.

UniPalm Ltd   The operator of Pipex in the United Kingdom.

University of California at Berkeley   *See* UCB.

U.S. Sprint   Operator of SprintLink.

usenet   Mail address for USENET news error mail, newsgroup creation requests, etc.

USENET (Users' Network)   All computers that carry USENET news, which is a distributed conferencing system.

USENET news   The many-to-many conferencing system of USENET.

user agent   *See* UA.

User Datagram Protocol   *See* UDP.

Users' Network   *See* USENET.

/usr/local/etc/rc.news   The INN startup script.

UUCP (UNIX to UNIX CoPy)   A store and forward protocol used to link together UNIX systems over low-speed serial lines.

UUCP mail network   A mostly dialup, mostly UNIX network that uses the UUCP protocols.

Veronica   A resource discovery protocol that allows indexed searchs across many Gopher servers.

virtual circuit   A connection established between two nodes in an internetwork. Differs from traditional circuit switching in that the connection is not physically established, and may instead be created on top of a packet switched network.

Virtual Terminal Protocol   *See* TELNET.

vn   A visual USENET news interface.

vnews   An early visual USENET news interface.

WAIS (Wide Area Information Servers)   A distributed client/server protocol and implementations for searches of documents, with or without prior keyword markup.

WAIS-8-b5   An old, freeware version of the WAIS system.

waisindex   The WAIS command to generate indexes.

waissearch   A line-oriented interface to the WAIS system.

waisserver   The server process in the freeWAIS distribution.

WGs (Working Groups)   Groups of people that produce specifications.

WIDE (Widely Integrated Distributed Environment)   A research and academic backbone network in Japan.

Wide Area Information Servers   *See* WAIS.

Widely Integrated Distributed Environment   *See* WIDE.

Working Groups   *See* WGs.

World dot Net   An Internet provider.

WWW (World Wide Web)   A hypertext-based resource discovery protocol.

X Window System   A portable windowed user interface for bit-mapped displays.

X.500   The ISO-OSI Directory and Naming Service.

xover   The NNTP extension that news readers use to access the news overview database. *See* nov.

xrn   A variant of rn for use with the X Window System.

Xwais   The WAIS client for use with the X Window System.

zone   A subtree of the DNS naming tree where all nodes are under the same naming authority.

zone database   The DNS database that contains resource records for a zone.

Index

4.2BSD (Fourth.2 Berkeley Software
     Distribution), **26**

A

A (Address), **85**
A news, 126
AARNET (Australian Academic and
     Research Network), **54**
Acceptable Use Policy (AUP), **55**
active, 136
address, 22
Address Resolution Protocol (ARP), **76**
Advanced Research Projects Agency
     (ARPA), **19**
AFS (Andrew File System), **12**, 166
Alex, 14, 166
alias, 8
Alias (Cname), **86**
alt, 123, 139
American National Standard (ANS), **35**
American Telephone and Telegraph
     (AT&T), **67**
Andrew File System (AFS), **12**, 166
anonymous, 167
anonymous FTP, 11, 65, 166, 241
ANS (American National Standard), **35**
archie, 14, 166, 241
ARP (Address Resolution Protocol), **76**
ARPA (Advanced Research Projects
     Agency), **19**
article, 9

AT&T (American Telephone and
     Telegraph), **67**
AT&T Jens, 55
AUP (Acceptable Use Policy), **55**
Australian Academic and Research Network
     (AARNET), **54**

B

B news, 126
BARRNet (San Francisco Bay Area
     Regional Research Network), **35**
base Gopher, 175
Because It's Time Network (BITNET), **28**
Berkeley Internet Name Daemon (BIND),
     89
Berkeley mail, 116
BIND (Berkeley Internet Name Daemon),
     89
bionet, 123
bit, 123
BITNET (Because It's Time Network), **28**
biz, 123
bridge, 154

C

C news, 126
California Education and Research
     Foundation (CERF), **35**
California Education and Research
     Foundation Network (CERFnet), **67**

Carnegie-Mellon University (CMU), **12**
CCITT (International Consultative
    Committee on Telegraphy and
    Telephony), **43**
CERF (California Education and Research
    Foundation), **35**
CERFnet (California Education and
    Research Foundation Network), **67**
CERT (Computer Emergency Response
    Team), **145**, 168
CIAC, 168
circuit switching, 20
CIX (Commercial Internet Exchange), **35**,
    53, 183
clari, 123
ClariNet, 123
Clearinghouse for Networked Information
    Discovery and Retrieval (CNIDR), **171**
CMC (Computer Mediated
    Communication), **7**
CMU (Carnegie-Mellon University), **12**
Cname (Alias), **86**
CNIDR (Clearinghouse for Networked
    Information Discovery and Retrieval),
    171
CO (COmmercial plus Research and
    Educational), **35**
Commercial Internet Exchange (CIX), **35**,
    53, 183
comp, 122–123
Computer Emergency Response Team
    (CERT), **145**, 168
Computer Mediated Communication
    (CMC), **7**
Computer Science Network (CSNET), **28**
Computer Systems Research Group
    (CSRG), **26**
Configure, 134–135
connectionless protocol, 23
connection-oriented protocol, 22–23
CoREN (Corporation for Regional and
    Enterprise Networking), **36**, 54
Corporation for Regional and Enterprise
    Networking (CoREN), **36**, 54
Corporation for Research and Education
    Networking (CREN), **28**
CREN (Corporation for Research and
    Education Networking), **28**
cron, 138
CSNET (Computer Science Network), **28**

CSRG (Computer Systems Research
    Group), **26**
ctlinnd, 136, 139–140
curses, 127

D

DARPA (Defense Advanced Research
    Projects Agency), **25**
datagram, 23
dbm, 136
DCA (Defense Communications Agency),
    26
Defense Advanced Research Projects
    Agency (DARPA), **25**
Defense Communications Agency (DCA),
    26
Defense Information Systems Agency
    (DISA), **26**
Demon Internet Systems (DIS), **35**
Department of Defense (DoD), **19**
Department of Energy (DOE), **32**
dig, 96
DIS (Demon Internet Systems), **35**
DISA (Defense Information Systems
    Agency), **26**
DNS (Domain Name System), **5**, 15, 29, 81
DNS Mail System, 29
DoD (Department of Defense), **19**
DOE (Department of Energy), **32**
domain name, 81
Domain Name System (DNS), **5**, 15, 29, 81
duplicate, 125

E

EARN (European Academic and Research
    Network), **28**
EBONE (European Backbone), **32**, 55
EC (European Commission), **32**
EInet (Enterprise Integration Network), **36**
electronic mail (email), **7**
elm, 116
Emacs, 127
e-mail, 7
email (electronic mail), **7**
Enterprise Integration Network (EInet), **36**
enterprise IP network, 31
/etc/rc.local, 131
EUnet (European UNIX network), **35**, 55

European Academic and Research Network (EARN), **28**
European Backbone (EBONE), **32**, 55
European Commission (EC), **32**
European UNIX network (EUnet), **35**, 55
expire, 126, 138–139
expireover, 135

F

Federal Networking Council (FNC), **32**
Fido, 29
FidoNet, 29
File Transfer Protocol (FTP), **10**, 11
finger, 163
FIRST (Forum of Incident Response and Security Teams), **234**
FNC (Federal Networking Council), **32**
Forum of Incident Response and Security Teams (FIRST), **234**
forward domain, 60
forward zone database, 84
Fourth.2 Berkeley Software Distribution (4.2BSD), **26**
FQDN (fully qualified domain name), **81**, 111
Free Software Foundation (FSF), **123**
freeWAIS, 171
FSF (Free Software Foundation), **123**
ftp, 167–168
FTP (File Transfer Protocol), **10**, 11
ftpd, 168
fully qualified domain name (FQDN), **81**, 111

G

gateway, 154
GIX (Global Internet Exchange), **36**
Global Internet Exchange (GIX), **36**
gn, 175
gnu, 123
GNU (GNU's Not UNIX), **123**
gnus, 127
Gopher, 15, 175

H

handle, 64
High Performance Computing Act (HPCA), **34**

history, 136
HKS (Hong Kong Supernet), **35**
Hong Kong Supernet (HKS), **35**
host, 21
HPCA (High Performance Computing Act), **34**

I

IAB (Internet Architecture Board), **32**
IAB Standards Process, 34
IESG (Internet Engineering Steering Group), **34**
IETF (Internet Engineering Task Force), **32**
IIJ (Internet Initiative Japan), **55**
IIKK (InterCon International, KK), **55**
inet, 124
inetd, 147, 167, 172, 177
inews, 126
info, 138
INN (InterNet News), 119, **126**
innd, 126
    and checking it out, 140
    and emergencies, 139
    and INN architecture, 129
    and news administration, 136
    and news implementations, 126
    and news user agents, 127
innxmit, 125
InterCon International, KK (IIKK), **55**
Inter-Exchange Carriers (IXCs), **43**
International Consultative Committee on Telegraphy and Telephony (CCITT), **43**
International Organization for Standardization (ISO), **23**, 43
internet, 25
on the Internet, 31, 41
the Internet, 25
Internet Architecture Board (IAB), **32**
Internet Engineering Steering Group (IESG), **34**
Internet Engineering Task Force (IETF), **32**
Internet Initiative Japan (IIJ), **55**
Internet Mail System, 30
InterNet News (INN), 119, **126**
Internet Protocol (IP), **24**, 44
Internet Registry (IR), **64**
Internet Relay Chat (IRC), **10**
Internet Research Steering Group (IRSG), **34**

Internet Research Task Force (IRTF), **34**
Internet Society (ISOC), **32**
Internet Standards, 34
InterNIC, 67
IP (Internet Protocol), **24**, 44
IR (Internet Registry), **64**
IRC (Internet Relay Chat), **10**
IRSG (Internet Research Steering Group), **34**
IRTF (Internet Research Task Force), **34**
ISO (International Organization for Standardization), **23**, 43
ISOC (Internet Society), **32**
IXCs (Inter-Exchange Carriers), **43**

J

JAIN (Japan Academic Inter-university Network), **55**
Japan Academic Inter-university Network (JAIN), **55**
Japan UNIX Network (JUNET), **55**
John von Neuman Computer Center Network (JvNCNet), **35**
JUNET (Japan UNIX Network), **55**
JvNCNet (John von Neuman Computer Center Network), **35**

K

Kermit, 56

L

link, 21
list, 136

M

mail, 7, 116
Mail Exchanger (MX), **85**, 103
mail forwarder, 29
Mail User's Shell (MUSH), **116**
mailbox, 8, 99
mailer, 8
mailing list, 8
mailx, 116
makegroup, 139
makehistory, 136

Martian packets, 59
in the Matrix, 31, 40
the Matrix, 30
MCC (Microelectronics and Computer Corporation), **36**
message transfer agent (MTA), **8**, 99
Metropolitan Fiber Systems (MFS), **54**
MFS (Metropolitan Fiber Systems), **54**
MH, 117
Microelectronics and Computer Corporation (MCC), **36**
MIME (Multipurpose Internet Mail Extensions), **8**, 115
misc, 123
moderated, 122
moderator, 122
MTA (message transfer agent), **8**, 99
mthreads, 135
Multipurpose Internet Mail Extensions (MIME), **8**, 115
MUSH (Mail User's Shell), **116**
MX (Mail Exchanger), **85**, 103

N

nameless host, 59
Nameserver (NS), **85**
NASA (National Aeronautics and Space Agency), **26**, 32
National Aeronautics and Space Agency (NASA), **26**, 32
National Center for Supercomputing Applications (NCSA), **179**
National Information Infrastructure (NII), **36**
National Institutes of Health (NIH), **32**
National Research and Education Network · (NREN), **34**
National Science Foundation (NSF), **27**, 32
NCC (Network Coordination Center), **64**
NCSA (National Center for Supercomputing Applications), **179**
NCSA Mosaic, 179
NEARnet (New England Academic and Research network), **35**
netfind, 164–165
Network Coordination Center (NCC), **64**
Network File System (NFS), **12**, 166
Network Information Center (NIC), **67**
Network Information Service (NIS), **16**
Network Job Entry (NJE), **28**

Network News Reading Protocol (NNRP), **125**
Network News Transfer Protocol (NNTP), **10**, 124
Network Solutions, Inc. (NSI), **67**
New England Academic and Research network (NEARnet), **35**
newgroup, 139–140
news, 123, 130, 138
news overview (nov), **135**
news.daily, 139
newsgroup, 9–10, 122
news.newsgroups, 123
NFS (Network File System), **12**, 166
NIC (Network Information Center), **67**
NIH (National Institutes of Health), **32**
NII (National Information Infrastructure), **36**
NIS (Network Information Service), **16**
NJE (Network Job Entry), **28**
nn, 127
NNRP (Network News Reading Protocol), **125**
nnrpd, 125, 129, 137
NNTP (Network News Transfer Protocol), **10**, 124
nntpd, 125, 133
nntplink, 119, 125, 133, 138
node, 22
non-service provider, 62
NorthWestNet, 35
nov (news overview), **135**
NREN (National Research and Education Network), **34**
NS (Nameserver), **85**
NSF (National Science Foundation), **27**, 32
NSFNET, 27
NSI (Network Solutions, Inc.), **67**
nslookup, 96

O

OBS (Online BookStore), **180**
Online BookStore (OBS), **180**
Open Systems Interconnection (OSI), **23**, 43
OSI (Open Systems Interconnection), **23**, 43
overchan, 135

P

packet, 21

packet switching, 21
patch, 134
path, 22
PDNs (Public Data Networks), **43**
Performance Systems International (PSI), **35**
Pine, 116
Pipex, 35
Pnews, 135, 140
point of presence (PoP), **73**, **184**
Pointer (PTR), **87**
points of presence (PoP), **47**
Point-to-Point Protocol (PPP), **43**, 78
PoP (point of presence), **73**, **184**
PoP (points of presence), **47**
POP (Post Office Protocol), **113**
Post Office Protocol (POP), **113**
Post, Telephone, and Telegraph (PTT), **43**
PPP (Point-to-Point Protocol), **43**, 78
Prospero, 14, 166
protocol stack, 45
protocol suite, 45
PSI (Performance Systems International), **35**
PTR (Pointer), **87**
PTT (Post, Telephone, and Telegraph), **43**
Public Data Networks (PDNs), **43**

R

RARE (Reseaux Associés pour la Recerche Européenne), **32**
RCP (Remote Copy Protocol), **12**
readnews, 127
rec, 123
reference model, 42
relaynews, 126
Remote Copy Protocol (RCP), **12**
Remote Login Protocol (RLOGIN), **12**
Remote Spooling Communications Subsystem (RSCS), **28**
repeater, 154
Request for Comments (RFC), **34**
Reseaux Associés pour la Recerche Européenne (RARE), **32**
Reseaux IP Européens (RIPE), **32**, 64
resolver, 90
resource record, 83
Resource sharing, 10
reverse domain, 60
reverse zone database, 86
RFC (Request for Comments), **34**

RIPE (Reseaux IP Européens), **32**, 64
RLOGIN (Remote Login Protocol), **12**
rn, 127
root node, 82
route, 22
router, 21, 154
Royal Signals and Radar Establishment
   (RSRE), **26**
RSCS (Remote Spooling Communications
   Subsystem), **28**
RSRE (Royal Signals and Radar
   Establishment), **26**

S

San Francisco Bay Area Regional Research
   Network (BARRNet), **35**
sci, 123
secondary nameserver, 91
sendmail, 99
   and aliasing, 106
   and example mail system, 104
   and gateway configuration, 110–111
   and gatewaying mail, 108
   and header address rewriting, 106
   and mail routing, 105
   and news implementations, 126
   and the post office protocol, 113
   and sendmail basics, 104–105
   and site mail addressing, 107
sendmail.cf, 104
Serial Line IP (SLIP), **78**
server, 22
service provider, 62
SGML (Simplified Generic Markup
   Language), **15**
Simple Mail Transfer Protocol (SMTP), **8**,
   100
Simplified Generic Markup Language
   (SGML), **15**
SLIP (Serial Line IP), **78**
SMI (Sun Microsystems, Inc.), **12**
SMTP (Simple Mail Transfer Protocol), **8**,
   100
SOA (Start of Authority), **85**
soc, 123
SPIN, 55
SprintLink, 35
Start of Authority (SOA), **85**
subdomains, 82

Sun Microsystems, Inc. (SMI), **12**
swais, 171, 173
syslog, 132

T

talk, 123
TCP (Transmission Control Protocol), **24**
tcpd, 164
TCP/IP (Transmission Control Protocol /
   Internet Protocol), **24**
TELNET (Virtual Terminal Protocol), **10**, 12
templates, 63
Texas Higher Education network (THEnet),
   35
TFA (Transparent File Access), **12**, 166
TFTP (Trivial File Transfer Protocol), **144**
THEnet (Texas Higher Education network),
   35
ticket, 145
tin, 127
TISN (Todai International Science
   Network), **55**
to, 138
Todai International Science Network
   (TISN), **55**
top-level domains, 82
translator, 154
Transmission Control Protocol (TCP), **24**
Transmission Control Protocol / Internet
   Protocol (TCP/IP), **24**
Transparent File Access (TFA), **12**, 166
transport protocols, 24
Trivial File Transfer Protocol (TFTP), **144**
trn, 119, 127, 140

U

UA (User Agent), **7**, 99
UCB (University of California at Berkeley),
   26
UDP (User Datagram Protocol), **25**
UniPalm Ltd, 35
University of California at Berkeley (UCB),
   26
UNIX Seventh Edition, 29
UNIX to UNIX CoPy (UUCP), **5**, 29
U.S. Sprint, 35
usenet, 131, 139
USENET (Users' Network), **29**

USENET news, 9
User Agent (UA), **7**, 99
User Datagram Protocol (UDP), **25**
Users' Network (USENET), **29**
/usr/local/etc/rc.news, 131
UUCP (UNIX to UNIX CoPy), **5**, 29
UUCP mail network, 29
UUNET (UUNET Technologies), **35**

V

Veronica, 15
virtual circuit, 22
Virtual Terminal Protocol (TELNET), **10**, 12
vn, 127
vnews, 127

W

WAIS (Wide Area Information Servers), **14**,
    170–171
WAIS-8-b5, 171, 179
waisindex, 173–174
waissearch, 171

waisserver, 172
WGs (Working Groups), **34**
WIDE (Widely Integrated Distributed
    Environment), **32**, 55
Wide Area Information Servers (WAIS), **14**,
    170–171
Widely Integrated Distributed Environment
    (WIDE), **32**, 55
Working Groups (WGs), **34**
World dot Net, 35
World Wide Web (WWW), **15**, 175, 179
WWW (World Wide Web), **15**, 175, 179

X

X Window System, 127
X.500, 14
xover, 135
xrn, 127
Xwais, 171–172

Z

zone, 82
zone database, 82